# Value . . . and What Follows

# Value . . . and What Follows

Joel J. Kupperman

New York      Oxford
Oxford University Press
1999

Oxford University Press

Oxford   New York
Athens   Auckland   Bangkok   Bogotá   Buenos Aires   Calcutta
Cape Town   Chennai   Dar es Salaam   Delhi   Florence   Hong Kong   Istanbul
Karachi   Kuala Lumpur   Madrid   Melbourne   Mexico City   Mumbai
Nairobi   Paris   São Paulo   Singapore   Taipei   Tokyo   Toronto   Warsaw

and associated companies in
Berlin   Ibadan

Published by Oxford University Press Inc.
198 Madison Avenue, New York, New York 10016

Oxford is a registered trademark of Oxford University Press

Library of Congress Cataloging-in-Publication Data
Kupperman, Joel.
Value . . . and what follows / Joel J. Kupperman.
p.   cm.
Includes bibliographical references and index.
ISBN 0-19-512348-4
1. Values.   I. Title.
BD232.K845   1999
121'.8 — dc21          98-12126

1 3 5 7 9 8 6 4 2
Printed in the United States of America
on acid-free paper

# Preface

My serious work on value began in the early 90s, although I had published a bit on it as early as 1970. Closer investigation made me realize one of the reasons why so many ethical philosophers avoid the study of value (axiology): so little of any use that is precise or global can be done in it. Ever since Aristotle, honest ethical philosophers have admitted the low degree of precision in their subject. But at the axiology end, the problem becomes most acute.

This is an argument for guarded estimates of what can be accomplished in axiology, but not for ignoring it entirely. A sense of what it is important to attain or avoid in life matters to all of us as human beings, and dim philosophical light is better than none. The trick is to remain faithful to imprecision without being vague.

Further, it is important to other areas of ethics that axiology not be pursued in too simplistic or unargued a way. One example can be found in the history of consequentialism. The classical utilitarians (Mill with more reservations and qualifications than Bentham) opted for a value system that is both simplistic and preposterous. Undoubtedly one motivation was to reduce the imprecision and complexity of the theory. G. E. Moore rejected the simplistic value system, engagingly presenting an assortment of major values in the final chapter of *Principia Ethica*. But Moore's rendering of the evidence for these value judgments, what he calls "intuition," is a non-answer masquerading as an answer. A consequentialism that both examines the bases for judgments of value and avoids simplistic generalizations can become a much more plausible, albeit much less precise-sounding, theory. It also need not conflict with "virtue ethics," especially if it also abandons the assumption that every good outcome is to be reached by a direct route.

It should be clear that much of the philosophical literature on value has seemed to me not to be very helpful, although there are some bright spots (most notably the work of James Griffin). The recent literature on the emotions, in contrast, is a pleasant surprise to anyone who does not know it. There can be few areas of philosophy in which there has been so much recent progress. The work of Robert Solomon and Claire Armon-Jones especially can be singled out, along with Gerald Gaus's investigation of the role of emotions in judgments of value. This advance in philosophical understanding of emotions provides a chance for investigations of value to be less sketchy than those of Alexius Meinong and Moore early in the century.

The first draft of this book was completed in a research year, 1995–96, during which I enjoyed the hospitality of California Institute of Technology. Let me express my gratitude to the Earhart Foundation for a grant to support this work, to the University of Connecticut Research Foundation for a travel grant, to Susan Davis at Cal Tech for her energy and kindness, and to Jim Woodward not only for these qualities but also his role in creating a collegial philosophical atmosphere from which I benefited. Jonathan Bennett, Diana Meyers, and Kwong-loi Shun made helpful comments on one or more papers that were preliminary studies for part I of this book. Part II revisits territory that occupied me in the 1980s; R. M. Hare and J. J. C. Smart made helpful comments on papers written during that period. Despite the manifest differences, part II owes much to their work. The final version of this book benefited from the comments and suggestions of Wayne Sumner and another (anonymous) reader, and of my editor, Cynthia Read.

# Contents

# PART I

# AXIOLOGY

# Values

Axiology is the study of value in the following narrow sense. Throughout this book, the words "value" and "values" will refer to what is worth having or being, taken purely for its own sake, or what is such that (taken by itself, apart from anything it causes) it is preferable that it exist rather than not exist. Negative values will be what it is advisable, if one discounts all causal relations, not to have or be, or what is such that it is better that (taken by itself) it not exist.

This sense of "value" should be placed in relation to two contrasts prominent in the history of philosophy. One contrast, from Plato onward, is between what is good as a means and what is good as an end. By value I will mean goodness as an end: what is worthwhile or desirable for its own sake. A second contrast is between what is good as an end, given a certain context, and what is good as an end regardless of context. Kant (1785/1981, 7) points toward this contrast when he speaks of the good will as the only thing that is good without qualification. The suggestion is that there are other goods, such as the good qualities of intelligence, wit, and judgment, as well as happiness and other "gifts of fortune"; but that these are desirable only conjoined with moral worthiness in the form of the good will. The importance of context will be discussed at various points in this section; but on the whole the book will not be as much concerned with this contrast, and "value" throughout will mean goodness as an end in the context in which something occurs or is posited.

In short, values in the sense used here are goods that by their nature would enhance a life or a world or negatively are things that by their nature would make a life or a world less desirable. Secondarily, I will speak of someone's values as what that person thinks are goods.

This narrow sense is distinct from an increasingly popular broad usage in which values include what is morally or socially acceptable, and someone's values include judgments of morality or of the acceptability of social policies. Some values in this broad sense might rule out activities that are nevertheless thought of as rewarding. "It would be wonderful but it would be wrong" is a coherent thought. Only the first half of this refers to what is meant by values.

A word should be said at this point to the reader who wonders whether some kind of rejection of morality is being built into the structure of this inquiry. In the middle section of this book it will be abundantly clear that this is not the case. My working assumption though is that what we think of as ethics is a patchwork of questions and judgments of a variety of kinds. Morality is important, and it may turn out in the end that there is some slight overlap between questions of morality and questions of value. But by and large, questions of value are not (taken by themselves) moral questions; and we can become much clearer about the relations and connections if we begin by examining questions of value separately.

## From Ordinary Thought to Philosophy

It makes sense in philosophical ethics to begin with ordinary speech and thought, both because this helps to locate the subject of discussion and also because it is always possible that ordinary thought has taken in something that philosophers miss. Ordinary people sometimes say, "That is really good," in a tone that suggests that whatever it is might well be savored. Sometimes what one is encouraged to appreciate is connected with what is morally admired or is thought of as a triumph of justice. This is not always the case, and indeed much of the popular resentment of people who are thought of as immoral and successful appears to be built around the idea that they have something good that they do not deserve (and indeed that they may have gotten by breaking the rules).

Someone's values (in the sense of this book) are conveyed by sentences that begin "What I would really like is . . ." or "What I have come to appreciate/enjoy is . . . ," as well as by those that begin "What I have come to think is really important is. . . ." They also are conveyed by envy, pity, and the sense that someone has been unlucky or lucky. We typically envy someone only if that person has something we are somewhat inclined to view as worthwhile (and would have liked to have). Equally, it would not make sense to consider someone lucky if what she or he had got seemed pretty worthless.

All of this suggests that value judgments are implicit in emotions and in judgments (like those of luck) that might not at first seem evaluative. People also sometimes say what their values are, but such statements can reflect more what one is supposed to value than what one does value. Actions may "speak louder than words" as a representation of someone's values. But actions too need not be definitive of values. Habitual or compulsive behavior may point toward goals that the agent is genuinely skeptical of the worth of. There is finally the special case of self-loathing people who think that they deserve very little and make sure that this is what they get. It would be simplistic to infer what they (genuinely) think valuable from what they seem to be trying to get.

This presentation of what a person's values are departs from a pronounced tendency in recent ethical philosophy to analyze people's beliefs in terms of the sentences they affirm or would (if the question arose) affirm. Further, some philosophers would want to distinguish between what (in my thoughts and emotions) I am willing to endorse and, on the other hand, what goes through my mind that

I am not willing to endorse. The suggestion is that many of the values implicit in my actions and emotions (especially, say, envy) are not *my* values. Something like this is implicit in the equation that has been suggested between what someone's values are and what that person desires to desire (see Lewis 1989, 116).

This is an appealing point of view, not least because of the things in our lives that we would like to disassociate ourselves from. It is certainly true that some actions and emotions (along with the valuing that is implicit in them) will be less characteristic of a person than others. It is also true that some episodes of thought and feeling will hardly be under the direct and immediate control of the person who has them. If one assumes that we have some significant degree of control over who and what we are, then these (especially if they are uncharacteristic) will seem not to be really ours. Nevertheless, there is something schizophrenic in any claim that thoughts and emotions that occur in our minds are not really ours. And to say that if we do not endorse them they cannot be ours opens the door to humbug and self-deception. It would become possible for someone to claim a set of values as his or her own on the basis of explicit affirmations even if the tendency of his or her whole life was in a different direction.

We need to get away from the notion that a person can be assumed to have a single unified set of values, or that there is a unified source of evidence of what someone's values are. Virtually everyone has areas of ambivalence, and moments in which one cares about certain things in spite of oneself; and we can get different readings in different contexts. Explicit judgments, emotions of various kinds, and actions can point in a number of somewhat different directions. No single source of evidence is necessarily conclusive. For some people there will be a fairly high degree of convergence. Sometimes, though, there are conflicts that are sharp enough (as in the case of self-loathing alcoholics who envy those who have kicked the habit, but who also enjoy being drunk) that there is little or no room for any kind of clear answer.

If we ask what most people value most, the answers will fall mainly under three headings: ongoing features of one's life (e.g., love, sets of personal relationships, a sense of success or achievement), particular experiences (e.g., moments of heightened awareness, or of euphoria or ecstasy), or things (e.g., money, expensive or attractive objects — perhaps only as a means, but very possibly for their own sake as well). There are of course other kinds of possibilities. One might value the sheer existence of a redwood forest, or the fact that there is more justice in South Africa than there once was. But, for most of us, the strongest emotions and most energetic activities are likely to be directed toward personal goods and evils; and envy and pity will be directed toward the personal goods and misfortunes of others. We envy people for their success, their money, their ecstasy. We pity them for their loneliness, their poverty, and their suffering.

Many philosophers have tried to impose order on this rather chaotic map of human values. Features of one's life hardly will be valued, it is argued, unless they are gratifying; a similar comment applies to things. This may seem to suggest that the root of value is experience, and specifically the positive kind of experience that involves enjoying or liking something. The existence of the redwood forest and of greater justice in South Africa look like untidy values in relation to this approach; but the values can be held to be reducible to those of the positive experiences that they include or make possible.

In one form the focus on positive experience gives us hedonism, the view that pleasure (or the balance of pleasure minus pain) is the only good. A more subtle, and harder to analyze, view is that happiness is the good. Both of these views are far too simple; but it is worthwhile, before examining why, to try to see why each has some inherent appeal.

It can be argued that pleasure or the thought of pleasure (or, in a negative way, pain or the thought of pain) is involved in any strong appetite or strong motivation. Further, pleasure and pain are agents of psychological conditioning, so that there is some general tendency for people to continue to want or strive for what has been found pleasant, and to lessen their appetites and motivations that are directed toward what has been found to be unpleasant or painful.

The first of these proto-hedonistic theses comes close to John Stuart Mill's assertion, in chapter 4 of *Utilitarianism*, that we desire pleasure and only pleasure (which he thinks is a strong argument for his further claim that pleasure is the good). Mill's claim about what we desire is explicitly about appetite and not about motivation: he recognizes the obvious fact that people are motivated to do or achieve all sorts of things that they know will give them no pleasure (and that the thought of gives no pleasure). There are some things that we want to do simply because we think them right or fitting, or because we are used to doing them. But Mill might agree that such motivations will not become strong unless they take on a connection with pleasure or the avoidance of pain (either in the thought of what would be done or achieved, or as an expected feature of it). This might be particularly true (along the lines of the second proto-hedonistic thesis) in cases of strong, sustained motivation. It may be too much to expect someone to continue trying hard for something who does not think it will be really gratifying or that it will avoid real pain, if the thought of it is not especially pleasant and the thought of not getting it is not especially painful. These points about motivation and desire might seem especially important to someone who accepts what James Griffin recently has called a "taste model" of how we find out about values (1996, chapter 2).

Do we all desire pleasure and only pleasure? Mill's claim has been treated as obviously false by philosophers who have pointed out that we desire a wide variety of things, many of which seem to have little or no connection with pleasure. The issue is complicated by the fact that the word "desire," which in Mill's day clearly stood for an inclination (usually one that is strongly felt) of a specific kind, has been increasingly used generically to stand for any inclination whatsoever. As in the case of "value," one needs to distinguish between a narrow use and a broad use. The narrow, traditional meaning of "desire" is a strong inclination directed toward something (typically, but not always, something that one could have or be connected with) such that not getting (or losing) what one desired would entail frustration or disappointment. Buddhist texts put part of this point by insisting that desire entails attachment, and they go on to claim that desire (because desires are not always fulfilled, and even when they are fulfilled lead to a spiral of further desires) is the root of suffering. In any case, someone who mildly is inclined toward A rather than B, but who really does not mind when only B is forthcoming, cannot be said (in the traditional meaning of "desire") to desire A. "If it's all the same, I'll take A rather than B although B would be fine" is not an expression of desire. Other words that are close in meaning but not synonymous would have to be used, such as the noun "mild preference" or the verbs "would like" or "fancies."

My suggestion is that Mill's claim that we desire pleasure and only pleasure is true in the following respect. In any case in which "desire" in the narrow sense is the appropriate word, one thinks that what one would like will involve pleasure, or at least there is the unarticulated ("implicit") expectation that it will, or (as in the case of martyrs who know that martyrdom will be unpleasant but look forward to it all the same) the thought of it is pleasant, or one expects that it will avoid pain, or the thought of not getting it involves pain. This last alternative deals, I think, with the cases of desires associated with compulsive behavior: even if there is no pleasure in them, disruption of the compulsion can seem painful.

One should note that this argument takes away from Mill at least as much as it gives. It treats the claim in question as true in virtue of linguistic conventions, specifically those that govern (or used to govern) the word "desire." Mill in effect points in this direction when he remarks (1861/1979, 38) that "desiring a thing and finding it pleasant, aversion to it and thinking of it as painful, are . . . in strictness of language, two different modes of naming the same psychological fact." Mill nevertheless thinks that his claim about desire and pleasure contributes to a "sort of proof" of hedonism. This can be the case only if desire is thought of as *the* value sense, analogous (as Mill suggests in the second and third paragraphs of chapter 4) to the five physical senses. But clearly (as was suggested early in this chapter) there are many ways besides desire in which we can be said to value things. These include reflectively thinking some things valuable as a result of examining the psychological framework of our experience. Many philosophers in both Europe and Asia (including Spinoza, Schopenhauer, and more than one school of classical Greek philosophy) have developed an ideal of a life they contend is of great value in part because it lacks desires (in the narrow sense). If Mill thought that his claim about desire and pleasure established the truth of hedonism, he needed to argue that sources of judgment of value other than desire were illegitimate or could not provide genuine evidence. This argument is conspicuously missing.

There are, however, well-known and compelling arguments that pleasure (while, at least in most instances, good) is not *the* good. One is the thought experiment proposed in Plato's *Philebus*: one is asked to imagine oneself as a mollusc, with the very limited life that this involves, but in a continuous state of pleasure. If pleasure really were the good, then one should prefer such a life to an ordinary human life that involves less pleasure. Few people, though, have this response, which at the least suggests that most of us think there are important goods other than pleasure (that would be lacking in the life of the titillated mollusc). Like all thought experiments, this is in no sense a proof of any proposition about what is really valuable. But it would seem to carry some considerable weight, at least as a reminder of judgments of value that are implicit in our ordinary thought.

The second argument opens with an examination of the varieties of gratification. Philosophers, especially if they equate having an austere and impoverished set of categories with precision, sometimes talk as if "pleasure" and "gratification" are for practical purposes synonymous. Mill in *Utilitarianism* sometimes talks as if the two most conspicuous kinds of gratification, pleasure and happiness, are equivalent; although in other works (especially his essay on Bentham) it is abundantly clear that he is sensitive to the differences. One difference is that pleasure typically is keyed to a shorter time frame than is happiness. It is true that people sometimes speak of a few moments of happiness; but it is also common to speak of a summer of happiness, happy years at such and such, or even a happy life, whereas most pleasures (especially those that are looked forward to most keenly) are fleeting. Another difference is that one's ability to accept oneself as one is seems crucial to happiness in a way in which it is not to pleasure. Someone who has a very low opinion of herself or himself cannot be happy (at least in a central and familiar sense of the word), but there is no reason why such a person could not experience many pleasures.

One complication in the discussion is that it is not the case that everything that can be termed pleasure or happiness is entirely alike, and there is more than one sense of "being pleased" or being "happy." Many people think instantly of sensual gratifications when they hear the word "pleasure," but one can be pleased also by the elegance of a mathematical proof or by hearing that a loved one is doing well. The differences among pleasures can be striking, which is why the general view on the value of pleasure held by a philosopher like Plato is "It depends." Pains also vary greatly. Some are directly and primarily physiological (there are pain nerves in the body in a sense in which there are not pleasure nerves), but there is also the pain of separation from a loved one or of realizing that one has just acted like a fool. To be happy is sometimes to have an immediate (and very possibly transitory) feeling of well-being, perhaps in response to (and intentionally related to) something that has just happened (e.g., "That makes me very happy," or "I am happy about . . ."). But there is a sense—common in everyday life and central in both philosophy and psychology—in which a person's happiness largely consists of a disposition to have feelings of well-being more often than people usually do, along with one to make positive assessments of one's life. Such happiness is global in that it is about life or the whole world rather than about some specific event or thing, even though specific events can have a causal role in bringing it about. When people speak of the pursuit of happiness, they mean "happiness" in this sense.

If we take care not to use words in the most broad and generic way possible, we realize that there are many words for kinds of gratification, and that happiness, pleasure, delight, exhilaration, joy, bliss, ecstasy, and euphoria (to name just a few) are not equivalent categories. (Equally we can distinguish between pain and suffering—not all pain involves suffering—and also misery, distress, desolation, sadness, dejection, etc.) Each of these terms covers a range of cases: not all ecstacies, for example, are entirely alike. There are areas of overlap, in that many states fit two or more categories. Indeed, occurrent positive states in general could be said to qualify, by and large, as pleasures, although the word will seem odd and out of place in relation to something that is strong, sustained, and global. (In this way we can understand the fact that many Buddhist and Hindu texts recommend giving up pleasures, and at the same time promise bliss as a reward of enlightenment.) The central ("paradigmatic") cases of pleasure will be occurrent, brief feelings that are caused by a specific thing or event and are intentionally directed toward a thing or event (usually the same one that brought about the pleasure). Happiness in the dispositional and global sense is clearly distinct from pleasures.

Once we see all this, the simple thesis that pleasure is the good comes to look preposterous. It would be possible, after all, to have a life with many pleasures, very few pains, and also not much happiness in the global and dispositional sense. A strategy that not-very-happy hedonists often adopt is to think as little as possible about oneself or the shape and general nature of one's life, but instead to concentrate on the objects of desire and aversion. The chances of success need not be very great, but someone who pursues this strategy might be lucky and generally get what was wished for. A life full of worldly success, good food and wine and sexual gratification, and no instances of painful diseases or severe loneliness or rejection could be abundantly full of "good times" and fun and yet would be compatible with not being an especially happy life. Also, despite all the pleasure, it could be devoid of joy, bliss, or even ecstasy. Viewed against this background, the thesis that pleasure is the good loses its appeal.

Thoughtful people have usually found the thesis that happiness is the good more appealing. Often it is attributed to Aristotle, although some classical scholars are quick to say that Aristotle's term (*eudaemonia*) for the good does not have quite the same meaning as the English word "happiness." "Well-being" is often suggested as an alternative translation; and this helps one to understand both Aristotle's view that eudaemonia can be augmented or diminished by events after death (in that the success or failure of what someone was committed to legitimately affects our sense of the success or failure of that person's life) and also the way in which Aristotle uses "eudaemonia" as an umbrella term for a number of different kinds of values that can (in his view) have some importance. Putting Aristotle to the side, though, we can see some plausibility in the thought that nothing in life is good without happiness, and also that if one is happy nothing else really matters.

Part of the appeal of the view that happiness is the good rests in its relatively non-judgmental quality. Many philosophers, including Aristotle, have held that someone who genuinely believes that his or her life is going well, or is of reasonably high value, can be wrong; and that general propositions of ethical philosophy can provide a way of seeing the error. This willingness to be judgmental often has been combined with an elitism of values (again very evident in the weight in eudaemonia that Aristotle assigns to contemplative activities of a high degree of rationality). To be elitist and judgmental is now very counter to the Spirit of the Age. To hold that happiness is the good, on the other hand, seems to close the door on elitism (absent any strong correlation between rationality and how happy someone is) and largely closes the door on judgmental attitudes. We still might question on psychological grounds someone's claim to be happy: for example, "She says that she is happy, but if you watch her and listen to her you will get a very different impression." But apart from this, the view that happiness is the good is wonderfully democratic in its unwillingness to challenge people's assessments of their own lives.

Further, it would seem that everyone — or at least virtually everyone — would much prefer to be happy rather than unhappy. It might be argued, indeed, that everyone desires happiness; but a claim that happiness is *the* key element in desire seems less plausible than the comparable claim for pleasure, in that people often desire things with not even an implicit expectation that they will make them happy and indeed with no particular thought of happiness at all (or happiness in the thought of what is desired). If we adjust our focus to another source of evidence of people's values, namely what they prefer when they are asked (or are given an actual choice), and if we further require that the outcome for one's happiness be an explicit element, the case for the centrality of happiness looks much stronger. There is a line of thought often attributed to Aristotle (despite the complications in the meaning of eudaemonia) to the effect that other things are valuable only as means to happiness, and that happiness is the ultimate end about which it makes no sense to ask, "What is it good for?" My impression is that most people find this an accurate analysis of the way in which their preference for happiness is related to their other preferences.

The strength of this must be conceded: to the extent that general preference counts as evidence, happiness is (to say the least) a very important value. But does everyone always prefer happiness, and is happiness always an end and never a means? There are cases, beloved of the romanticists, in which creative artists preferred not to be happy (or at least, preferred not to be very happy), because they thought their work would go better if there was a mixture of suffering and dissatisfaction in their lives. On the other hand, people who care deeply about the excellence of their performances (whether in athletics, the arts, or intellectual pursuits) sometimes will have the thought that they will perform better if they are happy than if they are not all that happy, and will devote a bit of energy to the more banal details of life accordingly. This would appear to be treating happiness as a means.

We are discussing the value of happiness in the dispositional and global sense. It is important to bear in mind that someone's disposition to make positive assessments of her or his life (and self) is an important factor in that person's happiness. Might such positive assessments be unwarranted? This is a question the door to which (as we have seen) many people would like to close. On the other hand, I have not seen any clear argument anywhere that the question is illegitimate or somehow meaningless. In a democratic, pluralistic society (especially one that values good manners), there can be strong reasons for saying that we should rarely if ever indicate to anyone that we question that person's assessment of his or her life. But what is rude or disruptive in direct interrogation may be entirely in order in quiet conversation with friends, or as a thought that is not voiced at all. These are ideological issues about which it is difficult to generalize, but risks of social abrasion need not be the only factors to be considered. Another (which will be discussed later) is that people who grow up largely unacquainted with the idea that a person's self-assessment of his or her life is open to challenge may well lack a sense that their own choices of way of life are meaningful or important. To be thoroughly non-judgmental may be conducive to a kind of nihilism.

In any event, there are choices that test the limits of a non-judgmental stance. Suppose that someone who is intelligent, dedicated to demanding pursuits, and not entirely happy is offered a frontal lobotomy, with the prediction that this operation will lead both to near-idiocy and entire happiness. It is said that someone who has had the operation will be, in the expressive New England phrase, "happy as a clam." (It is not material to the example whether the operation actually has these effects; we are imagining someone who believes that it does.) If happiness is the good, then such a person should choose to have the operation; and if it is true that everyone simply prefers more happiness to less happiness, she or he will.

But surely few, in the circumstances described, would choose the operation. It would be possible to refuse it without being judgmental: one might deny making any judgments about the relative values of life as an intelligent person and as a near-idiot, and simply report not being in the mood for such a drastic change. However, in most cases such an account of the decision would not ring true. Most of us, one hopes, are anxious not to be patronizing to, or dismissive of, near-idiots; but in our hearts we think that their lives are very likely not as good as would be the case if they were intelligent. Why else would we feel sorry for them, especially those who started life with normal intelligence and then were brain-damaged as the result of an accident?

The assessment of happiness is complicated by the fact that happiness (in the dispositional and global sense) typically involves not only dispositions to make certain kinds of judgment of one's life and self, but also a variety of positive affects over a period of time. We generally feel good when we are happy. In the respects in which happiness is like a mood, it is like a very good mood. Then there will be specific occurrent positive states. To be happy is not only to be generally upbeat; it is also to be prone to happy thoughts and feelings about various things. Who can be against happiness if it involves all of this? Even romanticist artists who wanted to suffer, and thus not to be very happy, could be argued to have some (distant) vision of happiness in mind. Perhaps there are cases (like that of the frontal lobotomy) in which attaining more happiness is not desirable, but it still looks very plausible to say that (ceteris paribus) happiness is always good. It may not be *the* good, but (taken by itself) it is very good.

Even this position though may overstate (at least for many cases) the value of happiness. We need to put happiness in context. In the context of near-idiocy, it does not look so wonderful; although, surely, it is much better to be a near-idiot and happy than to be a near-idiot and unhappy. Such a comparison looks more uncertain in the case of a vicious sadist. "Is that a life to be happy with?" one may ask. There still is an argument of sorts for saying that even the happiness of a vicious sadist, taken in itself (apart from any contribution to moral knowledge or improvement), has more value than unhappiness would. After all, many people would be more likely to have a twinge of envy of the happy sadist than of the unhappy sadist, which suggests the thought that even here happiness has some value. But, whatever the merits of this argument, it does not support the view that happiness in this case has much value. In the end, a reasonable view of how much value happiness has may be like Plato's of how much value pleasure has: it depends.

Thus far we have examined and rejected two appealing lowest-common-denominator views of what has value: hedonism and the view that happiness is the good. A third, which claims much less, is that anything that has value is an experience (or an aspect of an experience) of a sentient being. Some philosophers have found this modest claim plausible, although G. E. Moore (1903, 83 ff.) rejected it. Robert Nozick (1974, 42–45) has proposed a clever thought experiment that undermines it in much the same way as Plato's thought experiment in the *Philebus* undermines hedonism. He imagines an experience machine: one can choose to enter the machine and have highly desirable experiences for the rest of one's life while, in effect, never *doing* anything again. If all value resides in experience, this should be very appealing . Our unease suggests that there are things in life that we value that cannot be reduced to experiences.

A great deal hangs on the rejection this indicates of the thesis that all value resides in experience. On one hand, there are issues in ecology: do we prize redwood forests merely for the experiences they cause, or does their existence have some intrinsic value of its own? There are also related issues in the epistemology of values (a thicket we will enter later). If values reside in experiences, then one route toward making judgments of value is very plausible: have (or imaginatively reconstruct) the experiences and see what they are like. There are of course many difficulties along this route that it would be premature to mention. But if there are values that do not reside in experiences, the difficulties multiply. It is hard to see how one can even take the first step of finding a route toward making judgments of these values. How would one begin to determine the intrinsic value of a redwood forest?

## Sorting Out Values

Thus far I have surveyed one way in which philosophy has attempted to tidy up the chaotic and disparate elements of ordinary thinking about values. Philosophers can claim that the untidiness is only apparent, in that there is a root element in all value: pleasure, or happiness, or (more generally) experience. I have argued that this is wrong.

Merely to say this, though, is one-sided. These answers have appeal not only because of neatness, but also because there is something to them. Both pleasure and happiness have central roles in our thinking about values. Pleasure, along with its near opposite (pain), looks crucial to an important element to be examined in any judgment of what someone values, namely motivation; and I have argued that pleasure and pain are in one way or another essential to desire. (Indeed, it could be argued that valuing pleasure and the avoidance of pain is at the heart of human nature, that we are "hardwired" to care about them, and that the project of much of ancient philosophy was to improve human nature by advancing the domination of other values over these.) Virtually everyone wants happiness, not only because of what it is like to be happy, but also because to be happy contains as one of its ingredients a disposition to make positive evaluations of one's life (and self). So the appeal of happiness is virtually guaranteed: of course one thinks it would be better to be happy, because one will (when happy) think that it is better. As for experience, it could be argued that it is all that we are acquainted with the value of. In short, even if it is simplistic to regard pleasure, happiness, or experience as *the* root of all value, the philosophical theories that have advanced their claims cannot be totally dismissed and have some merit.

It would be wrong, though, to leave any impression that all, or even most, of the ethical philosophy devoted to value (in the narrow sense of this book) has been straining to find a common denominator of values. Ethical philosophy has included a large variety of investigations related to value. There are persistent questions (which will be pursued in the following chapters) about the ways in which values enter our lives. Also, many great philosophers have not looked for a common denominator but instead have been concerned (among other things) to suggest guidelines for a hierarchy of values. Classic examples are the ordering of values at the end of Plato's *Philebus*, and Aristotle's judicious insistence (*Nicomachean Ethics*, book I) that good fortune of one's family and in the endeavors of ordinary life has some weight in eudaemonia but not as much as the exercise of virtues (especially intellectual virtues).

Sometimes values dear to the average person emerge as a tug or an undertow to be found even in the best kind of life. This is implicit in the tripartite model of the soul presented in Plato's *Republic*. It will always be necessary for reason to control appetites, and indeed there is no suggestion that unruly appetites will be banished from even the best life. In the *Phaedrus*, where the soul is compared to a charioteer driving an obedient and an unruly horse, there is no suggestion that the charioteer simply kill the unruly horse. Similarly, Confucius (fifth c. B.C.E./ 1938, IV. 5, 102) observes that "wealth and rank are what every man desires; but if they can only be retained to the detriment of the Way he professes, he must relinquish them." There is no suggestion that an enlightened man will lose all desire for what he relinquishes. Indeed Confucius elsewhere says (VII. 11, 125) that "[i]f any means of escaping poverty presented itself, that did not involve doing wrong, I would adopt it." This has to be read, in the context of the pervasive and strong demands of Confucian ethics, as saying that, while the desire not to be poor should be overriden by other values, it will not (and should not) go away. Finally, there is the remark (IX. 17, 42) that Confucius has never seen anyone whose desire to build up his moral power was as strong as sexual desire. This may shed some additional light on the famous account of his ethical progress that culminates in the saying that "[a]t seventy, I could follow the dictates of my own heart; for what I desired no longer overstepped the boundaries of right" (II. 4, 88; see also the remark of Sophocles quoted in book I of the *Republic*).

One difficulty in discussions of value is that the descriptive language we have for what we value or disvalue is broad and inexact, and the terms that are readily available turn out to fit cases that differ significantly in value. Is a life marked by selfishness undesirable, or inferior to one that is less selfish but otherwise similar? Nietzsche, in a section of *Thus Spake Zarathustra* ironically entitled "On the

Three Evils," points out, both for selfishness and for two other examples, that generalizations fail in the face of the variety of instances (Nietzsche 1883–91/1978, 186–91). Indeed, we can see that the "selfishness" of a creative, work-absorbed artist might be much more positive than the "selfishness" of a petty profiteer or a family tyrant. One reason that Nietzsche's preoccupation with value is pursued in oblique utterances is that anything resembling a formula can be misapplied by someone who is insensitive to significant differences among cases. Camus makes a related point (1955, 51) when, after presenting some models of very good kinds of lives, he observes that a recommendation of the models does not include assurance that imitations of the models are to be esteemed. Nuances matter.

This difficulty with language points toward one of the ways in which context, especially the context provided by an individual life, matters in the assessment of value. My position can be presented in contrast to Moore's doctrine of "organic unities" (1903, 27 ff.), the claim that the value of a combination may be different from the sum of the values of its elements. Moore presents this doctrine in a way that suggests that we generally can assign value to an element independently of what it is found in combination with. His principle does its work at the level at which we reckon the value of the combination. In some cases that seems to me to be right. It is arguable especially that if we accept the existence of higher goods, then we must join Moore in rejecting the assumption that the value of any whole must be the sum of values of its parts (see Lemos 1993, 495). But it seems to me reasonable that sometimes, when we look back at the value of the individual element, we might say (as Moore would not), "What value it has depends on the context in which it occurs." The intrinsic value, if any, of the existence of a redwood forest is an example. If one believes in such values, independent of the experience of sentient beings, it would seem plausible to assign more value to the existence of a redwood forest in location X if there are very few redwood forests elsewhere than if the rest of the world were covered by redwood forests. It is also plausible to assign greater value to a few moments of careless abandon and euphoria in the life of someone who is austere and disciplined than in a life that is generally heedless and disorganized.

The importance of context to value exacerbates what is in any case a serious problem. If, as Aristotle says, every subject has its due degree of precision, and that of ethics is not great, it must be admitted that the precision generally to be expected in discussion of value is very low indeed. There are two strategies that a philosopher who believes in, and wishes to convey, a hierarchy of values can pursue in an attempt to mitigate this. One is not to rely entirely on general characterizations of the hierarchy of values, but instead to fill in meaning by presenting a concrete (and highly contextual) example of someone whose life was marked by the highest values. Thus, much of the meaning of Plato's ethics is in the portrait of Socrates that emerges; the students who compiled *The Analects of Confucius* pursued much the same strategy. A second strategy is to indicate one's hierarchy of values in a way that allows for elements of irony and a pervasive sense of the personal and elusive nature of what is being talked about. This is the strategy of Nietzsche and Camus.

Nevertheless, despite the irony and the elusiveness, hierarchies are in evidence. Camus consistently extols the value of lucidity of active experience, as Nietzsche does those of strength, independence, and creativity. Nietzsche's relativism, so evident in relation to morality, is not in evidence here. Both Nietzsche and Camus plainly believe that some lives are much more worth living than others, regardless of the levels of satisfaction in the lives they hold to be less desirable. Do they give arguments for this? It is hard to say. The answer is more clear in their analytic counterpart, in the final chapter of G. E. Moore's *Principia Ethica*, which extols an assortment of major values that Moore knows about through "intuition." Earlier Moore had made it clear that to speak of "intuition" is simply to speak of what cannot be argued for.

When philosophers do argue for a hierarchy of values, the reasons given or evidence appealed to can be quite diverse. Some arguments appeal to general assumptions about what will or will not have value, for example Aristotle's *dicta* that a good human life must partake of what makes humans distinctive (rationality) and that the best way of life is that closest to that of the gods. Some philosophers (e.g., David Hume) reconstruct values in terms of the basic tendencies of human psychology. Plato, in his rejection of the life of a democratic man (and even more extreme rejection of the life of a tyrant), grounds his argument in what can be expected to work in the harmonious functioning of a human mind. Many philosophers, at one point or another, have appealed to what we can be expected to value. Some of the most telling appeals in the history of ethical philosophy, from Plato's thought experiment of the highly pleased mollusc to Nozick's experience machine, have taken this form.

I will consider in later chapters how much weight such appeals should have (and why). But let us note now that they complete a circle, from ordinary thought to philosophy and back again to ordinary thought about values. The ordinary thought at the end may be informed by philosophy, although it is noteworthy that both Plato and Nozick appear to expect even beginners to agree with the point of their thought experiments. Perhaps what philosophy does for many valuers is not to eliminate values or to replace them with values previously never thought of, but rather to lessen what is seen as the importance of some values and to emphasize others in the context of a systematic presentation of a hierarchy. Reasons can play a part in this transformation, or it may be simply a gestalt shift in the image of what has been familiar.

In any case, human valuing gives us our starting points in the investigation of values; and it gives us much that counts at the end. This limitation is a constraint on the ethical philosopher, whose claims about value must engage with people's values or the views they are inclined to take of the philosopher's examples. But we should take the limitation also as a reminder that there is a subject matter, and a set of issues, that will not go away. Even philosophers who would reject any claim that there is evidence about what is valuable, and who would reject any form of "realism" about values, still have values. This is a stubborn given in any discussion.

# 2

# Emotions and Values

The previous chapter pointed out that one indicator of what someone's values are is that person's emotions. We must, for example, have some tendency to see as good what we envy in others' lives. The relation is reciprocal. If Bloggs thinks that being locked in a room is one of the worst experiences in the world, this (plus Bloggs's sense that being locked in a room is a possibility) is good evidence for thinking that Bloggs is afraid of being locked in a room.

Such commonsense observations suggest that there may be an especially close connection between someone's emotions and values, and that we can understand values better if we understand this connection. Philosophers, in the twentieth century prominently including Alexius Meinong (1917/1972) and Gerald Gaus (1990), have made this point. To pursue it we need to get a clear view of what emotions are. This view can help us to see the degree to which values are both formed and revealed in emotions.

Some readers might suspect that this inquiry will lead us to a view that values are inherently subjective and personal. This is always a possibility. But the assumption that it is a likely outcome owes a great deal to long-standing confusions about what emotions are. The history of western philosophy is full of sharp contrasts between reason and emotion. Reason, especially in classical philosophy, tends to subsume a broader range of abilities than one might at first think; but the presumption throughout is that reason can give us truth, or at least enables us to derive some truths from other truths. Emotion, in contrast, is not disciplined or autonomous (emotions can sweep over us from nowhere, or from the dim recesses of the mind), and is not connected in any reliable way with truth. When ethical philosophers in the mid-twentieth century developed an emotivist theory of ethics, this was widely seen by philosophers (including the emotivists themselves) as deprecating the claims of ethics to truth in any "objective" sense and as undermining claims that certain choices were *really* right and certain things *really* good.

The story of emotivist ethics is a complex one. Charles Stevenson, the leading emotivist, devoted great ingenuity and subtlety to successive refinements of the theory, over time accommodating (as any skilled polemicist will) what looked like the strongest objections of its detractors. Thus he was able to do a sort of justice to the fact that ordinary people commonly expect that an ethical judgment ought to be able to be supported by reasons (Stevenson 1963, 83 ff.); he also could isolate a sense in which one could meaningfully say that an ethical statement is true (1963, 214–20). (According to Stevenson, to say this was to agree with the statement.) These accommodations took place within a framework in which it remained the case that ethical judgments expressed attitudes rather than beliefs; so that, however we might speak of them as "true," they could not be true in the way in which, say, claims in the sciences and social sciences are often true. Ethical judgments supported by reasons still were regarded as expressive of attitudes, but as expressive in a more intricate way than ethical judgments that were unaccompanied by reasons.

As J. O. Urmson (1968) pointed out, attitudes, in which Stevenson (despite the name of his theory) anchored the expressive function of ethical utterances, are distinct from emotions. It is possible to have an attitude without any emotion at all, Urmson suggested: for example, someone serving on a committee may have a favorable attitude to a proposal or a candidate without having any feelings in the matter at all or indeed really caring.

This suggests two points. One is that the word "emotivist" reveals a rhetorical strategy, presumably one that trades on the long history of philosophical deprecation of emotion. Perhaps the strategy was not entirely candid, but more importantly it invites the possibility that we reconsider the philosophical deprecations of emotion—as one of Stevenson's students, Robert Solomon, did.

Second, we need a clearer understanding of what an emotion is, and also what attitudes, moods, feelings, and so forth, are. Only thus can we understand such things as the difference between emotions and attitudes, and also how either emotions or attitudes might play a role in ethical judgment. This understanding can lead us, also, to some sense of whether emotion is always, or generally, disengaged from truth.

## The Elements of Emotion

Many ordinary people think of emotions as feelings, as occurrent mental states that typically are either positive or negative. It may be that something like this is at both the origin and the core of our concept of emotion. The first non-obsolete sense of "emotion" given in the *Shorter Oxford English Dictionary* (SOED) is "agitation of mind; strong mental feeling." It is natural to suppose from this, and also the Latin etymology of the word, that at an early stage the principal and most prominent examples of what were called emotions were felt agitations or disturbances.

As John Stuart Mill says (1843/1884, book 1, chapter 8, 7, 99), "A name is not imposed at once and by previous purpose on a *class* of objects, but is first applied to one thing, and then is extended by a series of transitions to another and another." Not all feelings are agitations. Even Gilbert Ryle's famous list of feelings (1949, 84), which includes a striking variety of agitations, also includes glows. Glows resemble felt agitations in many respects (e.g., in the ways in which they are very noticeable and can engross someone's consciousness) even though they are not agitations. Similarly, there is the possibility that some agitations or glows might not register on the person who has them, and in that sense not be felt, even though in other respects they are like felt agitations or glows. In short, even if the paradigmatic cases of emotion involve felt agitations, cases of other sorts may resemble these (or resemble cases that resemble these) enough to be considered emotions.

Philippa Foot (1958–59) and Solomon (1976) deserve credit for having pointed out that familiar and central cases of emotions, even if they involve feelings, are not just feelings but rather take objects and involve a judgment (which may be implicit rather than explicit) of these objects and of one's relation to them. Foot's telling example was pride, which has a limited range of possible objects. Bloggs cannot be proud of the fact that the sun rises every day, unless he somehow has beliefs that allow this to be viewed as an accomplishment that somehow reflects credit on him. Both Solomon and Ronald de Sousa (1987) have argued, turning the dominant traditional view on its head, that emotions have to be regarded as cognitive, in that what is essential is not feeling but instead an element of judgment that can be correct or incorrect. To be afraid, for example, centrally is to judge that the object of one's fear is dangerous. This judgment may or may not be accompanied by feelings of the sort that we might associate with fear.

My own view of emotion owes a great deal to Claire Armon-Jones's *Varieties of Affect* (1991), which treats emotion in a way closer to Solomon's and de Sousa's "cognitivist" approaches than to the traditional anti-cognistivist view, but which rejects the strongest claims of the cognitivists. In particular, Armon-Jones points out that there are many cases in which we in no sense judge the object of fear to be dangerous; we know that the snake will not hurt us, or that there is no danger in being in a small enclosed space, but we are afraid nevertheless. There is an element of "seeing as" in these situations: one can see something as dangerous while knowing full well that it is not. If we want a general formula for the element of judgment, or something like judgment, in emotion, Armon-Jones suggests "construal" (1991, 31 ff.). To be afraid of something is to construe it as dangerous.

This seems to me to be very right. I would want to go beyond Armon-Jones though in denying that even the element of "construal" is to be found in every case of what could be reasonably termed emotion. That is, there are cases in which someone simply feels, say, terror, even though there is no object of the terror and, hence, no judgment or construal of an object involved. We would nevertheless be willing to consider this terror to be emotion. One defense of a "cognitivist" or quasi-cognitivist view is to hold that there is an object even in such cases — namely the world — along with a judgment that the world is (at that moment) dangerous. But this seems an ad hoc attempt to save a philosophical position. The person who is terrified of . . . he or she knows not what . . . is not focusing the terror on the world; the terror is not focused on anything.

While we juggle the claims of feeling and of judgment or construal to be central to emotion, we should consider a third element. This is motivation, interpreted broadly to be our inclination or tendency to seek or avoid something. Take again the example of fear. In a typical case, someone who suddenly sees a tiger in the wild will have a sudden surge of feeling that many will immediately associate with adrenalin, along with a disposition to say (and agree with others who say) that the tiger is dangerous. There will be another element: a strong inclination to flee, or (if we are talking about someone with a gun) to shoot the tiger. The motivational element can be crucial: anyone who says that fear is *simply* the judgment that something is dangerous will need to contend with cases in which someone makes the judgment but is indifferent to the danger or glories in it.

My view (more fully argued in Kupperman 1995) is that neither feeling nor judgment or construal, nor motivation is essential to emotion, although paradigmatic cases of emotion will involve all three. There are cases of, say, anger or fear in circumstances so pressing that the person who is angry or frightened has no time to *feel* anger or fear. The warrior after the battle may agree to having been angry or afraid, but plausibly deny having these feelings during the heat of action. There are psychoanalytic cases, also, in which a patient can be brought to agree that he or she has loved or hated someone or has been angry, even though (as part of the repression) there had been no noticeable feelings of love, hate, or anger.

This evidence leads to the conclusion that feeling, albeit a typical element of emotion, is not essential. One way of moving to a weaker thesis is to distinguish between feeling (which involves occurrent experience that is attended to or noticed, or can be remembered later) and affect (which need not be conscious experience but can be observed and possibly can be measured). Perhaps feeling is not present in every case of what we would consider to be emotion, but the fallback position is that at least affect is. The person who was in love or angry without feeling it will have been noticeably excited and uncertain in the presence of the beloved or the object of anger, or will have been flushed, or will have had a higher than normal pulse rate, or all of these at once.

This may be true. We need, however, to regard this as primarily an empirical hypothesis rather than an analysis of the concept of emotion, in that there could turn out to be cases of what we would consider to be emotion in which empirical research will fail to disclose affect. Perhaps, in some of the cases in which X resents Y (as we can tell from X's behavior) but is genuinely unaware of it, we will not be able to find physiological changes in X or psychic changes that X with honest effort could become aware of. It may be that some of the stronger emotions, such as love and hate, do conceptually require affect: that is, if there turns out to be no affect, we might regard the claim that X loves (or hates) Z as too strong. Even if this is so, we cannot generalize that all emotions require affect. In this sense, it would appear that affect (like feeling) is not essential to emotion; and it may be that (like feeling) it is not present in every case.

Motivation, like feeling, is generally present in core cases of what we would consider to be emotion. Clearly the primitive instances of agitation that are at the origin of the concept of emotion are by and large ones in which the subject feels impelled to do something about the agitation. If it is unpleasant, one seeks to eliminate it; and people usually seek to prolong or repeat agitation that is pleasant. The agitations characteristic of such emotions as love, hate, and fear have their own characteristic accompanying motivations, which sometimes are more complicated than mere approach or avoidance.

The largest and most conspicuous group of cases in which this normal connection between emotion and motivation fails are those of sentimentality. In these, emotion is often disconnected from action or any tendency toward action. "The only activity which the sentimentalist manifests naturally is," Michael Tanner (1976–77, 134) points out, "the activity of rendering himself more passive." Sentimentality in some contexts emerges, in Tanner's account, as a self-indulgent strategy. Feelings can be "of a kind that inhibit action, because they themselves are enjoyable to have, but if acted upon, one would cease to have them, and one doesn't want to" (139).

Thus motivation, like feeling, is not essential to emotion. I have already argued that this is true also of intentionality, in the form of either judgment or construal. It remains to say that each of these three elements, while not essential, is near essential in that (1) if one of the elements is missing, we will be reluctant to term something as an emotion unless the other two elements are pronounced, and (2) cases that lack one of the elements are treated as atypical and as needing explanation or analysis. Thus an emotion, such as "blind" terror or rage, that lacks intentionality typically will involve strong feeling and motivation. It also presents itself as somehow incomplete, so there is a tendency to attempt to supply the missing element, saying, "There must be something that she (or he) is frightened of/ angry about," or positing some default object of the emotion such as the world or life. Cases in which feeling is missing require explanation. Perhaps the subject was too preoccupied (often in the context of activity tied to strong motivations) to notice or have what otherwise would have been felt, or perhaps there were psychological mechanisms of censorship that blocked what would have been a kind of awareness in the form of a feeling. Cases in which motivation is missing also require explanation. "If she (or he) cares about such and such, why isn't she (or he) doing something?" we ask. Even after an explanation is forthcoming, there may be a tendency to view such cases as verging on the pathological, or at least as revealing a lack of wholeheartedness in someone's emotional life.

## Varieties of Emotional States

One of the difficulties in any discussion of emotions is in finding sharp boundaries. Moods are not the same as emotions, but it may not be immediately clear where the category of emotion leaves off and mood begins. Is joy an emotion or a mood? Or might there be cases of joy that are moods and cases that are emotions, and perhaps cases that are difficult to classify one way or another? A similar difficulty applies to the relation between emotions and attitudes. There are problems in relation to states that may extend over a period of time, such as happiness or misery. Perhaps they always involve emotions, but can we speak of happiness or misery as emotions? Might there be cases for which this is plausible, as when someone *feels* happy or *feels* miserable, and cases for which it seems implausible (e.g., the constant misery of someone who has been poor and hungry for so long that she can hardly remember anything else)?

Let me suggest the term "emotional state" as one that includes both emotions and also anything, like this constant misery, that involves emotion but that we would tend not to label in itself an emotion. Happiness of the global and dispositional kind, then, fits under the heading of emotional state that is not an emotion, as do (by and large) cases of suffering or of long-term misery. Perhaps many cases of short-term misery might also fit under this heading, in that even relatively brief misery is a complicated network of dispositions to have a variety of distressing thoughts.

An attitude is a tendency to respond (or not to respond) in a certain way to something. Most attitudes have a specific object or objects, to which one has a characteristic response or a response that follows from the attitude. Some attitudes are emotional states. One's attitude toward racial discrimination, for example, might be one of abhorrence. To abhor discrimination typically is to have emotions of anger or disgust on certain occasions; but abhorrence in itself would not normally be considered an emotion. Armon-Jones (1991, 5) uses the phrase "standing emotions," but this is (as she recognizes) an extension of the ordinary use of "emotion"; and the same job can be done by "emotional state." Urmson (1968) is surely right in saying that attitudes are not emotions in any ordinary sense of the word, and also in suggesting further that attitudes need not involve emotions. An attitude of indifference is a prime example of the latter. In the end, all we can say is that many attitudes (especially many of those that are positive or negative) do involve emotions, but that some attitudes do not. If our favorable attitude toward something consists merely in a mild inclination to vote "Yes," so that feeling is absent and motivation also is very weak, we would be very unlikely (as Urmson says) to be said to have emotions in the matter.

There is a tendency to view emotions as being closer to occurrent states (often ones that are felt) than attitudes are; conversely, even attitudes that are emotional states will be thought of as dispositional and more likely to have considerable duration. But particular cases are not easy to sort out. "Jack loves Jill" generally is held to describe Jack's emotion, but what of "Jack adores Jill" or "Jack approves of Jill"? There are feelings of adoration and of approval, as well as of love; but in all three cases (Jack's love, adoration, and approval) what is described is not simply a matter of having certain occurrent states. Nevertheless, my sense is that many people would be more comfortable in labeling love an emotion than they would in so treating adoration, and that approval is even further along the continuum that extends from emotions to emotional states that are not emotions (including those emotional states that are attitudes). Perhaps the fact that feelings and motivations associated with love often are strong makes it easier for us to place it, alongside such occurrent states as being angry or delighted, in the category of emotion. Approval would be classified as an attitude more often than as an emotion, even in cases in which there are feelings of approval rather than merely a tendency to vote "Yes" on what is approved.

It may be that there is a similar continuum from emotions to moods. Moods are less linked to specific objects than attitudes typically are. Nico Frijda (1993,

381) has spoken of three criteria for distinguishing moods from emotions: longer duration, lower intensity, and diffuseness or globality. Joy at, say, the birth of a child would be clearly an emotion; but the global joy that might overtake someone while standing in a field of daffodils would seem like a mood in its diffuseness, although if its duration were short and its intensity were high it would in those respects seem like an emotion. (My judgment is that there are at least some cases in which the short duration and high intensity would outweigh the diffuseness, providing more instances of emotions that do not in any normal sense have intentionality.) A fourth factor relevant to classification as a mood is that moods are frames of mind (see Armon-Jones 1991, 83). As Ryle put it (1949, 93) moods are like the weather, coloring the agent's actions and reactions. Again, brief, high-intensity global joy would be unlikely to have this characteristic to any pronounced degree, in that it would tend to engross someone's mind rather than provide a setting for other feelings and reactions.

Even if we restrict our attention to what are clearly emotions (rather than emotional states that are not emotions), generalizations are hard to come by. If one begins with agitations as examples of emotions, it is very tempting to associate emotions with strongly positive or negative responses, as well perhaps as urgency of action. But, besides Ryle's glows, there will be undramatic emotions of tranquility and emotions associated with agape or with mild compassion. The Japanese *amae* (the feeling of mutual interdependence with another) is worth mentioning, as is the Utku Eskimo *naklik* (the feeling that accompanies wanting to nurture and protect another) (Jerome Kagan 1984). In both cases, what is felt has enough connections with motivation and construal to qualify clearly as an emotion.

Emotions sometimes sweep over people. This is characteristic of passions, in the current sense of the word (which is narrower than some older senses). But emotions sometimes develop only gradually as the culmination of a long process of study and judgment. There is no incompatibility between judicious assessment, with fine analysis of relations and implications, and a culminating state in which one despises what one has assessed or feels strong affection for it.

Sometimes an emotion will present itself as just the way one happens to feel. "I like/loathe such and such; that's just the way I am," people will say. There may be no suggestion that others ought to feel much the same way, or that it would be appropriate for anyone either to defend or criticize the emotion. Many emotions are personal in this sense. But some emotions are very different from this. Notoriously, as David Hume pointed out, moral emotions present themselves as appealing to what is, or should be, a shared perspective (Hume 1739/1978, book 3, part 1, section 2, 472). One is morally indignant about what one assumes others should be morally indignant about; and it would sound oddly weak-minded or desperately non-confrontational if someone reporting moral emotions said, "That's just the way I am." It is arguable both that this appeal to a sharable vision is essential to morality and that moral emotions are unique among types of emotion in generally having this feature. But certainly there are emotions of other kinds that sometimes implicitly appeal to a sharable vision. For many people, this is true of emotions that are linked to etiquette rather than morality; in some instances aesthetic emotions will present themselves in this way, as will some instances of admiration that is directed to other than moral qualities.

We have already seen that most (indeed, nearly all) emotions have an element of judgment or construal of some object or objects. It is not easy to find emotions in which an element of judgment does not evaluate its object(s), either positively or negatively or (in the case of some emotions of detachment) neutrally. Familiar emotions judge their objects to be charming, adorable, morally admirable, unacceptable, potentially harmful, outrageous, disgusting, and so forth. Such evaluations can fit a variety of categories: moral, aesthetic, pertaining to etiquette, or practical in some very broad sense. Or they may be simply indicators of personal likes and dislikes.

Some emotions have an element of judgment (or at least construal) of value in the narrow sense of this book. To fear something, for example, is to see it as involving, or as being able to bring about, something of negative value. We fear animals that can devour or maim us. It would make sense to fear an animal that might tickle us only if we think that being tickled is a terrible thing. The phenomenology of emotions of this sort, and of their relations to the value judgments that we are prepared to avow, is complicated. Sometimes we argue people out of emotions. When Bloggs tells us that he is afraid of X, we ask, "What's so terrible about X?"; and it sometimes happens that, after discussion of X and its ramifications, Bloggs is no longer afraid of it. There are cases, also, in which people come to have emotions of admiration, fear, loathing, and so on, only as a result of a reasoned investigation of their objects; when one comes to see how good, or bad, they are, other elements of emotion (feeling and motivation) may naturally develop around the original core of value judgment. On the other hand, there are cases in which people articulate a judgment that something is highly undesirable only after finding themselves in the grip of negative feelings about it along with a strong motivation to avoid it. The relation between "reason" and emotion can look very different in these cases from the way it looks in the cases in which feeling and motivation follow the process of judgment.

Much of this discussion will frustrate the reader who looks for general formulas that will bring enlightenment. But, if I am right, general formulas are usually misleading in this territory, in which labels such as "emotion" are used to cover a wide range of cases among which there are significant differences. Those who provide general formulas can disagree among themselves if they focus their attention on cases in different parts of the range: different examples lead to different oversimplifications. We need to look in detail, with some variety of examples, at the relations among the elements of emotions that are linked to value judgments.

## Emotions as Judgments of Value

Let us begin with a case at one extreme of a continuum. Imagine an artist who is offered a job, involving mainly time-consuming routine office work, in a family business, with the promised reward of financial security. As the time for beginning her duties nears, she finds herself dreading it. Two elements of her emotion of dread seem fairly straightforward. There may well be feelings of unease or anxiety, as well as the harder-to-describe feelings that often go along with a sense of being trapped or confined. There will be negative motivation, manifested perhaps in hesitation to make a firm commitment to the new job or perhaps to discuss the subject at all. The third element in her dread, that of judgment or construal, may be less straightforward. Perhaps she does simply say to herself, "This will give me a life that I don't think will be all that good." Very possibly, though, she does not articulate any judgment of this sort; no judgment rises to the surface of her thinking about her possible new career, although there are her negative feelings and her negative motivation. It might be urged, nevertheless, that a negative judgment is implicit in all of this; we certainly could say, along the lines suggested by Armon-Jones (1991, 31), that she "sees" or "construes" the new career as confining and as of low value.

If a negative judgment is implicit in the artist's feelings and motivations, what does this really say? Part of the point may be that we expect an articulate judgment of (negative) value to develop as a natural outcome of the emotional turmoil, like a bubble rising to the surface of a troubled liquid. We normally do think in terms of connections of this sort, although it is not always clear whether the connection between the feelings and motivations, on one hand, and the articulate judgment, on the other, is meant to be causal, or rather is the kind of relation that a natural continuation of a story or a piece of music has to what went on before, or whether it is of some hybrid or intermediate character.

What if the articulate judgment never develops, and we are left saying merely that the artist sees or "construes" the office job as undesirable? Thus far this element has been presented as an element of emotion that is separate from, although often found in conjunction with, the elements of feeling and motivation. But it could be argued that in some cases the separateness is an illusion, that the artist's construal of the office job as undesirable consists just of her negative feelings and motivations. Sometimes the undesirability of the job takes a particular form, and there is a visual emphasis on clocks slowly ticking on bare walls along with general associations of the job with closed spaces and lack of freedom of movement. All of this would make the artist's response a full-blown instance of "seeing as." In a case in which the negative judgment is more generic, and there are negative feelings and motivations of avoidance that have not taken any form that suggests a specific kind of negative judgment, it still could be claimed that there is a separate element of construal or judgment in this respect: the artist will have a disposition, if suitably pressed, to say, "This will not be good for me." But is this more than to say that the elements of feeling and motivation, which are already present, can give rise to an element of judgment?

Whatever one thinks about the separateness of the element of judgment or construal in cases of this sort, it is clear that feelings and motivations sometimes precede articulate judgments of value, and also that the value judgments may merely record, as it were, what was implicit in the feelings and motivations. There is a great deal of latitude in how one takes such cases. One might say, with Pascal, "The heart has reasons that the reason knows not," and regard feelings and motivations as sources of knowledge of values. Alternatively, one might view such cases much as Stevenson and A. J. Ayer would have viewed them. The origin of value judgments in feelings and motivations would be taken as one more indication that, in the end, they must be taken as merely expressions of how people feel.

To speak of this latitude in how one takes the cases is not to declare philosophical neutrality. There are serious issues of whether, and in what respects, it makes sense to speak of knowledge of values or to espouse a kind of "realism" with regard to values. These will be taken up in the chapters following this one. It is important, though, to be candid about the nature of the philosophical issues. Much in them is a matter of the interpretation of real-life cases of values; and, when interpretations compete, it often is naive and simplistic to view as flatly and simply "true" the one that appears to be more perspicacious and revealing , or to view as flatly and simply "false" the one judged to be inferior. Moreover, an interpretation may seem more plausible, and may work better, for some cases than for others. This is one of the reasons that variety of examples is so important.

Two points need to be made in relation to the case of the artist. One is that even value judgments that develop only as a result of feelings and motivations are open to reasoned argument. A friend might convince the artist that the office job would involve more latitude and call for creative energy than first appeared possible, and her feelings and motivation might change as a result. Even a judgment that originates apart from evidence and reasoned examination of its object will not be exempt from a relation to evidence and such reasoned examination.

Of course, the artist can respond to evidence and argument by saying, "This is the way I feel"; and that will end the discussion. People who are rationalists about life sometimes dismiss such responses, but they can have a justification. There are cases in which "This is the way I feel" is an expression not only of blind feelings but also of closed-mindedness about evidence. But sometimes it instead is an outgrowth of a sense that the factors that justify one's response are so subtle and removed from the common categories of descriptive discourse that they would be virtually impossible to articulate. In these cases the feelings are not truly blind, and the close-mindedness can be mainly on the part of those who fail to understand the perceptions that are linked to them.

The most extreme cases, and the easiest to deal with, are those in which it is abundantly clear that feelings and motivations are not based on defensible judgments or perceptions. An example is when someone says, "I know that snake could not harm me, but I am afraid of it nevertheless." But to recognize such cases is merely to grant that people may have feelings and motivations that, in the view of their friends or of impartial bystanders, are unreasonable, and that make continued argument both useless and churlish. It is not to deny the relevance of evidence and reasoned examination of the objects of emotion.

A second point is that many cases in which a value judgment is linked to feelings and motivation differ significantly from the case of the artist. Sometimes, indeed, the reason has reasons that the heart does not know . . . at first. Someone who is indifferent to the plight of a group of disadvantaged people may develop compassionate emotional responses as a result of detailed examination of their situation and of their responses to it. It is sometimes argued that, in cases of this sort (in which emotion appears to follow reason), there was an emotional element all along in the form of a general predisposition to respond compassionately to certain kinds of situations. Hume is the best known philosopher who has advanced a view of this sort, along with the related claim that (even in cases in which "reason" does much of the work) "sentiment" pronounces the final ethical judgment. Even if one agrees with Hume on all of this, there still will be many cases (as Hume recognized) in which most of the psychological movement in the direction of a final judgment is rational. Also, some cases of the sort now under discussion could be argued to come close to being mirror images of the cases in which the element of judgment or construal in an emotion consisted merely of a disposition — if suitably pressed — to articulate a judgment of a certain sort. That is, compassion that grew out of rational study of the circumstances of disadvantaged people might be rather matter-of-fact, with rather few occurrent feelings. It is often said that the most effective helpers of the unfortunate are, by and large, not those who have abundant feelings about them but rather those who in a clearheaded way size up what is needed and briskly set about to provide it. For a person of this sort, the emotion of compassion could consist largely of certain kinds of judgments (and a strong motivation to act accordingly) in certain kinds of situations. It would be open to the emotivist philosopher to insist that the value judgment, "What is happening to these people is terrible," must be regarded as simply expressive of the emotion of compassion. There will be some truth to this: the judgment will express (both giving vent to, and revealing) the emotion. But it looks especially implausible in cases of this sort to regard the emotivist's analysis as the whole story, and indeed it may seem out of focus.

## Values, Personal and Otherwise

Many think of value judgments not only as expressive of emotion but also as in some sense personal. There are of course many senses in which a value judgment can be said to be personal. First, all judgments are personal in the sense that everyone arrives at judgments in her or his own way, within the contexts of individual psychologies. Even if someone else's judgment is accepted on trust or on authority, each of us must make such a decision; and the decision will be made in the context of one's own psychology. Second, the elements of motivation and feeling that may accompany or flow from a value judgment will have individual ramifications in people's personal lives. The responsibility for arriving at, or reconsidering, a value judgment also will be personal.

There is a further sense in which value by and large is, and should be, personal and relative: your happiness will be more important to you than to anyone else, and normally your psychological equilibrium should be much more your concern than anyone else's. It is easy to say that the objects of your concern have value for you in a way in which they may not for someone else. But this is merely another way of saying that they matter to you in a way in which they may not matter to someone else. People who say this frequently will go on to say that of course their happiness or their psychological equilibrium, "in the scheme of things," has no more value than anyone else's. This comment suggests strongly that there is a central and primary sense of value—the one indeed on which our investigation focuses—in which it is not relative. This leaves room for partiality, for the victory of your team, your country, or your child having (in the secondary sense) a special value for you, even though you may recognize (barring genuine superiority on the part of your team, country, or child) that "in the scheme of things" victory for a rival team, country, or child will have about as much value. For almost everyone partiality has an important role in creating a meaningful, situated human life. But in the heat of partiality, people sometimes forget what would be a reasonable assessment if the personal perspective were put to the side, just as they sometimes come to think that God favors their team.

Here again we must take care not to overgeneralize about the relation between value in the secondary sense of value-for and value in the primary sense. When such and such experiences had enormous value (i.e., value in the secondary sense) for someone, it is an open question whether we would judge them to have significant value in the primary sense. Sometimes the answer is "Yes," as when experiences (as "defining moments") play a major role in crystallizing or anchoring a rich and integrated sense of self. They can be the high spots of a very good life. In other cases, though, as when Bloggs tells us that it has great value for him to have visited all fifty of the American state capitals, we reasonably judge that what mattered a great deal to someone really did not have all that much value (in the primary sense) in that person's life. Bloggs himself, after he has found something more meaningful to do with his life, may come to agree with that judgment.

Our concern in any event is with value in a sense that is transpersonal in not simply being keyed to one person's perspective. This concern leads to the issue of whether there is something like truth about values that is transpersonal and "objective," an issue that will be considered in later chapters. For the moment, we need merely to examine what kinds of claims value judgments can be taken as making, putting to the side the question of what kind of validity (if any) they might have. Can we regard some (or all) judgments of value (in our primary sense) as making claims that extend to everyone's life?

There are two factors that complicate this issue enormously. One is the variability, from person to person, of the nature of what is evaluated. The other is the importance of context to value.

Much of what one judges the value of lies outside oneself. Examples earlier used were the existence of a redwood forest, or of greater justice in South Africa. In these cases, there is no obvious reason why each of us could not arrive at value judgments of the same object; and, furthermore, it is possible that many of us will have very similar visions of what is involved in the existence of the redwood forest or in greater justice in South Africa.

Probably, though, most value judgments will be of elements in a life, as we have experienced them. Even if we insist that we are talking about the value of such and such in anyone's life, it is arguable that the object of the judgment is the value of such and such in the form in which we have experienced it. There will be the strong possibility that something that fits the general description of such and such could yet be significantly different from what we are familiar with in our own lives and in those of people we know well. This is particularly likely in the lives of people who are very different from us and our friends: people within our own culture who have different outlooks and ways of life, and especially people from cultures that seem alien. A claim about the value of X, if it has any validity, looks likely to have more in relation to X of the sort that we are familiar with than in relation to unfamiliar forms of X.

As I argued in the first chapter, context can matter. (For opposing views see G. E. Moore, 1903, 30, and Noah Lemos, 1994, 40–47.) A highly positive judgment of moments of careless abandon looks more plausible in relation to lives that we might judge to be excessively rigid and controlled than in relation to those that, in contrast, seem unfocused and entirely undisciplined. Similarly, the value of the redwood forest would seem different in a world crowded with redwoods than in ours.

When we experience something that would normally be described as X in a context that would normally be described as Y, it is more than likely that "X" and "Y" will be broad categorial terms (or conjunctions of such terms) that cover a range of cases among which there can be significant variations. Any generalization that we are inclined to make about the value of X in context Y will be vulnerable on that count. There are two strategies that we could follow in attempting to minimize this difficulty. One is to pile on descriptive labels that are as specific as we can make them, to the point of being tedious. The other is to give up on descriptive labels and to rely instead on demonstratives. We might claim that "[a]nything very like this in a context very like this has such and such a value."

The form of this claim mimics one used by R. M. Hare (1963) in explaining the universalizability of moral judgments. Hare's thesis is that any particular moral judgment implies a universal moral judgment, one that fits all cases that are in relevant respects very similar to the case initially judged. The thesis has, in my view, survived attack very well and is valid. Are all value judgments universalizable in the way in which moral judgments are?

If one looks at the two sorts of judgment formally and logically, there will be no apparent reason that they should be treated differently. Hare's argument, put untechnically, is that what is morally right (or wrong, obligatory, permissible, etc.) has this feature because of what it (descriptively) is like, and, hence, that anything which is very similar in all relevant respects will have the same moral feature. The absurdity of assigning different moral properties to two things that are descriptively very similar could be compared to that of claiming that, of two pictures that are virtually identical, one is beautiful and the other is ugly. It is easy to see how a similar argument could be produced for values.

Nevertheless, I want to suggest that there are significant differences between value judgments and moral judgments, not formally and logically but rather in the real-life uses and implicit conditions of the two kinds of judgment. First, moral judgments generally have the function of helping to protect individuals from one another (or perhaps, occasionally, from themselves) and of maintaining a social order that includes elements of cooperation and trust. This imposes constraints on morality that go beyond what can be derived logically. Formally and logically, it could be asserted without absurdity that something that would be morally wrong for you and me would be permissible for Bloggs, who as it turns out is a brilliant and sensitive artist with special needs. There is nothing in Hare's thesis of universalizability that rules out the possibility that a relevant difference between Bloggs's moral position and ours is that Bloggs is such an extraordinary person in respects that are relevant to the moral judgment at hand. Nevertheless, there would be a general tendency to resist moral special treatment of this sort. An obvious factor is that we are generally suspicious of other people's claims to be extraordinary. But what is most important is that any viable morality, even one initially espoused by a lone individual or a small group, must be workable for an entire society. It verges on contradiction to advance a moral claim while granting that no society could accept it without generally unfortunate consequences. Increased tensions and deeply felt divisions count as unfortunate.

Thus, part of this requirement is that one's morality must be a plausible candidate for acceptance throughout the society, so that virtually no one feel left out, slighted, or discriminated against by the moral order that it would represent. To allow moral special treatment is to encourage a sense that the morality is for "them" rather than for us. In short, around the logical core contained in Hare's thesis of universalizability, there is (for morality, and also for the law) a functional penumbra, which leads us to think that morality (and the law) should apply "irrespective of persons."

The second difference between moral and value judgments that is relevant to our present discussion is this. When something is spoken of as, say, morally wrong or obligatory, there is no ambiguity such as is often present in value judgments that something is good, wonderful, awful, and so forth. Often it will not be immediately clear whether the goodness or awfulness of a thing is meant to be as an end, as a means, or some combination of the two. It also may be unclear whether the goodness or awfulness is meant to obtain in any context ("without qualification" to borrow Kant's words), or is context dependent.

Hence, while anything that is in relevant respects descriptively like X will have the same moral standing (for anyone), it is not true that anything that is in its nature like Y will be as good for anyone, if we are talking about goodness in context or goodness as a means. What works well in the circumstances and context of one person's life may not work so nearly well for another. Most people are very aware of this variability; and consequently, when they claim that something is very good or awful, often they turn out to mean very good or awful in the circumstances and context of their lives. Such judgments are personal in a sense in which a genuinely moral judgment is not personal.

What if we restrict ourselves to judgments of value in the sense with which this book is primarily concerned: that is, judgments of value as an end, rather than as a means? Are these ever personal? To put the question in this way eliminates from consideration the causal means-ends relations that are so variable. But relations of context remain. What is a bright spot in one life, connecting very well with persistent features of it, may seem largely irrrelevant to another life or even jarring in that context. One could argue that the element that adds nuance and complexity to one life but is jarring in another is not really the same in the two cases. Perhaps so, but it remains the case that often a statement about its value that refers to the element but does not include reference to the contexts cannot plausibly claim to have transpersonal validity.

My attempt here is to provide an analysis that does justice to the respects (which many people would think obvious) in which judgements of goodness, awfulness, and so forth, are personal, while not making too much of them. There is no reason to assume that all such judgments are personal in the sense now under discussion. It may well be that some experiences that we think are awful would be awful for anyone. Also, if an environmentalist claims that in the context of the present ecology of our planet, and apart from any causal effects on human life and experiences, and so forth, it is better that there are redwood forests in California than that none exist, this presents itself as a claim to transpersonal validity, in which factors of causal relations and of context are already discounted.

It might be said, nevertheless, that such a statement is personal in the sense that it represents the point of view of a person or of a group of persons. This is a very broad sense of "personal," and one might wonder whether the statement that the earth is round (as opposed to flat) is personal in this sense. We think that the earth is round, but there are a few people who (they say) still believe that it is flat. Some would contend that these two cases are very different, in that round-earth people have a method and evidence by which they can support their claims, whereas people (like the ecologist) who make value claims lack such a method and such evidence. But to say this is to beg the question, which we will consider in later chapters, of whether axiology too has methods of inquiry and sources of evidence. It may be that the answer is "No," and that this difference is such that we can be led to speak of all value judgments as at best personal (in that there is no relevant transpersonal knowledge to be had). But no one is in a position to say this without argument. At the moment all we can say is that there are some value judgments, including that made by the ecologist, that present themselves as claimants to transpersonal validity. Other examples, including judgments of ways of life and of experiences, will be forthcoming as we proceed.

When we look at the specific remarks that people make about what seems to them to be good, awful, and so forth, nothing like a neat picture emerges. A reading of Gaus (1990) is very persuasive in moving toward this conclusion. People like or dislike things often in terms of whether they cause pleasure or displeasure; the mechanisms of pleasure or displeasure are variable enough that they would not recommend to others what they themselves find good, or perhaps they would recommend it to some people and not to others. "You might try this if you like such and such" is a common sort of remark. Even cases in which this would be said are not all alike. Perhaps the immediate subject is goodness as a means to pleasure, but one can ask also about the goodness of the pleased experience (which is not usually taken as a means to something else). People will generally regard pleasure as "nice," as a good thing; but an experience that is pleasant may be more highly recommended, even if there is some trouble in coming to have it, than other experiences that are equally pleasant. Sometimes the difference among these cases is akin to the difference between, on one hand, liking something in a way that involves admiring and appreciating it, and, on the other hand, simply liking it.

This distinction is related to the difference between saying, "X is nice, if you like that kind of thing" and "If you can manage to experience X (in some appropriate way), it is wonderful." The latter smacks more of a value judgment that is intended to have transpersonal validity even if an appropriate experience of X is not available to everyone.

It is possible to take claims to transpersonal validity as symptoms of a philosophical disease, a craving for something approximating "a view from nowhere." The roots, though, seem to go deep, into the structure of the emotions. To like, to fancy, or to desire something involves no commitment to claims about its value. We often think, of course, that what we like, fancy, or desire is (or would be) good to have or to experience. But there is no contradiction in admitting that one likes, fancies, or desires something while denying both that any value attaches to whatever it is and that much value attaches to the pleasure it gives. A similar comment applies to disliking or not caring for something. To admire or to despise or feel contempt for something is at the opposite extreme, in that it would seem contradictory to say, "I admire X but neither it nor the experience of it has much value" or "I despise X, but that's just me: I'm not saying that there is anything really wrong with it." These emotions, which are not the invention of philosophers or scientists, present themselves as incorporating transpersonal claims about value. Again, this is not to say that such claims are ever warranted; the issue remains open and will be considered in the next chapters.

# 3

# Are There Senses of Value?

A broad use of the phrase "sense of value" is as an inclination to accept certain values. I will use the phrase more narrowly, adopting a more "cognitivist" interpretation of what a sense of value would be: it would be a mode of awareness of value. Is there such a thing? One possible answer, which cannot be readily dismissed, is "No"—for the simple reason that there is nothing to sense: that is, there are no facts of what is valuable, nor are there judgments of value that are correct in some "objective" sense. Many philosophers would accept this answer, in part because it seems so difficult to construct any argument for value-facts or for objectivity of values. I will pursue this issue both in chapter 4, in an examination of arguments for holding that there can be knowledge of values, and in chapter 5, where I will consider whether there is any sense in which there are real values or certain things are really valuable.

We have already seen, in chapter 1, that there are many senses of value in the broad (and noncommittal) reading as sources of inclination to accept certain values. Why is it so tempting, despite persistent skeptical doubts, to think that there is a sense of value in our narrower (cognitivist) construal? Part of the reason is that most of us feel strongly drawn to certain beliefs about what is valuable. Indeed, we may accept these beliefs almost in spite of ourselves; and this suggests an analogy with the ways in which our five senses make us believe certain things about the physical world. Anyone who believes that there are truths about what has value must be attracted to the notion that there is something that gives us access to such truths in much the way in which the five senses give us access to truths about the physical world.

I have contended that the opening paragraphs of chapter 4 of Mill's *Utilitarianism* are to be read in terms of such an analogy, and as suggesting that desire is the value sense. We have seen reasons, though, for thinking this nomination of desire as the value sense most implausible. Here is another. The five senses not only are, at least in the general run of cases, sources of information about the physical world; they also typically present this information in a way that is saturated with intentionality and such that one has some tendency (unless there are countervailing reasons) to think, "Things are really like this." The phenomena of desire do not, by and large, present themselves so sharply and distinctively as an opening to what is really of value.

The point here is complex and has to do with degrees of similarity, and on both counts needs explanation. First of all, there are hallucinations, and there are moments when people do not have the slightest inclination to believe their senses. Hence, one needs locutions like "the general run of cases" and "typically." Even if there are hallucinations, in the great majority of cases we have reasons to think that our senses have told us something about the physical world, bearing in mind the possibility that they have told us something but we have misinterpreted it. Typically that is how sense experience presents itself, although there are special circumstances (especially when people are not in anything like a normal state of consciousness, or do not have what they would take to be a normal access to reality) when it does not. Second, to make these claims is not to discount the role of interpretation in sense experience. It certainly is not to posit a "neutral given." There are interpretative elements in even the most unreflective sense experience. One can say this without denying that usually sense experience tells us something (and presents itself as telling us something) about reality. Third, most people are, in most cases, more strongly inclined to think that something is desirable if they desire it. In that sense they take desire to provide evidence of value. The respect in which desire is not *very* like the five senses is the way in which the deliverances of the latter usually present themselves with an air of contact with what is really the case apart from us. People do not normally say, "I did not realize how good such and such was until I found myself desiring it." Occasionally, desire does present itself as a revelation of value, as when one realizes how valuable something is by missing it a great deal (and desiring that it be present). Most cases of desire, though, are not quite like that. In this respect, there are stronger candidates than desire for the designation of "sense of value": delight, for example. People do often have a sense of finding out how good something is when they delight in it.

The notion of a sense of value will seem bizarre to anyone who has in mind a very close and literal similarity with the five senses, which, after all, are physical and involve such things as nerve endings. There is no sense of value if by that one means something that has non-physical nerve endings. The verdict is less clear if one means any set of faculties or of relations to the world that function as a mode of awareness of value.

Let me spell out what is contained in this characterization of what would count as a sense of value. To function as a mode of awareness of value is not necessarily to be always, or even generally, a reliable guide to what has value: sight would count as a mode of awareness of what is visible even if most people had poor eyes and made many mistakes. But, unless the record of visual experience were very poor indeed, we would say that someone is in a better position to judge whether something is visible (or what its visual properties are) if she or he had had a relevant visual experience than if she or he had not. Similarly, any mode of awareness of value will put someone in a better position to make judgments of value than she or he would otherwise have been. Second, to be a mode of awareness is to involve, often, a sense of awareness, of an opening to that of which one might be aware. If there are senses of value, their deliverances often present themselves as awareness of value. Third, to be a mode of awareness is to yield judgments that will seem firsthand, in contrast to judgments that merely are accepted on the basis of authority. (The contrast between first- and secondhand judgments of value will be pursued later in the chapter.) Fourth, to agree that there are senses of value (in the construal under discussion) would be to accept some kind of realism about values: it is to say that some things are really valuable, and here are some ways in which we become aware of this.

To say that some ways in which we are related to values *seem* to meet the first criterion for a sense of value, and also meet the second and third criteria, is not to make a very large metaphysical claim. (The fourth criterion is a different story, which will be told in chapter 5.) Indeed, there might be room for lots of "senses." Francis Hutcheson, one of the most important of those philosophers who held that there was a moral sense, was willing to speak (for example) of a sense of honor and a sense of decency, and clearly left room for a sense of the ridiculous (Hutcheson 1728/1972, 256). Common speech assigns to most of us also a sense of humor, and this suggests a somewhat relaxed standard for what would meet the first three criteria for a sense of value.

## Senses and Emotional States

It must be stressed that at this stage, before we examine realism about values, any discussion of senses of value must be tentative. Also, we must remain firmly aware of the imperfection of the analogy with the five physical senses. There may be similarities between some of the routes we pursue to judgments of values and the ways in which the five senses lead us to judgments about the physical world, but it would be absurd to expect the analogies to be complete in every respect. Given this limitation, we can see also that there is no reason to assume that every question of the form "Does such and such qualify as a sense of value?" will admit of a clear-cut yes-or-no answer. The analogy with the deliverances of the five senses will work better (although never perfectly) for some cases of delight than for others, and better for delight generally than for desire generally, and better also for some cases of desire than for many cases of phobic fear, and so forth.

Let me suggest a generalization about the plausible candidates to be senses of value. They all will be emotional states. This answer may seem surprising, given the long (and sometimes illustrious) history of rational discussion of value. No one should deny that we sometimes can be brought to admire and cherish or delight in certain things, and to abhor others, by a dispassionate examination of the nature of things that includes a strong element of logical analysis. The point (which borrows both from Plato and Hume) is that someone who accepts an argument of this sort about what has value cannot be said really to "see" it unless she or he in the end admires, cherishes, or delights in what has been argued to be good and abhors what has been argued to be bad. Otherwise, the person who says, "X has high value" (without relevant emotional states), is merely *saying* that X has high value, without any sense of an opening to the value of X.

Before we explore the respects in which some emotional states can be senses of value, two disclaimers are in order. First, the claim is that there are significant similarities between the ways in which emotional states can seem to function as awareness of values and the ways in which the senses function as awareness of the physical world. There is no claim that the analogy is very strong; it is merely that it is not very weak. One respect, besides those previously noted, in which the analogy is imperfect is this. Types of emotional states cannot be treated as discrete modalities in the ways in which the five senses are. There is room for worries as to how, for example, the deliverances of what we desire accord (or fail to accord) with those of what we cherish or delight in; and these might seem a little like Berkeley's problem of how we synthesize the reports of different sense modalities or like Molyneux's Problem. But the separation is sharper and clearer among the modalities of the five senses, and, indeed (as we have seen), categories of emotional states can overlap.

Second, as I write the first draft of this chapter (1995), a great deal is being made of "emotional intelligence" and of education of the emotions; this amounts to an educational movement of sorts. The argument that I am about to give, that some emotional states seem strong candidates to be senses of value, is close enough to a theme of this movement that it could be taken as uncritical endorsement of what needs to be treated critically. A good deal that is positive can be said both about some emotional states as aspects of intelligence, and about education of the emotions. But it needs to be stressed that development of appropriate and sophisticated emotional responses requires an eye out on the real world, whose features provide whatever justification the emotions will have. Because of this relation to reality, some emotional responses (including those most revelatory of value) will be intelligent and others will be unintelligent. To focus on emotions apart from knowledge of the world is educationally dangerous. And if students are encouraged to be in touch with their feelings, in a way that suggests that emotions are beyond criticism, "education of the emotions" will become one more excuse for narcissism.

The most plausible candidates to be senses of value, in my view, are admiration, contempt, and abhorrence, with such emotions as delight, cherishing, and disgust not far behind. Contempt (and perhaps marginally one or two of the others) can be an attitude or an emotion; for the sake of simplicity, we will begin by looking at contempt as an emotion. People often have the experience of finding themselves feeling contemptuous of something in a way that is reflected in a value judgment. It is as if feeling contempt is a way of seeing the low value of the thing. Something like this is true of admiration and abhorrence, and often of delight, cherishing, and disgust.

There are, of course, differences among these emotions. Abhorrence usually takes as its object actions or patterns of behavior, especially those that might be subject to moral censure; although moral judgments that express abhorrence readily lead to (or incorporate) negative judgments of the value of the life that is abhorred. ("Who would want to live like that?" it might be asked.) Contempt and admiration, in contrast, are used as readily when there is no question of moral judgment as in moral cases. We can admire charm, aesthetic gifts, and a whole way of life that is based on these, while feeling contempt for, say, some people's boring, narrow attitudes. We also can experience contempt for someone's lack of moral principle, and admiration for someone who courageously carries through on a difficult moral choice. Delight, in contrast, rarely takes an object that is viewed in the context of moral judgment. This may say more about widespread human attitudes toward morality than about the logic of the concept of delight: it certainly is possible to delight in something morally positive, as when we are delighted by an unexpected example of moral virtue that gives various people their just deserts. Usually people delight in such things as loved ones, social interactions, beautiful scenes, wonderful meals, engaging music, and so forth. Often there is a sense that what one delights in, or the experience it provides one, is very fine, really good, or something of that sort: in other words, the delight involves a value judgment or construal. But often people will deny that they think there is anything especially good about either the object or their experience of it. One just happens to be delighted by such and such. Something like this is true of cherishing. The line between cases of delight or cherishing that involve value judgment or construal and those that do not is not at all sharp, in that usually someone who says, "I just happen to like, or care for, such and such," will be at least slightly inclined to regard the moments of feeling delight or of cherishing such and such as high points (or at least as moments better than most) of her or his life. Cases of disgust separate more sharply into those that do, and those that do not, involve value judgment or construal. Often we are disgusted by something in an almost instinctive or visceral way without having any inclination to regard it as having especially low value in some objective sense. An example is disgust at the fact that a cockroach had been in the now sterilized drinking glass (See Rozin et al., 1993.) But disgust can be linked to moral condemnation, as in the cases of unacceptable behavior that is extremely flagrant or inhuman; it can be linked to a negative assessment of a life, not only in the cases linked to morality, but also in cases in which someone's crude tastes and interests and sloppy style of life disgust us.

It might appear that any claim that (in some cases) emotions of the sort just discussed provide awareness of value suffers from circularity. If any awareness of value is involved, admiration, contempt, and so forth, *incorporate* it, rather than lead to it. Some cases of some of these emotional states, of course, do not contain judgment or construal of value. It is possible to cherish something without seeing it as having particularly high value, and to be disgusted by things to which one does not attribute particularly low value. But, in those cases in which the emotional states under discussion could plausibly seem to be awareness of value, the element of judgment or construal in them is clearly one of judging or construing something to have high or low value.

In weighing this objection, we need to be circumspect in the use of terms like "provides," "leads to," and "is a source of." Here is a case. Smith, who always has been hardworking and given to various forms of self-improvement, has a friend who is much more fun-loving. The friend has inherited money, and has abandoned intellectual and cultural pursuits for a life of idleness, and for gratification of her momentary urges (as long as they can be gratified almost instantly). Smith finds the idea of this alternative style of life appealing; but, after spending several days with her friend she comes, almost in spite of herself, to feel contempt for her friend's new way of life and what her friend has become. Smith thinks that she has become aware of the low value of this kind of life.

One can present the case in this way without necessarily agreeing that Smith's contempt is justified, and certainly without any claim that every intelligent or reasonable person would see the matter much as Smith comes to see it. Issues of how we sort out conflicting points of view, or of how we might justify one of them, will be taken up in later chapters. For now we are considering the way in which emotions can present themselves as openings to value, whether or not the emotions are in any sense justified and whether or not there are real values to be aware of.

Now (to return to the circularity objection) it will be said that Smith already judges her friend's life to be of low value (or "sees" it in this way) if she is to feel contempt, and, hence, it is nonsense to regard the emotion of contempt as providing some awareness of low value. This much must be conceded: if emotions provide or lead to value judgments, "provide" or "lead to" cannot be understood in a way that requires temporal priority. From this it can be argued, further, that there is no question of a general requirement of causal priority. Let us concede all this. The claim instead is this: the process of Smith's arriving at what she takes to be awareness of the low value of a certain kind of life is an emotional process. She "sees" (she thinks) the low value of the life because she has come to feel contempt for it. The "because" in the previous sentence should be taken as an enabling, rather than a causal, "because."

The force of the enabling "because" becomes clearer if we bear in mind that what we are talking about is not the formation of a value judgment ("That kind of life has low value") per se, but rather the formation of such a value judgment in a way that presents itself as realizing, becoming aware of, or "seeing" its correctness. The cases with which we are concerned can be contrasted with, say, Smith's being hypnotized and told, as a posthypnotic suggestion, that she is always to assent to the proposition "Lives of idleness and instant gratification have low value" and to any propositions that it implies, and with the case in which Smith comes to assent to the proposition because her parents and teachers drummed it into her.

Smith's contempt enables her not only to think or say, "Lives of this sort have low value," but also (at least in most cases) to be attentive to features of her friend's life that might be used to justify such a judgment, and to regard these as salient. Further, the motivational component that will be included in the contempt (we are precluding any hard-to-imagine case of contempt that is merely sentimental) typically will amount to a degree of commitment not to have a life like that of her friend. The sense of having seen for oneself the low value of such a life will strengthen any inclination to regard this as one's own autonomous choice. In some cases, in which what presents itself as a realization of value is especially forceful, so that people say, "It hit me between the eyes," the degree of commitment and the sense of having found one's own way will be especially strong.

All of this falls under the heading of how emotions can enable us to have a sense of value, if there are such things as senses of value. Sometimes, though, there are temporal as well as structural relations that can be explored. The process of having a full-blown emotion may proceed by stages. Someone may begin by having feelings that are so non-specific and separate (as yet) from judgments, construals, or motivation that no one would speak of them as emotions or elements of emotions. Smith may begin by having vague feelings of unease while she is with her friend. Similarly, she may begin by "feeling good," in a general sort of way, in the presence of something or someone that she comes to cherish or admire. Even if emotions typically include an element of feeling, there are feelings that are simply feelings. One can feel (the emotions of) contempt, disgust, anger, or fear; but also one can simply feel bad, or feel uncomfortable. Often we are in the dark about what causes our feelings, and they also will lack intentionality. If someone asks us what they "are about," it will be far from clear that they are about anything.

Feeling unease in the presence of a friend can admit of a huge variety of explanations, most of them having little or nothing to do with value. Still, persistent negative (or positive) feelings can seem to function as clues, indicating that perhaps something is really wrong (or right). This kind of thought has to be viewed with caution. At the root of vague feelings there may be what amounts merely to prejudice, or bad (or good) "chemistry," rather than anything that calls for a value judgment. Smith can assess her initial feelings of unease by trying to notice when they are strongest, and also by trying to focus on features of her situation to which she finds herself responding. A real perceptual and analytical effort can lead to a conclusion that "What really bothers me is . . . ," and it may make sense to identify the cause and the object of the feelings. At this point intentionality is in play, and the judgment or construal that it involves will normally be accompanied by a motivational factor. Smith has moved from mere feeling to emotion, in the process arriving at a sense that a certain kind of life has low value.

In cases of this sort, the early stages of the emotional process do have a causal role in the eventual formation of a judgment of value. But it is important to bear in mind that there are other cases in which almost all of the initial work is done by empirical investigation, logical analysis, and rational argument. Many cases are still different from both these groups, in that it is not plausible to view the development of the emotion in terms of a process in which there are early preemotion stages (either of inchoate feeling, or of empirical investigation, etc.); rather, the emotion seems simply to emerge full-blown. The circularity objection is disarmed in relation to these cases by understanding them as ones in which the elements of emotion together (including value judgment or construal) enable one to have a judgment of value of a special sort: that presents itself as an awareness of value.

It should be added that something like the circularity objection could also be brought against the claim that the deliverances of the five senses provide awareness of the physical world. On one hand, these deliverances are sometimes highly misleading. But when they are reliable, it could be argued that the awareness of the physical world is already contained in them, rather than being provided by them. Descartes, in effect, tries to drive a wedge between sense experience, on one hand, and awareness of the physical world, on the other, by distinguishing between ideas (which the senses give us) and judgments (in arriving at which our free will plays a role). Many philosophers have regarded this as too sharp a contrast, as underestimating the active and interpretative elements in sense experience. It also overlooks the way in which we may be, in much sense experience, "nearly there" in relation to a judgment of the reality of what we seem to experience. In much this way, when Smith feels contempt for her friend's life, she is "nearly there" in relation to a judgment that such a life has low value. She is so nearly there, that the value judgment may be taken as implicit in the emotion of contempt, much as your judgment that you have hands may be taken as implicit in your visual experience as you hold them in front of you.

The contrast between what we would be inclined to think of as firsthand, and as secondhand, judgment is not as sharp and as clear, either in relation to values or to the physical world, as we might like. An element of interpretation, which includes both the way in which we work with a repertoire of categories and also the way in which the field of what is experienced is arranged and demarcated, is found in both cases. What might seem an immediate revelation is filtered and prestructured. In addition, there is considerable psychological evidence that sense experience is suggestible (see Asch 1952, 450 ff.). It is notorious that what people think they "see" of values is highly suggestible, having a great deal to do in particular with early education. Philosophers are more often tempted to put down suggestibility as the whole story in relation to (what presents itself as) experience of values than in relation to sense experience. But incidents in which people undergo something like conversions in their values, claiming now to appreciate the value of what they had always been told was worthless, or to see the low value of what they had always been encouraged to want, suggest that this represents an attempt to ignore a problem area by means of quick overgeneralization.

We are most inclined to regard judgments of the physical world as firsthand when they seem to result from looking, tasting, smelling, hearing, or touching something without very strong influence of preconceptions on the report of what is then experienced. A very quick look, after which someone reports pretty much what he or she had expected to see, may not always seem to yield a judgment that we would consider firsthand. There will be, of course, many cases about which we will not be sure what to say, some of them appearing to be borderline cases. Much the same picture, to a degree, emerges in relation to emotional states such as admiration, contempt, and so forth, as sources of values. Perhaps there will be fewer instances of what looks clearly like firsthand judgment of value, if we bear in mind the childhood indoctrination that lies in the background of most people's experience. But, if we also bear in mind the account that some philosophers of science (see Kuhn 1963) have given of the ways in which holders of established scientific theories can resist new data, we will not overdraw the contrast in these respects between judgments of the physical world and judgments of value.

## Attitudes and Moods

Emotions come and go, and we normally expect some degree of stability in the sorts of value judgments that a person makes. Emotional states include not only such things as fear, hate, delight, and sadness, which we readily classify as emotions, but also moods and some attitudes. In addition, there are such states as suffering and long-term and global happiness and bliss, which are very difficult to classify but certainly yield occurrent emotions. It is natural to suppose that some of these states have a close relation to people's judgments of value, and, indeed (as we have seen), Charles Stevenson keyed ethical judgments in general to attitudes rather than to emotions.

Often what begins as an emotion becomes entrenched as an attitude. Smith will arrive at her contempt for a life of instant gratification (and at the judgment of low value that expresses this contempt) by feeling contempt, but over time her contempt may well become mainly a disposition to make negative comments and negative choices in appropriate contexts. We would certainly then speak of her attitude of contempt. As Urmson pointed out in his commentary on Stevenson, attitudes often do not involve emotion at all. It is barely imaginable that, over time, Smith's attitude will manifest itself entirely in negative comments and choices, without any occurrent emotions, although in the entire absence of occurrent emotions we would, I think, hesitate to use as strong a word as "contempt."

Arguably the transition just sketched, from emotion (perhaps with a sense of discovery) to an attitude that typically involves some occurrent emotions, is a frequent pattern in people's emotional lives. One example might be the course of "true love," although the opening stages are so dramatic that people tend to speak of love at any stage as an emotion and never as an attitude. Being in love on a long-term basis typically has its own network, deep and complex, of subtle emotions; but these will not be the agreeable shock to the system that falling in love is. Falling in contempt (so to speak) similarly can be much more dramatic, and seem much more revelatory, than a long-term attitude of contempt.

What is most dramatic and revelatory need not be most important. Ethical life requires strongly entrenched attitudes. We need to count on other people, and they need to count on us; and even in those areas that seem most personal and least subject to moral or social disapproval, someone whose values fluctuate is not likely to have a sense of a successful and coherent life. Therefore, any account of how people make ethical judgments that they will stand by, and of how they become responsible moral agents and pursue happiness, will emphasize attitudes more than it does occurrent emotions.

Our present inquiry, though, is into the ways in which people might think that they are discovering for themselves the correctness of judgments of value. Emotions come to the forefront in this story. It will look at first as if attitudes, even those that involve emotions, play a relatively small part. There may be occasional cases like the following. Smith realizes that for years she has had an attitude of resentment toward people like Bloggs, who engage in long pointless conversations; and it comes to her that there really is something lacking in a life (like Bloggs's) that centers on such things. This is not quite the experience of direct contact, of an opening to something that presents itself as really the case, that we encountered in the earlier case of Smith's contempt for her idle friend. But people do sometimes say, "I now realize that my attitude of such and such was telling me something," and they may have a sense of access to what is really the case, although the access would be protracted and indirect rather than immediate and direct. Sometimes, also, people think that their attitudes tell them something about values that they already had known, serving as reminders of what they had come to judge earlier. In these cases there is a sense of renewed access to what really has high, or low, value. It is like revisiting a familiar scene and confirming one's sense of its features.

Moods similarly can provide a sense of access. Usually, of course, good moods and bad moods will seem (as Gilbert Ryle said) like the weather; and they will seem similarly unenlightening about anything beyond themselves. But sometimes moods will seem to point beyond themselves to the goodness or badness of conditions with which they are associated: this is especially common in the cases of exhilaration or euphoria as a mood, or depression as a mood.

Here is one reason why moods and attitudes sometimes can loom large as sources of judgments of value, and can seem to provide a veiled sort of access to what has high or low value. This is that many of the features of people's lives and of the world that, in the end, we may come to think have significantly great (or little, or negative) value are difficult to focus upon at first, largely because it is difficult to articulate what is important about them. This difficulty is especially common in personal relations or in the adjustment to a culture or a society. It can be hard to say what it is that rubs you the wrong way, or just what it is that makes you so depressed after you have been with Bloggs. Many people become quite adroit at staying on the right side of rules of propriety, including moral rules, while cumulatively having both a low quality of life and a rather distressing effect on that of those who spend a lot of time with them. It is easy to ignore, or to dismiss as an illusion, what one lacks words for. This is one reason that moods of depression or exhilaration, especially when there is a pattern of them, or inchoate feelings of unease or well-being, sometimes (although by no means always) can be taken as revelatory of value.

Suffering and happiness or bliss of the global kind also can be taken as revelatory of value. Such states, of course, always incorporate judgments or construals of value. To suffer is, among other things, to see one's life or what one presently has as being of very low or negative value. It is to do this in a context in which one also feels very bad, there is a sense of limited (or no) control over what bothers one, and there is no end in sight. In some cases, though, the value construal or judgment is actually prior to the suffering. Someone begins by hating her or his life, develops a sense of powerlessness about it, and settles into a state of suffering. Even in cases in which a value construal or judgment is not prior to suffering, it can seem so obvious or automatic that we would not normally think of the suffering as revelatory of value. Someone whose body is horribly mangled in an accident, for example, will be unlikely to seem to discover anything new about value.

The cases in which suffering or global happiness or bliss will seem to provide an opening to value will all be ones in which there is an element of surprise, or at least of not being prepared for the reality that such and such would involve suffering, happiness, or bliss (or for the degree of suffering, happiness, etc.). A struggling artist tries out a well-paid career of office work, and after a while is surprised at how unhappy she is. A previously successful person sinks into poverty, develops a series of painful medical problems, and thinks that this kind of life is even more awful than one would have expected.

The great axiological novels of the eighteenth century, *Candide* and *Rasselas*, are about the awareness of value as it might develop in the context of a search for happiness. Without assuming that everyone who is happy has in fact a very good life, one can think that we often learn a lot about value by finding out what will make us happy and what fails to do this. Many of the things that, in advance, seem likely to make us happy turn out to be lacking in various respects. Lack of happiness can be as revelatory of value as happiness.

To make this statement postpones a number of difficult questions. There is the metaphysical question of whether there is something like a value reality to which emotional states sometimes give us access. If they do give us access to something of this sort, how does it happen: what is the connection between the values and us? Also, it is easy to be struck by the great variability in the value judgments that express what people think they are aware of. Perhaps they do not have access to the same realm of values? In some cases, like that of the struggling artist who becomes an office worker, it may be that values that are revealed are in some sense personal. But we have still not become clear about what sense this might be. Can intelligence (or something like it) be a significant factor in what seems like awareness of value? We have seen that the most dramatic (seeming) openings to value are those provided by (some) occurrent emotions. But we need to explore whether, and how, something like intelligence might function in having these emotions.

# 4

# Knowledge of Values

To speak of knowledge of values is to claim that there are cases in which a judgment of value is not mere opinion. The difference between knowledge and opinion has been a subject of philosophical investigation for more than two thousand years, and the investigation has intensified in the last few decades. Many philosophers agree that there are three criteria for what counts as knowledge, as opposed to opinion: (1) that there be confidence in what is believed, or at least that it not be thought of as a guess or an offhand estimate, (2) that someone who has knowledge be indeed in a position to be confident (e.g. have very good evidence, or very good reasons, or a clear view as an eyewitness); and (3) that what is believed in fact is true, correct, or right. My statements of the first two criteria are not intended to be at all precise, in part because there have been great difficulties in arriving at exception-proof, moderately precise statements of these criteria. Indeed, even in the loose formulations just provided, they have problems. What of someone who does not think he knows the capital of Nevada, and when pressed says "Carson City," which is the right answer? There is not much confidence there; and yet we sometimes say, "You knew that all along" , especially when the subject's record of correct answers in such matters is very good, and especially if he had just looked at a map of Nevada on which the state capital is highlighted. Criterion 2 needs adjustment in order to deal with puzzle cases in which someone has what we would normally consider extremely good evidence for believing that P, but in which unbeknownst to that person the evidence is (in some freakish way) misleading in that it is disconnected from whether P is true or not, but in which P turns out to be true after all. In these cases, sometimes referred to by the name of the philosopher (Gettier) who first discussed them, the subject gets the right answer not as any kind of rational achievement, but by luck. We do tend to say, "In the light of the way in which your evidence was in fact disconnected from the truth of P, you didn't really know P." Perhaps criterion 2 should be amended by adding the proviso that the correct answer not be gotten by luck, although this is not nearly precise enough to satisfy most philosophers who have worked on these problems. The philosophical literature on this subject has all of the fascination of lost causes. Why, one wonders, should there be any assumption that a key term in a natural language, namely "knowledge," can be explicated in a moderately precise set of necessary and sufficient conditions?

In what follows I will not make any such assumption. The words "knowledge" and "knows" are used in a variety of ways. My concern will be with a central use in which typically to ascribe knowledge to X says something about the degree of confidence that X has or ought to have, and usually says something to the effect that this confidence is merited in some way that connects X to the truth or rightness of what X knows. A good way of putting some of this is to say that if X knows P, then it is (in the general run of cases) because of experience, reasons, evidence, or whatever else that put X in a better position to make judgments about P than X otherwise would have been. There is finally a third criterion, something about the truth, correctness, or rightness of what is known. The shape that this should assume in relation to values is one of the things that will be discussed in the next chapter. In order not to clutter this chapter with constant qualifications, let me say now that its subject is what *would* be knowledge of values *if* the third criterion (in some form) is met. The reader should bear in mind the tentativeness that this entails.

## Knowing That Pain Is Bad

It may seem obvious that, if anything is generally known about values, it is that pain is bad (i.e., in itself undesirable). It may not surprise the reader, though, that even this assumption is open to question. I will survey objections, beginning with one that would occur only to philosophers, and moving on to some that are rooted in practices of a culture or subculture.

Knowing that pain is bad might seem like knowing that one is in pain, both because the subject is pain and because of the immediacy. Some philosophers, though, most notably Wittgenstein (1953, no. 246, 89), have denied that it is appropriate to speak of knowledge that one is in pain. Knowledge is an achievement, which presupposes the possibility of failure; but how could someone be wrong about whether she or he is in pain? Many people would say that it is similarly impossible to go wrong about whether pain is bad, and thereby would concede that any objection to claims to knowledge that one is in pain would apply with equal force to claims that we know that pain is bad.

On the other hand, the two cases are not entirely similar. People do not normally hesitate about whether they are in pain. But many might hesitate about whether slight pains or even moderate pains, say those endured as part of long distance runs, really are bad. In some contexts, perhaps, they play a part in and contribute to an appealing experience. There is an instinctive tendency to avoid pain, it will be said; but what does that prove about the intrinsic undesirability of these minor pains, especially in the context of a gratifying sense of fitness to which they may add piquancy? Probably, though, virtually everyone—at least in our culture—would agree that excruciating pain is bad, and that anyone who had experienced such pain would not hesitate to say either whether it was present or that it was a very bad thing indeed.

Not everyone would agree. A sense that even great pain does not have the significant negative value that most of us would ascribe to it seems to be at work in traditions found both within the samurai class in Japan and among some American Indian tribes. These include the infliction of pain on others in ways that horrify outsiders, but they include also self-infliction of extreme pain. Sitting Bull missed the battle of Little Big Horn, at which Custer and his men were killed, because he had not yet recovered from self-inflicted wounds to his arms and could not fight. The predilection of samurai for the very most painful mode of suicide is well known. One needs to be hesitant in reading opinions into practices; however, these practices suggest a view either that great pain is not as bad as most people think it is (and perhaps, in certain contexts, is not bad at all), or alternatively that even if it is bad there are some things (such as courage or self-control) that are more important. If the view is the latter, then great pain might be sought as a means to the greater goods involved in enduring the pain. If it is the former, then in certain unusual cases great pain could be held to play a positive role in something that has a value that most of us would not appreciate.

Here is a clearer objection to the claim that pain is bad. It is that we think that pain is bad because, especially when it is great and continues, it is associated with suffering. But what is bad is the suffering, and it may be a confusion on our part to think that the pain in itself is bad.

Some traditions, notably that of Buddhism, draw a sharp distinction between pain and suffering. A value premise of Buddhist thought is that suffering is bad: this is treated as so obvious, as a judgment so inherent in the experience of suffering, that it would not be surprising if some Buddhists denied (in the spirit of Wittgenstein) that the badness of suffering is something that we can be said to know. Buddhism is often presented as therapy that enables people to avoid suffering. The realities of sickness, old age, and death are such that pain is inescapable; but, the Buddhists contend, someone who no longer believes in a substantial self, and thanks to that has lost all desires, need never suffer. (The reader should bear in mind here the narrow sense of "desire" discussed in chapter 2. The sense in which Buddhists hold that one does not have a self also is not as straightforward as it might appear [see Kupperman 1991, chapter 2].)

In Buddhist texts this is often presented, in the way in which philosophical arguments are often presented, in an abstract and schematic form. There are ample indications, though, that the loss of desires, along with immunity to suffering, are less matters of a single, immediate decision than they might sound. Instead they require a lengthy and demanding progression of self-discipline. An illustration of how this might work in the end is the story Alexandra David-Neel (1929/1971, 16) tells of a Buddhist monk who was knifed by a disciple who stole the temple money he was carrying. The dying man, who was in great pain, cut short questioning; he preferred not to suffer, and wanted to control his thoughts by maintaining a meditative state. Self-discipline and concentration, in short, can sever the usual link between pain and suffering. This may seem exotic, but much of the childbirth training given to expectant mothers centers on a similar idea. The point is not only that mental discipline makes a difference. It is also that a sense of control makes a difference, in that suffering (as was noted in the last chapter) is at home in cases in which someone feels a lack of control over what bothers her or him.

Let us look more closely at the Buddhist attitude toward pain, so that we can see whether (1) it gives room for plausible doubt about the claim that pain is in itself bad, or (2) suggests that this should be replaced by a more qualified claim. Serious Buddhists are very scrupulous about inflicting pain on any living thing. They may choose to avoid experiencing various pains themselves, where this is feasible; but rarely is there a strenuous avoidance of pain, and the care in avoiding pain may seem less than the care in not inflicting pain on others. One factor in this distinction between pain-for-others and pain-for-oneself surely is the link with suffering: after all, pain involves suffering for the great majority of human beings and all other animals, but not (it is held) for someone with a prepared mind. Perhaps their view is that pain is in itself bad if and only if it is accompanied by suffering. Alternatively it may be that pain merely is bad (for most people and all animals) as a means (to suffering, which is intrinsically bad).

It certainly is possible to hold that what is (in itself) bad in all this is suffering, and that the view that pain is in itself bad is a superstition about value. A Buddhist philosopher might agree that we are "hardwired" to think that pain is in itself bad, but hold that this is a mistake that an intelligent and disciplined person can come to see through in the process of overcoming the value tendencies of normal human nature (as a way of overcoming the normal human condition of life that is full of suffering). This is a possible view; but I do not think that it is the most plausible construal, even within a Buddhist framework, of most people's experiences of pain — especially of great and continuing pain. When the ordinary undisciplined person or animal experiences pain, and suffers, what will seem awful in the experience is in large part the pain. Thus, the most reasonable way of putting the Buddhist view is not as the claim that pain is bad only as a means to suffering, but rather as the claim that pain need not be bad; that it is in itself bad only in the context of an unprepared mind that will suffer.

This is a construal both of what most people's immediate experience seems to tell them, and also of how it would best be incorporated within a Buddhist framework. If this is accepted, and if further we think that Buddhists are right that even great pain need not be (in itself) bad, then we can replace the claim that pain is in itself bad by a qualified claim. This is (1) that pain is usually in itself bad, and (2) that great pain is almost always in itself bad. This qualified claim is consistent with the tendency of people like long-distance runners to say that their minor pains do not seem (even in themselves) undesirable, with Buddhist claims that even great pain is not bad for someone with a prepared mind, and with assertions that might be made by people who have undergone self-inflicted extreme pain or are about to commit hari kiri that great pain can have (in the context of great mental discipline) positive value. The reply is that even minor pains are not like this for most of us most of the time, and that great pains especially are not like this (and are highly undesirable) in the context of the lives of the great majority.

This shows how claims that pain is itself bad can be qualified and protected. However, we have not seen a telling argument that pain (especially great pain) is intrinsically undesirable. It is just that virtually everyone regards it as obvious. The possible objections that were canvassed, though, show that the answer need not be regarded as obvious. One positive result is that this strengthens the case for saying that, *if* pain is bad, it could make sense to speak of people as knowing it. But it leaves the question of *how* they would know it.

Perhaps the answer is that, if there is knowledge that pain (some pain, anyway) is bad, this is not arrived at by argument or reasoning. The second criterion for knowledge (as opposed to opinion) had to do with being in a position to be confident of one's judgment. In some cases reasoning or evidence will put some-one in such a position. But there are other cases, as when someone is an eyewitness with good eyes and a clear view, in which a claim to knowledge will rely neither on reasoning nor on one's having weighed evidence. Smith simply knows what happened on that day because "I was there, and I saw it." Could Smith know that pain is (generally speaking) in itself undesirable in a comparable way?

If the answer is "Yes," then one of the differences between knowing that pain is bad, on one hand, and most knowledge based on direct experience, on the other hand, is simply that the experiences relevant to a judgment of the badness of pain are very widely shared, whereas the experience that puts Smith in a good position to say what happened on that day may well be unique or virtually unique. Knowl-edge that pain is bad would then seem to be as universal as any knowledge of value one could imagine.

If we look at the way in which we ordinarily discuss judgments of value (and we continue to put to the side issues concerning realism), it does seem that rele-vant experience often confers a warrant, in that we commonly think that someone is in a better position to make a judgment of value if she or he has had relevant experiences than would otherwise be the case. Someone who characterizes a week-end of uninterrupted sensory deprivation as awful (to take a simple and easy ex-ample) is especially likely to be listened to if she or he has had the experience. There are complications of a number of sorts in less simple and easy cases, which we will consider shortly; the point for now is that experiences that enable someone to say, "I know what it is like," also place that person in a stronger position to be confident of judgments of value. In the case of pain, virtually all of us know what it is like. This, rather than argument or evidence, is what supports the claim that virtually everyone knows that pain is (generally) bad.

The argument that experience can put someone in a position to be confident of a judgment of value should be put in a larger picture. I will argue later that, in some cases, other people's testimony reasonably can substitute for personal experience. On the other hand, a second element is required for the relevant experience to be experience *of* value: an appropriate construal of what is experi-enced (e.g., as awful, admirable, wonderful, etc.). In most (but not—as we will see in chapter 5—in all) cases this construal will be part of an emotional state that informs one's own (or another person's reported) experience; and usually we will think that someone is in a good position to be confident only if the construal is part of what seems an appropriate emotional state. A value judgment that is based on relevant personal experience and on a related emotional state that one arrives at on one's own (instead of its being merely the result of indoctrination) can seem firsthand and a kind of witnessing. This will still leave open the question of whether the emotional state is justified or appropriate: witnesses do make mistakes.

The case of pain, however, is one in which there is widespread agreement that, in the context of most people's lives, emotional responses of wanting to avoid pain are appropriate. If we are willing to treat this as obvious, then the claim of near universal knowledge (that pain is generally in itself of negative value) seems to have strong support indeed, and to be extremely plausible. Much the same assessment applies to the variant claim that great pain is almost always in itself bad. Not everyone can say, "Look; I've experienced great pain, and I can tell you it was awful"; but those of us who have not had the relevant experience generally take the word of those who have.

Strong support, however, is not proof. It is not only value anti-realists, along perhaps with a few fringe Wittgensteinians and Buddhists, who would dispute these claims to near universal knowledge. There is room for a general skepticism about judgments of value. Even if some form of value realism turns out to be warranted, it may be that our access to real values is so unreliable, so suggestible or controlled by hardwired animal instincts, that there are rarely or never strong grounds for confidence in judgments of value. In one way, this skeptical response is least plausible in relation to widely accepted value judgments about pain, simply be-cause of the experiences accompanied by near consensus that support them. On the other hand, there is room for the suggestion that these judgments cannot be taken seriously because they merely reflect something hardwired into human na-ture (which, however, thoughtful people can largely overcome). It is not entirely clear to me how we are to evaluate either this skeptical suggestion, or the opposing claim that analysis of the criteria of what counts as "truth" leads to the idea that what we are predetermined to think true must be true (in that our word "true" has meaning only within the framework of human thought). In the absence of (as it seems to me) compelling arguments on either the general skeptical side or the staunchly anti-skeptical side, we are left with a sense that there is room for skep-ticism about judgments of value, but that the skeptical response may be least plausible in relation to widely shared judgments about pain.

Are there other judgments of value that have similar claims to be widely known? One candidate might be the judgment that suffering is bad. This judgment needs to be approached with caution, for a number of reasons.

One is that it may seem close to being tautologous, in that X is not suffering unless X is experiencing his or her state as in itself undesirable. Because of this, there is room (as already has been noted) for an argument that it does not make sense to speak of knowing that suffering is bad, in that this is hardly something one could go wrong about. However, one's own suffering and the suffering of others represent distinct cases. There is a contradiction if Bloggs says, "I am suf-fering but in itself it is not undesirable," in that the person who suffers must take the experience as in itself undesirable. But it may be that there is no contradiction in saying, "You are suffering (hence you are taking your experience as in itself undesirable), but I doubt that it is in itself undesirable (even if your negative attitude is included in the psychic state to be evaluated)."

Second, whether there is ever any plausibility in saying that someone is suffering but it is in itself not undesirable, it is often plausible to speak of a particular episode of suffering as good as a means. It was a commonplace among romanticists that suffering can be conducive to creativity, especially among artists, poets, and composers. Beethoven was as great as he was, in this view, because of the ways in which he had suffered and in which the suffering then found expression in his music. Nietzsche's often-quoted praise of suffering I think can be interpreted in this way. But one does not have to be a romanticist, or to be referring principally to the lives of creative individuals, to think that it is in general undesirable for someone never to have suffered. This judgment—that virtually any adult would be better off if she or he had at some point suffered—might be interpreted as a positive judgment of the intrinsic value of suffering (at least of limited episodes of suffering) within the larger context of an entire life. But this, I think, would be a misinterpretation. To the extent that it is plausible to claim that it is in general undesirable never to have suffered, this is because of the ways in which having suffered gives one a sense both of what it is like to suffer (thus being conducive to compassion) and of the vicissitudes of life (thus being conducive to personal strength and resilience). Suffering, from this point of view, can be good as a means for almost anyone. It should be added, though, that even if suffering can have these benefits, they usually do not require much suffering, and that it is highly arguable that most of the suffering that human beings endure in their lives has no redeeming features. The case for deploring animal suffering is, if anything, even stronger, in that it is hardly ever plausible to say that suffering brings benefits to an animal.

Third, there are the cases of miscreants, who many of us might judge deserve to suffer. Is their suffering good as a means? One might say this, if one thought of deserved suffering as a form of rehabilitation or ascribed to it other utilities. But there is no contradiction if someone expresses extreme skepticism about the prospects of rehabilitation and of other utilities caused by someone's suffering, but still maintains that it is better that the miscreant suffer than not suffer. To say this is not to talk about suffering as good as a means; it is to talk about suffering as good in the context of a social order.

Fourth, we need to distinguish between the claim that suffering is bad, as a general claim (either unlimited or limited as to context) made in the abstract, and claims about the badness of suffering that have to be understood as about the badness of *this* experience (and ones like it) that one places under the heading of suffering. Someone who had never before really suffered might discover just how awful it can be by having an experience that would be labeled one of suffering.

This last point seems to me to provide clear cases in which someone could claim to be in a good position to make judgments. To have had relevant experiences that would be generally considered to amount to suffering gives someone warrant to say, "Take my word for it; it is really awful." The possible Wittgensteinian response that there is no knowledge here, because there is no chance of going wrong and hence no achievement, is undermined by the fact that the relevant question is not only "Is it bad?" but also "How bad is it?" There can be a sense of discovery in the experience of the suffering, along with an apparent realization that previously one had underestimated the badness of at least some forms of suffering.

This possibility can be contrasted with the general judgments in the abstract of the badness of suffering, particularly in relation to the issue of whether the suffering of miscreants can be (if considered in the broad context of a just society) good in itself. No one should deny that there are important questions here, with ramifications not only for retributivism as a philosophical view of punishment, but also for practical policies within a criminal justice system. The position one takes, if widely accepted, could change the lives of convicted criminals. Nevertheless, this sense of the importance of the issue is consistent with general skepticism of claims to know the right answer: either as made by "hardliners" who think that deserved suffering can be (within an appropriate social context) good in itself, or by "softliners" who think that it can never be. Admittedly, there are arguments on both sides, but this fact does not entail that any of them is compelling or provides a warrant for great confidence. The relation to experience that we found in the case of the person who discovers how awful certain forms of suffering are appears to be lacking in these cases. Everyone would agree that the immediate experience of suffering is one that no one, even a convicted criminal, should want to have for its own sake. That is, within the restricted context of an individual life we can agree that suffering is in itself bad. But the issue we are discussing concerns the value (positive or negative) of deserved suffering within a much larger context, and can be settled only by comparative evaluations of societies in which such suffering is—or is not—inflicted beyond the point at which it might be justified as a means to various desirable consequences. One can certainly have relevant experiences of having lived in such societies. But the experiences are likely to have at best a highly tangential relation to the issue at hand, and as a result there does appear to be a great deal of room for axiological and political agnosticism on this issue.

Finally, let us look at another strong claimant to the status of something that we know about value: that bliss is in itself desirable. As a general claim this is a stronger candidate than similar propositions about the value of pleasure or of happiness. This is because bliss, unlike pleasure, does not take an object. When the hedonist claims that pleasure is always good, there is room for the objection that the value of pleasure very much depends on what someone is pleased about or by. Happiness of the global and diffuse sort does not take an object; but even so, it typically involves episodes of being happy about various things, and furthermore presupposes a moderately positive evaluation of what one is. We may hesitate to praise or even envy the happiness of a highly smug villain whose happy state is based on enjoyment of acts of sadistic villainy. Bliss, whoever experiences it, is not subject to such colorations.

There is room here, too, for the objection that there cannot be knowledge that bliss is good because the proposition is a truism, and for the reply that there are instances in which someone discovers, as a matter of personal experience, just how good bliss can be (thus perhaps revising a previous estimate and arriving at a judgment that does not look entirely like a truism). One difference between bliss, on one hand, and pain (and probably suffering), on the other, is that most of us have not experienced it. People who have experienced bliss are, by normal standards, in an especially good position to judge its value.

What about the rest of us? This is to inquire whether in matters of value, as in matters of sense experience, other people's testimony can put one in a good position to make a judgment. There is no general answer that is highly plausible. Even in matters of sense experience, we distinguish between trained and untrained observers, between people who are alert and clearheaded and people who are not, and perhaps in general between people who are trustworthy and people who are not. Distinctions of this sort can loom large in some cases (when what might have been witnessed was complex or subtle or simply not that easy to see) and not in others (e.g., a murder committed on an uncrowded street in broad daylight). Similarly, as we shall see, there is more room for skeptical treatment of testimony as to values in some cases than in others.

Bliss, along with pain and suffering, seems to be at the lower end of the scale here. That is, there is considerable consensus among those who have experienced bliss. It would seem odd to suggest that there are some types of people who are ill-equipped to appreciate bliss or to see through it critically. There may well be some who are ill-equipped to experience bliss, but that is a different matter. Because of all of this, it seems reasonable to allow the testimony of those who have experienced bliss to stand in for personal experience, and to ground confidence that bliss is generally in itself of high value.

## Knowing That the Contemplative Life Is Good

By the contemplative life I mean the one praised most highly by Aristotle in the *Nicomachean Ethics*. Many elements are relevant, in Aristotle's account, to the eudaemonia of such a life. But the exercise of intellectual virtues, of inherent human rationality, in contexts separate from those of practical decision, is most highly emphasized: hence the label "contemplative."

Our concern here is with (putative) knowledge. Could anyone be said to know that the contemplative life is in itself very good? If so, how? Aristotle clearly would answer, "Yes," to the first of these questions. His answer to the second is not so clear. On one hand, there are well-known arguments for the contemplative life, having to do with its close connection with the rationality that is the essence of human nature, and with the fact that it is (among the kinds of life of which we are capable) closest to what we imagine the life of the gods to be. Are these arguments the source of confidence that we can have knowledge, rather than mere opinion, about the excellence of the contemplative life?

It may well be that Aristotle thought so. Let us grant that there are many branches of knowledge, including both the natural and social sciences, in which someone can be in a position to be confident of a judgment (and to have knowledge of its correctness) on the basis of having produced or thoughtfully accepted an appropriate and cogent argument. Argument also can play a major role in our position to be confident of some moral claims, although that does not mean necessarily that it has an entirely similar role in relation to values.

Aristotle's arguments about value do not appear all that strong. It is far from clear that the privileged value of the contemplative life follows from the rationality of human nature: the fact that almost all humans have some degree of rationality could be used to argue merely that any acceptable human life requires some degree of rationality. The thought experiment of asking what the life of the gods would be like is a good way of getting us to think what life we would choose if we had great powers and very few obstacles, but not everyone would answer this in the same way. The answers passed down by Homer are not very much like Aristotle's.

Two other lines of thought in the *Nicomachean Ethics* are relevant to the issue of how the claim made for the contemplative life might be warranted. Aristotle's dialectic requires him to canvass rival views. He considers hedonism, which he attributes to the common people, and also the widespread opinion of the better sort that what matters most in life is one's reputation. In each case he has an argument against the rival view. What is presented as an argument against hedonism might at first look more like an insult: this is a view suitable for cattle (book I, 5., 1095b). (We will come back to this shortly.) The argument that follows against the opinion of the better sort is more intriguing. Reputation is all well and good, but it is not entirely within one's control; the suggestion is that a false rumor or a misleading appearance could destroy someone's reputation regardless of his or her desert. Therefore, it cannot be the highest good.

There is something appealing in the assumption that the highest goods in life must be within one's control, and will not be subject to luck. It appeals not only because we like the sense of control over our lives, but also because it is close enough to a maxim of prudence to be mistaken for it. This is that the attractiveness of what we cannot control (and hence is subject to risk) should be discounted when we decide what to seek. Suppose for the sake of argument that an excellent reputation would be worth 10 eudaemonia units in Bloggs's life and that Bloggs, instead of pursuing "that bauble, reputation," could devote his energies instead to achieving a heightened exercise of his intellectual virtues, which will be worth 6 units and is entirely within his control. Suppose also that there is a 50 percent chance that Bloggs's search for an excellent reputation will miscarry, because of the efforts of his rivals or the prurient interest of the media. Then we should advise Bloggs to pursue heightened exercise of his intellectual virtues (yield, 6 units) rather than the excellent reputation (average expected yield, half of 10 units). But this does not mean that the excellent reputation, assuming one gets it and keeps it, is not worth more than the heightened exercise of intellectual virtues.

Some other argument is needed. Further, Aristotle is not in the best possible position to use an argument that counts its vulnerability against an ideal. This is because the package that he endorses as the highest degree of eudaemonia assigns some modest weight to elements other than exercise of virtues: for example, the success and well-being of one's family and community. King Priam (book I, 9., 1100a; also I, 10, 1101a) is presented as a classic image of someone who exercised virtues but had very bad luck in other areas of life. The assessment of his fate is a good indicator of the degree of invulnerability Aristotle thinks someone who accepts his view of eudaemonia will have. Priam, despite the tragedies surrounding him, cannot be termed lacking in eudaemonia. But neither could he be esteemed to have it in the highest degree.

Aristotle presumably did not know that his flank was exposed, in relation to the system of thought advanced two hundred years previously by Buddha. Buddha preached, in effect, complete invulnerability. Loss of desires, and of the attachments that these imply, must lead to the elimination of suffering. The way of life that this implies is austere in many ways, including a renunciation of what would normally be thought of as pleasures. (It is possible to think that this cure of human suffering is worse than the disease.) But there is the promise of bliss when one has become liberated, no longer self-concerned, and no longer driven into the future by desires and anxieties. To become largely indifferent even about this goal is a sign that it is near, but in any case it is presented as within our control.

It is pretty certain that Aristotle would have rejected this line of thought if he had known of it. But what then is his argument against the view of the better sort worth? In the absence of some independent argument as to the importance of invulnerability, the appeal to it does not seem compelling.

Even if I am right in saying this, one possible response is that Aristotle knew this, and that we need to look at arguments about value, such as Aristotle's, differently from the way in which they customarily have been viewed. Consider a comparison with arguments about aesthetic value. In a typical case, someone reads a novel or a poem, sees a painting, or hears a piece of music, and immediately has a sense of value: that is, part of one's enjoyment, boredom, or irritation is a judgment that "this is really good [or awful, or mediocre as the case may be]." This response typically occurs before reasons or arguments are articulated. Occasionally someone who has a theory of what counts as good literature, art, or music may, as it were, infer the value of what is experienced. But this is rare, and indeed it is at least as common that an original artist will create something that deliberately violates established norms but nevertheless comes through to members of its audience as really good.

This is not to suggest that critical reasons and arguments are totally worthless or phony, but merely that they have a less direct heuristic role than one might think. After Bloggs finds himself thinking that the music is awful, he may well look for reasons, especially if he has friends who seemed to love it. The reasons advanced may be frivolous and totally unconvincing, or they may in some cases have a genuine connection with structural or melodic features of the work at the root of Bloggs's experience (and that quite possibly could have been improved). Sometimes, as when plays are continuously revised in the process of early readings and performance, critical arguments have important diagnostic functions. In virtually every instance, though, it would be wrong to read a reason that supports an evaluation as having a complete and self-contained meaning separable from experience of the particular work being evaluated. Aesthetic reasons and arguments, in short, point outward and complete their meanings in the experiences of the work of art (see Isenberg 1953).

Everything that Aristotle says about eudaemonia can be read in much this way. In particular, we need not read his point about the vulnerablity of reputation in the self-contained and schematic way indicated above. It instead can be taken as pointing to something that we can experience ourselves (or witness in the lives of others), namely, that to care a great deal about reputation is to introduce into one's life a strong element of anxiety and uncertainty, along with heightened attention to the fleeting and superficial things that determine reputation. Aristotle's likely reply to a Buddhist observation that his ideal, too, involved a degree of vulnerability would be, I think, that a modest degree of concern for reputation could play a part in a well-balanced, excellent life; only great concern would distort and trivialize people's experience.

This appeal to life experience lacks the impersonality that we normally assign to reasons and arguments. It is possible that someone who has become greatly concerned about reputation could be recalled, as it were, to a more balanced perspective by Aristotle's argument. But the argument would find no resonance among dyed-in-the-wool philistines. Their response to Aristotle might be curiously like Aristotle's response to the hedonism of the average person: "What can you expect," they might ask, "from an ivory tower intellectual?" The success or failure of reasons (either in axiology or in aesthetics) to carry conviction will always depend in large part on the general disposition of those to whom they are addressed. Some will like the music that Bloggs despises, and no reasons he can give will change this; and similarly some will prize the life of unbridled pursuit of reputation that Aristotle finds unbalanced and trivial. This lack of predictable consensus needs to be considered when we assess claims to knowledge. It can be used both in arguments that there is nothing real that people are arguing about (otherwise there would be more convergence of opinion), or alternatively that even if there are real (axiological or aesthetic) values we should treat skeptically any claims to know what they are.

One way of dealing with the lack of predictable consensus, in aesthetics and in axiology, is (so to speak) to impugn some of the witnesses of value. One might speak, for example, of that "depravation of taste" on which John Stuart Mill (1859/ 1978, 75) says we have no strong general reason to withhold judgment. Or one might discount the judgments of average people, because of what they are or how they live, as Aristotle does. To modern or postmodern ears all of this is likely to sound like the worst kind of snobbery; and, especially because my position is in many respects like Aristotle's, I should disassociate myself from his comment. Experience shows that many people who are in the most obvious respects "average" are often very keen and perceptive witnesses of values, often being more sensitive to salient features of what has (or lacks) value than I and many of the people I work with sometimes are.

A word should be said about "witnessing." It can be thought of as a nest of metaphors — connected both with bearing witness and with witnesses in legal proceedings — for what is involved when someone feels in a position to testify to the value (or disvalue) of something. None of the metaphors is to be thought of as a strict parallel. In particular, we should not think of witnessing value as exactly like what is called for in law courts, where witnesses are asked to "stick to the facts," which not only rules out inferences but also means that they must confine themselves to descriptions whose interpretative framework would be very widely shared (rather than venture interpretations of their own). Witnessing for legal purposes is

Wittgensteinian "seeing" with no overt element of "seeing as." There is no reason to assume that witnessing for other kinds of purpose (including ethical purposes) shares this feature.

A more basic point is that there is no reason, either in ethics or in relation to our knowledge of how the world works, to assume that experience merely reports to us some neutral substratum of what is experienced—which then further may be interpreted in various ways. Sometimes experience gives support to a way of seeing something. Direct experience that includes a sense of connections does not provide the last word about historical or sociological causation, but it counts for something. Similarly, people's claims to know through experience just how horrible something is cannot always be disregarded.

Let us return to Aristotle. What should be defended in his view is (1) that some people can be better aware of some values than others are, and (2) that there are some values that people are unable to judge with any reasonable assurance simply because they have not had the relevant experiences. The first point can be asserted apart from any facile generalizations as to who the good witnesses are and who the unreliable ones are. Indeed, this might depend on the value with which one was concerned. Very clever people can be conspicuous dunces in matters of personal relations, and it may be that there is no more reason to trust their value judgments in this area than to trust their general ability to make discriminations and see connections. Anyone who has gotten to know a wide variety of people, on the other hand, knows that there are some uneducated people who are remarkably good at taking in what the clever dunces miss, and who also seem to have a fine sense of the emotional and personal dispositions that contribute to a genuinely satisfying life. The clever dunce who is, say, a physicist may have, all the same, a fine awareness of the value of certain experiences of understanding or of creative work that are simply inaccessible to most of us.

A charitable reading of Aristotle's argument against hedonism is that those who accept it make poor witnesses, because their lives lead them to have a low degree of the rational capacities that are important in such matters. Even in this reading, the argument does not seem very strong. It also may remind some readers of the way in which Mill constructs his argument for the superiority of the higher pleasures, setting it up in effect so that only qualified aesthetes or intellectuals are equipped to judge. Nevertheless, I would like to suggest that we cannot entirely dismiss all arguments that are broadly like the one Aristotle uses against hedonism. Here is a case. Mr. Ecstatic Toad becomes a heroin addict, and especially values the experiences that immediately follow injection of the drug, not only because of the relief of craving that they provide but also because they seem to open up a heightened sense of reality. "This is the best that life can offer," he tells us. A fair-minded response might be that, while he might be right (normal people have no monopoly on truth), his testimony should be discounted, not only because his addiction creates a bias, but also because it is judgment made in what we would consider an impaired state. This is like Mark Johnston's point about what he calls "alcovalues" (Johnston 1989, 160).

My suggestion is that this is a reasonable response, and not that this amounts to an argument of some strength against the claim that heroin experience is highly valuable. We may simply not know whether the claim is right or not, but it is reasonable to have doubts. "Consider the source" is not an altogether foolish comment, whether we make it about Mr. Ecstatic Toad, Aristotle makes it about the average hedonist, or the average person makes it about a brilliant academic who is manifestly insensitive to most of the details of ordinary life but very confident of his or her value judgments in this area.

The case of the heroin addict also is merely an extreme example of a general difficulty in assessing value judgments. These judgments are not made by pieces of laboratory apparatus; they are made by people, who have to some degree committed themselves to forms of life. Thus, there is always a bias. It is impossible to assess in any general way what the bias will be. Some people will tend to overestimate values associated with their chosen path, perhaps in part as a way of reassuring themselves. Others may have the opposite tendency, being easily dissatisfied and likely to believe that "the grass is greener" in other forms of life. The habits of mind associated with the chosen way of life may affect what is noticed or taken in. Some ways of life can dull the mind or lower standards, which fits most people's prejudgment of the reliability of the heroin addict.

To bear this in mind is to lessen confidence in anyone's value judgments, including one's own. But this need not lead to the conclusion that we never have what amounts to knowledge of value. The case for saying that we know that great pain is usually bad has been made, along with similar cases for suffering and bliss. There are some widely experienced values also that are less elemental, but about which there is enough convergence among people who have had the relevant experiences and appear to have reasonably sharp minds, that it seems reasonable to speak of knowledge of them. Many of us know, for example, that Moore is right when, in the final chapter of *Principia Ethica*, he speaks of the experiences of love (for someone worthy of that love) as of high value.

What of the excellence of the contemplative life? Let us consider a claim for it somewhat weaker than the one Aristotle makes. He holds it to be the very best way of life that is available to a human being. Many who agree with Aristotle that some lives are in themselves more worth leading than others, and that someone who is satisfied with his or her life is not thereby necessarily living the best life that is available, would still want to insist that different lives can be excellent in different ways. Aristotle slights creativity in the arts; and it may be that there are excellences, and also that there are wonderful features in some human relations, to which he does not do full justice. So let us consider merely the claim that the contemplative life ranks as excellent among the possible kinds of human life, whether or not it is the single pinnacle of what human life can be.

It seems important to pursue this, in part to rectify an imbalance in the examples used. A focus on values that can be encountered and discovered lends itself to examples of values that come and go in a life. But it is arguable that the most important values in a life typically are stable and lasting, including, of course, those that spring from the character of the person whose life it is (see Kupperman 1991, chapter 6). The nature of a person's life also provides a context that colors and affects values that come and go in it. For all of these reasons, Aristotle centers his ethics on the evaluation of entire lives.

One difficulty in assessing a high evaluation of the contemplative life is this. We may think that we know that the contemplative life *can* be wonderful (which is how Wittgenstein, just before he died, characterized his life) (see Malcolm 1958, 100). But is it wonderful, or even very good, for everyone? Suppose that Bloggs, after reading Aristotle in a required college course, takes up the contemplative life, pursuing it for many years. He spends long hours in studying, thinking, and writing. But the rest of us, treating Bloggs's writing as, in effect, reports of his contemplative life, think that it must be pretty boring. Perhaps it is better than a life that centers on watching sports on television, but none of us is inclined to regard it as even a minor pinnacle of what life can be. Bloggs at least seems to enjoy his contemplative activities. Some of his classmates, it turns out, were equally convinced by Aristotle, tried the contemplative life, and abandoned it after discovering that they simply did not enjoy what they were doing. Did they, so to speak, misperceive the value of the life they tried?

It is possible to respond to the story of Bloggs's classmates by saying that, if they did not enjoy the contemplative life, this must be because they did not pursue it in the right way. It may be, though, that to all outward appearances they did what Bloggs and Wittgenstein did: they read, thought, and wrote, and gave these activities their full and strenuous attention. Two things are conspicuously lacking: enjoyment, which has the dual role of both appraisal of something as experienced and also element of the experience that (in its fuller form) can be appraised, and (very probably) what might be termed vocation. Vocation often is connected with aptitude, but this is not always the case. Bloggs has a vocation for the contemplative life but slight aptitude; some of his clever classmates might have had more aptitude for it but still found that they did not enjoy it.

Most people would say, from their own experience, that enjoyment is often a necessary condition for experiences or ways of life to be worthwhile. Enjoyment is arguably not a sufficient condition, or we should envy the sadistic killer who really enjoys the infliction of pain. Nor can we readily say that enjoyment is always a necessary condition. There may be some experiences that are fairly unpleasant but call forth resources that we did not know we had; such experiences often play an important postive role in a person's life story, not merely because of their causal work in character building but also because they seem at the time (and especially seem later) enormously meaningful. It is hard to deny value to these on the ground that they were not enjoyable. Of course, what was not enjoyable at the time can be enjoyable in retrospect; and the issue is further complicated by the fact that enjoyment can take subtle forms, which are very different from broad smiles and happy words. Did Wittgenstein enjoy his life? Biographical reports do not give a strong impression that he did. Yet his summary judgment that the life was wonderful suggests that in a subtle, deeply involved but far from euphoric way he did enjoy the tension of hard work on philosophy. Psychological research (see Csikszentmihalyi 1990) shows that there are deep satisfactions in sustained and absorbing performances of a high degree of competence, and these can be enjoyment of a high order.

It is difficult to judge what the value might be of a contemplative life that is not enjoyed. It might not be entirely negligible. But most people, trying to put themselves inside what such a life would be like, would judge that the absence of enjoyment—of some sort—is crucial. No one would praise or envy such a life.

The value of a contemplative life that is enjoyed, though, is less easy to generalize about, as the case of Bloggs indicates. It is consistent, indeed, with everything that Aristotle says to insist that the value of contemplative activity depends very much on how well it is done. This follows from the claim that the exercise of intellectual virtues is crucial plus the fact that intellectual virtue is clearly a matter of degree. So it does not really run counter to Aristotle's view if we reply to praise of the contemplative life by saying that, yes, Wittgenstein's life is a pinnacle of what life can be but Bloggs's (to judge by the outward signs) is not.

How can we know that Wittgenstein's life, or indeed anyone's life, is a pinnacle of what life can be? This leads to a second question; how can we know what anyone's life is like? To be in a position to evaluate anything we must know the nature of what we are evaluating. My argument earlier was that two things are required: relevant experience, and a construal of what is experienced (which in most cases will be part of an emotional state, such as admiration or delight). But surely the most relevant experience is of what it is like to be the person whose life we are considering, and surely this experience is not available to us.

It may seem that this requirement is no problem in at least one case, that of our own life. But this may be overoptimistic in view of the lack of clarity that many have about their lives, not to mention cases of outright self-deception. Furthermore, to think that one's own life is unusually good involves an implicit comparative element. Can we be sure that what seems so wonderful in our own lives does not occur, even to a greater degree, in the lives of most other people, or conversely that what we regret most in our own lives does not occur in a more distressing way in other lives? The problems of knowledge of what we are evaluating are not easily overcome, even in the case of our own life.

This suggests room for caution, and that there are many matters of value about which we can have opinions but not knowledge. The grounds for caution multiply when we are tempted to assess lives very different from our own. Even more extreme are issues like that of whether the existence of a redwood forest has value in itself or merely is a means to experiences that have value. I want to believe in the first alternative, but a desire to believe is not tantamount to knowledge. It is not clear what we have to go on in forming an opinion.

Of course, it is a general truth about human knowledge, even in favorable cases, that whatever the relevant experience and the grounds for confidence, they always could be bettered. There always could have been more observations, more expert witnesses. We never know what it is like to be someone (including ourselves) as well as might be the case, but this does not mean that we never know what a life (or an aspect or part of a life) is like well enough to have an informed judgment of its value.

Sometimes we know someone well, or salient facts are clear enough (in convincing detail) that there is room for confidence both about what a life is like and about its value. Many of us might think this in relation to the lives of Socrates and of Confucius, as revealed in Plato's *Dialogues* and in Xenophon's account, and in the *Analects of Confucius*. Even if one accepts that the differences between

Plato's and Xenophon's portrayals create some areas of uncertainty, these are not crucial enough that we should hesitate in thinking that Socrates had a wonderful life. A similar judgment applies to Confucius, even though he had his share of disappointments. In his case, we might be doubtful as to whether the life qualifies as what Aristotle had in mind as a "contemplative life." Confucius was a very profound and insightful thinker; but his thought lacks the dialectical constructions and the emphasis on argument that are so striking in Socrates, and political, social, and ethical concerns are always much closer to the surface. Whether it was a contemplative life or deserves its own category, it too was wonderful.

To know that Socrates' contemplative life was eminently worth living involves a sense of what it was like and an emotional complex, which typically will include admiration, a degree of delight in some of the things Socrates did and thought, and a wish or a preference that one's own life include some of the elements that are so pronounced in Socrates' life. The emotional character of all of this need not be (and probably in virtually every case will not be) very strong or passionate. Most of us are not carried away by delight in lucid philosophical investigation. But emotions that are not markedly strong can be genuine nevertheless, and can exert a great influence on a person's view of life. Furthermore, there is an important difference between a high opinion that involves mild emotions of admiration (with accompanying motivations), on one hand, and, on the other hand, a high opinion with which no such emotional elements are associated. The former bespeaks a degree of confidence and commitment of a sort that the latter lacks. In terms of the first of the three criteria for knowledge (as opposed to mere opinion), the former is more likely to qualify as knowledge than the latter (although, as will become apparent in the next chapter, it is difficult to generalize). Furthermore, if we admire and have grounds for our admiration (say for what went on in Socrates' life), we can satisfy the second criterion.

If there is knowledge of what is good, or not so good, in one's own life, the emotional complex will typically be different. Did Wittgenstein know that his own life had been wonderful, or was that a mere opinion? Our own inclination to say the former is strengthened by the impression that Wittgenstein in some sense enjoyed his life, was highly motivated in his pursuit of it, and indeed very probably would have suffered if prevented from thinking about philosophy. Perhaps the word "enjoyed" should be replaced by something that refers to a feeling of involvement, a sense that what is happening or is about to happen is intensely meaningful. People who have this seem, unless what happens is truly horrible, typically to like their lives. Their involvement gives them a confidence in, and commitment to, the view that the life is worth living. This satisfies the first criterion for knowledge (as opposed to opinion). Whether the second criterion is satisfied may be, of course, another matter. Even if Bloggs thinks that his contemplative life is wonderful, we may have reason to disagree.

None of this proves that we have knowledge of the value of contemplative lives, or of any other lives come to that. But it outlines a case for taking such claims of knowledge seriously. The limits on what should be claimed need to be emphasized. My suggestion is that often we are not in a good position to judge the value of a way of life, and furthermore that our general labels for ways of life cover such broad ranges of cases that judgments of individual lives should be viewed with great caution. Not all contemplative lives are very much alike, and for that matter there is no reason to suppose that all wonderful lives qualify as "contemplative." I have argued, though, that it is plausible to say, using the examples of Wittgenstein and Socrates, that we know that some contemplative lives are of very high value. Final determination of whether any claim to knowledge of value could be sustained, of course, awaits examination of value realism.

# 5

# Real Values?

Thus far we have explored reasons why one might think that there are (following a loose and imperfect analogy with the five senses) senses of value, and that there sometimes is knowledge of value. But none of this gets us anywhere unless there is something of which to be aware and to know. The phenomena of seeming-awareness of values and seeming-knowledge can be viewed through the lens of an "error theory" (see Mackie 1977). That is, it can be said that it is *as if* we sometimes are immediately aware of values and sometimes have knowledge of values; unfortunately, there are no real values, and therefore this is an illusion embedded in our practices of discussing and thinking about values.

## Moral Anti-Realism and Moral Facts

Because ethical philosophy in the last few decades has been preoccupied with morality, and has largely neglected axiology, there is a large literature on issues of moral realism and not much that is recent on value realism. The two sets of issues need not be entirely the same, but it is instructive to note that even the best writers on moral realism have had difficulty in specifying just what is at issue. Often there is a reference to "moral facts," usually by writers who want to deny that there are any such things. But no one makes clear what a moral fact would be, if there were such; indeed, such writers neglect the foundational work of explaining what a fact is.

There are at least two schools of thought on this. One, exemplified by P. F. Strawson (1950) and Bede Rundle (1993), treats facts as interpretative constructs of what is (or might be) experienced in the world. A fact itself, as Strawson says (1950, 135), is not in the world. Another, exemplified by John Searle (1995, 211), treats facts as conditions that obtain in the world. Facts in such a view are more complex (and often more difficult to point to) than things or events; but they are part of reality, and true propositions are those that correspond to the facts.

Both of these accounts seem persuasive (although I lean toward that of Strawson and Rundle), and as a result a philosopher can be reasonably in doubt as to what a fact is. But do we need to talk about facts in order to understand issues of moral realism and of value realism? Indeed, reference to purported "moral facts," on the part of moral anti-realists who do not bother to examine what a fact is, can be seen as a rhetorical strategy, appealing to a thoughtless tendency to assimilate "facts" to things (see Strawson 1950, 133) and to regard things as able to be experienced through the senses. If one thinks facilely of facts in this way, any suggestion that there are moral facts might well look preposterous. How the issue is framed has a great deal to do with the answers we are inclined to give.

Consider a case in which an anti-realist verdict is surely appropriate: that of witches. When many people believed in witches, it might have been possible for those who did and those who did not to reach some rough agreement on what some of the criteria were for being a witch if there were any. These would take in such relevant evidence as being observed to mutter curses, and some pattern of misfortune for those who had behaved slightingly to the putative witch. If there are witches, someone might have said, here is how we might know who they are. (The parallel with the previous two chapters of this book should be evident.) There is a further criterion for being a witch, which includes really having the power to affect people's lives in the way traditionally associated with witches. Indeed there are no witches, and this has everything to do with the absence of such powers in the real world, whether we wish to speak of "facts" or not. Even someone who rejects the correspondence theory of truth can say that, in the context of our core beliefs about the world and our conventions of language, we could imagine a universe in which there were witches, but that our universe is not like that. Is our universe such that, much as there are no witches, there are no moral obligations and there are no values? Or, conversely, are there some things that really have the binding quality traditionally associated with moral obligations, or that really have the desirability traditionally associated with values?

If the question is put in this way, there would not be many moral anti-realists or value anti-realists. Certainly there would not be as many as there would be if the issue is put in terms of facts. One is reminded of the exchange at the deathbed of Gertrude Stein, when Alice B. Toklas asked the dying woman, "What is the answer?" to which the reply was "What is the question?" The question at the heart of the debate between moral realists and moral anti-realists is far from clear, and by analogy this is true also of the central issue concerning value realism.

Someone who wants to be a moral anti-realist might say, "Of course there are moral obligations, and there are certain things that we really ought to do; but this is so in a way different from that in which there might have been witches (but are not)." One possible version of this response is to say that there are moral obligations but to treat them merely as equivalent to conventions that various societies establish, for social convenience or for other reasons. This is not a plausible view, though, in that it is generally taken as possible to dissent meaningfully (with some chance of being right) from the established morality of one's society, whereas if moral obligations were merely conventions the dissenter would be by definition wrong. Perhaps moral obligations are conventions, but not merely conventions. A sophisticated moral anti-realist could talk about morality as satisfying needs of social coordination, and could put all of this in a neo-Darwinian framework (cf. Gibbard 1990). This view would have the virtue of legitimizing dissent, in that it is always possible that a given society has not met the needs of social coordination as well as it might, or that it met these needs in a way that is now outmoded.

I have argued (Kupperman 1996) that this line of thought works better for some parts of morality than for others, and that in any case it would not work well for values (in the narrow sense specific to axiology and to this book). It is hard to view either Aristotle's praise of the contemplative life, or competing views such as hedonism, as answering to needs of social coordination in the way in which rules that protect life or govern what counts as legitimate treatment of property do. Let us continue to look at morality, though, and continue to look at what it is that the moral anti-realist is trying to deny. I have suggested that what is denied is not usually that there are genuine moral obligations. Perhaps it is, after all, the existence of moral facts in some specific and clear sense that I have failed to understand or that moral anti-realists have failed to explain.

Is it that there are moral facts in the sense of conditions in the world such that we genuinely have certain moral obligations? This would allow us to put the issue in terms of moral facts, while giving some explanation of what a moral fact might be. However this does not seem to be a plausible interpretation of the anti-realist position. For one thing, it would be said that the facts that underlie moral obligations are themselves ordinary and not "moral" facts. Also, most moral anti-realists probably would agree that if we have repeatedly promised Bloggs that we could come to his aid in his hour of need, and that hour of need has come, and there are no extenuating circumstances or conflicting demands on us, then we have an obligation to fulfill our promise. They would agree, presumably, that there are conditions in the world such that we have this obligation. Are these conditions (e.g., Bloggs's need along with the lack of extenuating circumstances, etc.) ordinary rather than "moral" facts? They are conditions that we perhaps cannot readily point to in the way in which we can point to a desk or a chair; but this is true of many facts, such as—to borrow an example of Bede Rundle's (1993, 10)—that the rate of inflation has fallen.

Perhaps, then, the nub of moral anti-realism is that, even though it is a fact that Bloggs is in what we would construe as need and that there are no circumstances of the sort that we would regard as extenuating, the moral obligation that these ground is not a fact. Why not, we might ask? Could one just as well say, while stable prices in this or that sector of the economy are a fact, that the rate of inflation has fallen is not a fact? Perhaps the difference between the two cases is that the move from Bloggs's and our circumstances to the judgment of moral obligation is normative, whereas the movement from various price levels to the decreased rate of inflation is not. But why this difference should matter is not clear, unless it is merely a matter of some prejudice against the normative. It might be said that there is room for disagreement in normative matters that one does not find in non-normative matters. But this by itself cannot be the story, in that economists who agree about the basic data of price levels might disagree about the rate of inflation, so that in the end we say that "the facts [i.e., some of them] are in dispute." When there is disagreement about whether we have a moral obligation to help Bloggs, why can we not say, "The (moral) facts are in dispute"?

If we look in the moral anti-realist literature for argument, as opposed to rhetorical strategy, there is one ingenious and persuasive family of arguments. It appeals to the causal connection that should obtain between anything that genuinely is a fact, on one hand, and, on the other hand, beliefs about it that we would (or should) consider to be knowledge. If it really is a fact that X, and Smith knows it, then it must be the case that X had a causal role in Smith's arriving at her belief that X; indeed, it must be the case that Smith would not have arrived at her belief unless X were a fact. In one form of the argument it is claimed that upbringing, temperament, and so forth, can provide a complete causal explanation of an individual's moral beliefs. Putative moral facts are not needed. Hence there are not any.

In one light this argument is puzzling, in that arguably we would not believe that we have a moral obligation to help Bloggs unless matters were such that we do. (This would be strongly supported by the assumption that this segment, at least, of our morality is reasonably enlightened and humane, that Bloggs's case, unlike some others, is clear, and that we have been clearheaded in assessing it.) In other words, a crucial part of the causal explanation of our belief that we have the moral obligation is that we do. The strength and persuasiveness of the anti-realist argument come in the reply to this kind of objection. It is that our belief that we have a moral obligation to help Bloggs can be causally explained by the purely descriptive facts that we might construe as constituting our promises and his need (and the absence of extenuating factors, etc.), along, of course, with our social conditioning, and so forth. The normative construals that we might place on all of these facts are not needed in the causal explanation. The normative then looks like a wheel that is not (causally) connected with the rest of the mechanism of our moral judgments. The facts that do play a part are that we said certain words to Bloggs, that he is now at a certain level of poverty, and so forth; putative moral facts fail the test of causality.

One reason that the philosophical debate between moral realists and anti-realists has come to look like a standoff is that it is not clear what grounds we have for preferring one or the other of the causal stories they tell. It certainly is plausible to say that we would not believe we had a moral obligation to Bloggs unless it were the case that (were the fact that) we do. If two causal explanations, in this case the anti-realist's and the realist's, each serve to explain someone's beliefs, do we automatically prefer the one that carries the fewest ontological commitments? The implications of an answer of "Yes" go well beyond ethics, in particular creating a presumption in favor of some kind of phenomenalism as against realism about the physical world. The moral anti-realist, of course, could insist that the issue of moral facts is special, that what is questionable is not so much the postulation of unnecessary facts as it is the postulation of unnecessary facts of a special and mysterious kind. But to insist that only a causal explanation in descriptive terms of moral beliefs is legitimate is in effect to prejudge as doubtful the status of normative construals of descriptive facts.

Also, a moral realist could argue that what typically seems most salient — and seems the source of our belief, when we find ourselves judging that there is an obligation to help Bloggs — is the normative shape of the situation. Our intuitive sense of causal connection, as when — to use an example of Anscombe's (1957, 16) — we immediately know that the face at the window caused our fright, is here of connection between the normative and our judgment of it. Because of this, some will want to insist that our sense of vivid awareness that such and such conduct really is obligatory or abominable, so that its moral requiredness or wrongness presses itself on our attention, should count for something in weighing the competing claims of descriptive-based and normative-based causal explanations of moral beliefs, in some cases creating a presumption in favor of the latter rather than the former.

Further, even though what the moral realist takes to be moral facts are grounded in ordinary facts, we need not assume that there are lawlike connections between the two. The relation might be a little like that for which Donald Davidson pioneered the phrase "anomalous monism" (see Davidson, 1970). Perhaps some "moral facts" do have lawlike connections (of the sort beloved of moral "rigorists") with ordinary facts, and some do not. If so, it still could seem plausible, although more cumbersome, even in the case of "moral facts" that do not have such lawlike connections to give a causal explanation of the associated moral beliefs in purely descriptive terms. Do we still insist that only the causal story in terms of ordinary facts is legitimate? An anti-realist still might argue, of course, that both the realist causal story (if one assumes, for the sake of argument, that there are moral facts) and the anti-realist causal story would be acceptable; but, in that we do not need the special "facts" and normative dimension provided by the former, the anti-realist story is all we need and is therefore privileged. But it can be argued in reply that sometimes the anti-realist causal story is likely to be far more cumbersome, and indeed messy, than the realist story, and that in the sciences we do not always prefer the explanations that posit the narrowest range of facts. Simplicity and a sense of immediate cogency also matter. And what could be simpler than explaining our belief that we have an obligation to Bloggs by saying, "We do have an obligation to Bloggs"?

There are other complications. One, which seems to me most serious, is that the anti-realist line of argument just discussed is embedded in a framework of rosy optimism about scientific explanations of our moral beliefs. It is the same kind of rosy optimism, distinctively found among non-scientists, that makes many philosophers treat determinism as if it were an obvious truth about the world. Now it is clearly true that people's upbringings, temperaments, and so forth, have a great deal to do with the moral beliefs that they *are likely to* have. But, except in cases so rare that we tend to refer to them under the heading of "brainwashing," we are unable at present to predict an individual's moral beliefs with entire certainty on the basis of these factors. Perhaps in the future, as we come to know more (and especially if psychology were to undergo some kind of Newtonian revolution), we will be able to make such predictions. But is there any reason to assume this, or to assume that the world is such that someone who knew all of the relevant descriptive details of an individual's life and was equipped with an optimal theory could (in principle) make such predictions?

A variant of the anti-realist causality argument escapes the force of this doubt. It is that there is a valid causal explanation of moral belief on the social level that renders it unnecessary to posit moral facts. This line of argument is most closely associated with Allan Gibbard. One of its merits is that it avoids speculative claims about what the sciences in the future will, should, or in principle could provide; it is grounded in known science. Another is that its causal explanations are neither cumbersome nor messy. The claim is merely that moral beliefs can be explained by the evolutionary advantages of certain forms of interpersonal coordination.

There is clearly a lot of truth to this. As my earlier remarks suggested, this may be nearly the whole truth as regards the part of morality that is related to ownership of property. It also works very well for the morality of political and social justice. It certainly is part of the truth even in relation to moral rules that forbid torture, maiming, and so forth. The fabric of trust, personal sense of security, and mutual regard is likely to be rather thin in a society that tolerates such practices. It might be argued that there is ample room for doubt that the evolutionary advantage account gives us anything like the whole causal story of such moral beliefs. But my skepticism about the evolutionary advantage account has been diminished by reflection that the mechanisms of human sympathy, which clearly are a large part of the story, might themselves be causally explained in terms of evolutionary advantage. Thus, it does look plausible to say that we could give a satisfactory, or at least largely satisfactory, causal explanation of moral beliefs on the social level without introducing moral facts.

To this it might be objected that, after all, even socially accepted moral beliefs are also personal moral beliefs, and that in almost every case what became socially accepted started out as the belief of a person or a small number of persons. Doesn't this put the anti-realist back in the position of needing causal explanations of individual moral beliefs? However, the anti-realist could reply first that moral beliefs that we would agree to be unacceptable do not need to be explained (in that we would perforce agree that "moral facts" play no part in causing them), and second that other beliefs have to be seen as moving in the direction of societal acceptance. A "true" moral belief that is held only by one or a few persons is to a socially acccepted "true" moral belief, in this view, as a caterpillar is to a moth. The moral anti-realist may not be able to explain how Bloggs came to have his opinion on the one moral issue on which he is ahead of his time, but there may well be an evolutionary advantage explanation of why *some* people would come to have that opinion.

If the evolutionary advantage theorist can give largely satisfactory explanations of what we would regard as "true" moral beliefs, does this establish the truth of moral anti-realism? Part of the appeal of the evolutionary advantage account is that it does appear to work well for the structure of morality, which includes its internal logic and the ways in which morality functions in a society such as ours. But, with regard to the content of morality, there is the complication that what is largely satisfactory may not be entirely satisfactory. Some parts of social morality can be well explained directly in terms of the need for social coordination, and other parts can be explained by reference to human attitudes (e.g., sympathy) that themselves might be given an evolutionary explanation. There remain other prevalent elements of social morality, whose roots are neither in sympathy nor (at least in any obvious way) in the needs of social coordination. Some moral judgments about sexual practices, and perhaps about treatment of the dead, seem to have this character. Whether any of these provide counterexamples to the evolutionary advantage account of morality would have to be argued on a case-by-case basis. Those who accept the account would have to argue, in relation to each apparent counterexample, either that the taboos that motivated the moral judgment could be analyzed after all in terms of needs of social coordination, or that the moral judgment represented something like an evolutionary false start, a prejudice that in the long run could not be sustained. At this stage it appears that the evolutionary advantage account of morality has considerable plausibility, whether or not it is entirely convincing. It does strengthen the case for moral anti-realism, even if this will turn out to be stronger in relation to some parts of morality than in relation to others.

The case, however, is hardly overwhelming. At most it can be claimed that the evolutionary advantage causal account of moral belief can explain the general character of our morality as well as a realist's causal account could. We still have to ask, if that is so, why the anti-realist's causal account needs to be regarded as privileged. Sometimes, as when people callously desert children, it may seem as if the normative element is the most salient feature of the situation as it presents itself to us, and of the process that brings about our moral judgment; and the causal account in which this normative feature ("It is abominable/inhuman") plays a central role in explaining our moral judgments will seem intuitively more compelling than the anti-realist evolutionary advantage account. In the absence of generally agreed upon standards for determining the merits of competing causal accounts, though, moral realists and anti-realists may have to agree to disagree.

## Value Realism and Value Facts

Could we construct an evolutionary advantage account of judgments about values? Here again we enter a debate in which it is likely that not all of the advantages will be on one side. But it is a different debate from the one about moral realism. For one thing, it can be argued that it is essential to the concept and function of morality that judgments that can be accepted personally be acceptable on the social level. It counts heavily against the claim that X is morally obligatory (or merely permissible, or impermissible) if one concedes that widespread acceptance of this moral judgment would turn out to be a social disaster. Such a social dimension is not essential to the concept of value (in the narrow sense of this book). X can be of high value even if it turns out that most people are not suited to the pursuit of X. There may be some slight communal advantage if large numbers of people share a view of what is most desirable in life; but it is not clearly disastrous if there is widespread disagreement about the value of, say, the contemplative life, as it would be if there were widespread disagreement about the permissibility of murder and torture.

Having said this, one has to concede that an evolutionary advantage account might work pretty well for some persistent beliefs about value. Most people's beliefs that other people's pains, like their own, are intrinsically undesirable could be explained in this way. Beliefs that are somewhat less widely shared, such as that intellectual activities, or success at demanding tasks, have special value, also could be understood in terms of the evolutionary advantage of there being at least some people who appreciated intellectual activity or meeting challenges. Whether such explanations would work well for very impractical activities, such as research in metaphysics, within the contemplative life is another matter. The special value that Aristotle assigned to such activities could not be readily explained in evolutionary terms. Neither could the very great value that some would assign to extremely subtle aesthetic experiences, from which society does not benefit in any obvious way.

The anti-realist, of course, can press a causal explanation of these and all value judgments in terms that include individual psychologies. The explanations that are actually now available (as opposed to those to be provided by scientific revolutions that might or might not be possible) tend to be less plausible in relation to values than in relation to morality, simply because the causal contribution of indoctrination typically is greater and more obvious in relation to moral opinion. Thus, while both varieties of the anti-realist argument about causality are available in relation to values (and cannot be entirely dismissed), they both look less plausible in relation to values than morality.

Anti-realist arguments that are older than the ones we have discussed might be more damaging to value realism. These center on the notion of verification. As popularized in A. J. Ayer's *Language, Truth, and Logic*, the anti-realist's argument is that a meaningful claim must be capable (at least in principle) of verification; normative claims (along with those of religion and metaphysics) fail this test. Hence, a statement that X has such and such a value is not meaningful and cannot be true or false. At best it expresses the emotion or attitude of the speaker.

Much of the power of Ayer's argument comes from his faithfulness to the core of scientific practice. What counts as verification in physics, chemistry, and biology is assuredly both impersonal and communal. Experiments and observations have to be able to be replicated, and in principle it should not matter who is doing the observing. It needs to be said, as a qualification, that sometimes most people would not be capable of the relevant observation. It may require a trained eye. But, at least in principle, some who are not qualified observers should be capable of being trained; and the presumption is that trained observers will and should agree.

Might something like this be true of some forms of knowledge — and of the observations at their base — and not of others? Nearly a century before Ayer, Kierkegaard in *Concluding Unscientific Postscript* (1846/1941, 176–77) drew a distinction between forms of knowledge in which the self or personal orientation of the knower was not essentially involved and forms of knowledge (in which he included ethical and "ethico-religious" knowledge) in which it was. A similar notion was implicit in Plato's model of the "divided line," at the highest level of which the knower becomes the known. Both were convinced that there are important forms of genuine knowledge that do not fit the pattern that Ayer and others have discerned in such sciences as physics and chemistry.

Two sets of claims about ethical knowledge are implicit in this. One has to do with a peculiar way in which such knowledge encapsulates motivations, so that (in ethics) to know is to care and to be committed. The other is that evidence in ethics is not impersonal and need not be communal: what is evident to one person at a certain level of ethical development need not be evident to another who is at a different level (or who has a different orientation or different commitments). Hence, if there is something like verification in ethics, involving occasions on which someone comes to "see" things for herself or himself, it lacks a central feature of verification in the sciences. What one person comes to see may well be invisible to others.

Ayer regarded such claims about special (and sometimes personal) forms of knowledge as preposterous. Moral realists and value realists can argue that Ayer has succeeded in showing that normative claims cannot be true *only* if one first accepts the assumption that any form of knowledge must be like knowledge in the "hard" sciences in the kind of verification that it requires. Ayer presents this as a dogma. Is there any reason to accept it?

The anti-realist can turn the question around: is there any reason not to accept it? After all, the successes and progress of the sciences have established them as paradigms of genuine knowledge. The burden of argument, then, might seem to fall upon those who wish to claim that there are radically different forms of knowledge, such as ethical knowledge.

Here again it may look as if we are witnessing a standoff between realists and anti-realists, with anti-realists perhaps having a slight advantage: the one that philosophical minimalists generally have, of being able to assign the burden of argument to their opponents. In any event, we need to probe more deeply, pursuing further the question of what knowledge of values would be if there were such a thing. How do values differ from the kinds of things about which physicists, chemists, and so forth, know?

## What Values Are

We may begin by recalling Wittgenstein's distinction (1953, 194 ff.), illustrated with a drawing of a duck-rabbit, between seeing and seeing as. The figure can be seen either as a duck or as a rabbit. These two experiences, which can occur in rapid succession, are very distinct from one another. But the lines of what is seen, along with the dot that represents an eye, remain the same. In this sense, what is seen is constant, although what it is seen *as* can change drastically.

This distinction looked more straightforward in 1953 than it does now. It has become commonplace among philosophers to say that there is no neutral given. Experience is mediated by the ways in which the field of experience is divided up, which items are treated as salient, and how connections present themselves. Both language and styles of perception play a part in this preinterpretation of direct experience. Scientific observation is not immune from this, and many philosophers of science have followed Kuhn (1962) in claiming that observations designed to test an established theory will be themselves mediated by methods and assumptions internal to the theory to be tested. If these highly influential lines of thought are correct, there is no such thing as "raw" unmediated seeing. All seeing is seeing as.

Nevertheless, the distinction has some meaning. It has come to look like the distinction in the arts between style and content, which has run into the similar difficulty that there is no such thing as content that is in no style whatsoever. It can make sense, however, to speak of two stories that depict what we would call (perhaps speaking loosely) the same sequence of events as having roughly the same content, especially if the same characters and incidents are salient in them. This can be correct in the context of a shared sense of what is highly similar (what the stories are about) and what is rather dissimilar (sentence structure, narrative rhythm, points of emphasis). In a comparable way, we can say that the constituent elements of what we see are much the same whether we see the figure as a duck or as a rabbit (and would be much the same for someone from a very different culture, one which lacked birds and rabbits, who looked at the figure), but that what the visual experience, so to speak, added up to would be very different among these cases.

The duck-rabbit highlights two different ways of regarding an experience, which are such that the role of interpretation in one seems minimal (and is easily ignored) and this role in the other can seem pronounced. In the first we try to abstract (but cannot entirely abstract) materials of the experience likely to seem very similar to different experiencers and to be moderately independent of such factors as temperament, aesthetic taste, and personal experience, and in some cases (like the duck-rabbit and like someone writing a story) are prior to any deliberate decision to structure the experience in one way rather than another. In the second we emphasize aspects of the experience that answer to these factors or result from deliberate structuring, and that therefore can make the experiences of different people (or of the same person at different moments) seem very different from one another.

One way of putting all of this is to say that all experience, along with the judgments that are drawn from experience, is interpretative but that some experiences and judgments are more interpretative than others. What seems highly interpretative can depend on the context, in that what is shared and taken for granted in one place or time can seem contestable and eccentric in another. That the temperature outside my office as I write is about eighteen degrees centigrade seems hardly interpretative at all. That the universe is finite but unbounded seems more interpretative. That Elizabeth Anscombe (1958), who had incurred grocer's bills for the delivery of potatoes, owed her grocer the money might seem hardly interpretative at all; indeed, it might seem to qualify, as she suggests, as a "brute fact." This might seem especially plausible if we have in mind the sense of "fact" in which someone might be told to "stick to the facts" as a way of discouraging anything conspicuously interpretative or inferential. Most moral or value claims though—especially if one does not share the outlook that is expressed by them, or is willing to suspend belief—will conspicuously be interpretations of the world on which they project evaluations.

My first suggestion, then, about values is this. To experience something as having or lacking value is usually, in most contexts, to have a highly interpretative experience. There are plenty of exceptions to this generalization. To experience great pain as bad will seem, both because of the immediacy of the value element of the experience and because its outlook is very widely shared, hardly interpretative at all. It may be that there are tight-knit religious communities in which most experiences of value or lack of value will seem this way. If most value experiences seem to us to be highly interpretative, this has a great deal to do with our pluralistic society and the related need often to stop and think about values.

This experience of value as interpretative still does not distinguish values from the objects of the general run of highly interpretative experiences that might be had by, say, rival sociologists or economists in relation to issues in which values were not a prominent element. A further feature of some value experiences is the close connection between the experience and motivation. This connection is not universal, but it is common enough that we associate this motivational implicature with experience of value.

The word "implicature" refers to what we might suppose, rather than what is entailed. It is important, in what follows, to keep in mind the differences between psychology and traditional formal logic, and especially that the former discloses connections that may turn out to obtain only for the most part or "normally," or merely sometimes. To see something (e.g., a set of experiences, a way of life) as having high value is often to be motivated to promote it for other people in general, or to make it available to the people one most cares about, or to have it for itself. The experience in which this presents itself will be interpretative in standard ways: the elements of what is experienced will arrange themselves in a certain way, with some of them seeming more salient than others and with a heightened sense of certain connections with other items of experience. But, in addition to this construal of what is judged to have high value, there can be positive feelings (which, depending on the surrounding elements of the experience, we might label as delight, admiration, or desire) and positive motivations of various sorts.

In short, seeing something as having high value can be an emotional package that includes motivation. It need not be. Bloggs can see a life of aesthetic refinement as — it seems to him — one of high quality, but "not for the likes of us," or "not my cup of tea." Some may want to object at this point that, if Bloggs's value judgment lacks accompanying motivation, then he does not really "see" the life of aesthetic refinement as of great value. It is hard to know how to reply to this; perhaps Bloggs sees but does not *really* see. The terms are so imprecise that the issue becomes hard to grasp. We will have a better sense of what is at stake, though, when we have understood what leads to the "prescriptivist" view that ethical judgments (or some favored group of ethical judgments) imply motivation.

At the root is the perception that ethics (including, of course, both axiology and moral philosophy) has the function of guiding us in our lives. How can it have this function if people are not motivated along the lines of the ethical judgments they accept? It is admitted that there are clear cases of people who say that they accept an ethical judgment but then behave in a way that would seem to run counter to it. But there are classic strategies to deal with such cases. In some, the people were motivated along the lines of the ethical judgment, but some contrary motivation (growing perhaps out of temptation) outweighed this (perhaps temporarily). Cases of *akrasia* are like this. Sometimes, though, people behave in a way counter to their ethical judgments with no sense of struggle, or of having been overcome by temptation, and so forth. These people commonly are said to have been insincere or hypocrites; and their acceptance of the ethical judgments in question is viewed as only apparent, involving either self-deception or pretense. Prescriptivism thus is saved from apparent counterexamples.

Prescriptivism is especially plausible in relation to moral judgments, but we need to understand why. We also need to reject two extreme views of the relation between ethical judgments and motivations. One is the strong prescriptivist view that a statement that A accepts ethical judgment E logically implies that A is motivated to act in accordance with E (even if these motivations may have been outweighed or overcome in the case at hand). At the other extreme is the anti-prescriptivist position that the two things (accepting E and being motivated accordingly) are entirely separate, so that there is no logical relation between a statement of A's motivation and one of A's ethical beliefs (or vice versa). There are cases, as we will see, that the strong prescriptivist view cannot cope with very well: the most dramatic are of satanic motivation. The major difficulty for the anti-prescriptivist is this. We have a variety of criteria for judging that A accepts E; it follows from a widely accepted view of what meaning is, that these criteria together constitute the meaning of "A accepts E." These criteria of course include what A says, especially in unguarded moments or under the influence of truth serum. But they also include A's motivations as revealed in behavior directly (or indirectly in gestures of frustration, satisfaction, or the like). Consequently, it simply does not seem true to say that A's ethical beliefs and motivations are entirely separate. Motivations are evidence for ethical beliefs, and here the status as evidence is not simply a matter of what usually occurs together: rather, it flows from relations of meaning between descriptions of motivation and descriptions of ethical beliefs. Because the relation is grounded in meaning and would obtain in all possible worlds, it seems reasonable to take it to be logical rather than empirical, even though it is weaker than entailment.

We can agree that A's motivation logically counts toward the ethical beliefs that we ascribe to A, while admitting that other factors could count more and point in a different direction. There might be cases in which a whole network of related moral judgments are made with most of the appearances of conviction, but with no corresponding motivation. Someone notes that such and such is morally wrong or morally obligatory, in a way that convinces us that there is genuine belief; but this seems to have no impact on his or her motivation (see Baier 1967, 142). Such cases appear to be rare, but there is no clear a priori way of ruling them out. More frequent are the cases of satanism, in which there is a special explanation (perversity) that helps to convince us that the acceptance of moral judgments is genuine despite contrary motivations. When Milton's Satan says, "Evil be thou my good," the statement (although paradoxical) is intelligible. Satan really does think that what he does is evil, being motivated to promote evil and to undermine or destroy what he judges to be good. Some may object that this case is both unique and fictitious. But surely there are ordinary human cases of perversity, and one need not look at satanists to find them. Ordinary people who belong to no cult will sometimes find satisfying the idea of doing something in part because it is wrong or a mistake. This is especially common in relation to such minor (and non-moral) lapses as overeating, drinking too much, and being deliberately rude to someone who is disagreeable. Much of the pleasurable excitement can be contributed by the sense of transgression. One might be reminded also of the Jules Feiffer cartoon character who became convinced that sex was not dirty and lost interest. Beside these cases we can place extreme and horrifying instances of crimes committed by people who were attracted (sometimes in a self-hating way) by the idea of sinfulness.

One reason why we are especially prone to associate moral judgment with corresponding motivation is that we are trained that way. A major function of morality is to coordinate social behavior, and there are strong practical reasons for a system of upbringing that insists that moral judgments are mirrored in conduct. As Jackson and Pettit (1995, 37) observe, to have beliefs about fairness in a way connected with motivation is the "canonical way." The practical reasons for expecting that value judgments will be mirrored in conduct are less compelling. Much less damage typically is done to others if Bloggs does not live up to his judgment of what the best kind of life is than if he does not live up to his judgments of how one should behave toward other people's property or personal safety.

It is also relevant that much of what people attach great positive value to is personal and idiosyncratic. One can think things to be highly valuable that would not occur to most people to be important. Someone who has come to find something of this sort important may be able to convince others that it has high value, without necessarily convincing them to care or that it is relevant to their lives. All of this seems less true in relation to judgments of great negative value, which often are directed toward experiences of acute suffering or misery or deprivation of various kinds that can be widely shared and will seem potentially relevant to the life of virtually anyone. Anscombe has suggested in talks that there is an asymmetry between pleasures and pains: that acceptance of pain requires a reason whereas eschewing a pleasure typically does not. Perhaps much the same asymmetry obtains (at least in some cases) between positive and negative values, between accepting something that one judges to have negative value, on one hand, and passing up something that one judges to have positive value, on the other? I will pursue this idea in the next chapter.

These considerations leave us with a weak prescriptivism. People's motivations logically count as evidence for claims about the ethical judgments that they accept. It is hence in the general run of cases reasonable to suppose that people's motivations are in accord with the ethical judgments that they accept. Because of the social function of morality, the supposition will be, in general, stronger in relation to moral judgments than in relation to axiological judgments. It also may be stronger in relation to negative axiological judgments than positive ones. With all of this in mind, we can say that to experience something as having positive (or negative) value usually involves not only a pronounced interpretative element but also a corresponding motivation.

This may seem a weak claim indeed. It can be stiffened by the following consideration. If we take seriously the (extremely plausible) idea that the function of ethical judgments is to guide us in our lives, then cases in which they fulfill this function inevitably emerge as more central than cases in which they do not. It can be argued the satanist's use of terms like "evil" and "good" is parasitic upon, and presupposes, a morality of ordinary people in which motivations generally fit moral judgments (rather than turning them on their heads). Similarly, the cases in which someone believes, without any corresponding motivation, something to be of high value are parasitic on those in which motivation corresponds to judgment; the practices of value judgment could not exist without cases of the latter kind.

What then are values? The preceding discussion has been of value experience and value judgment. Objects of the experience and judgment might seem to be presupposed, but we have not said what they are. This demand for the objects of value judgments and experience, though, is less innocent than it looks. It asks us to follow the garden path of our forms of discourse down to obscure regions of ontology. It is natural to speak of "values" in connection with our thought about and experience of what is or is not of value; and then it is easy to go from that to thinking of values as like things, furniture of a peculiar sort among the other furniture of the universe. But the objects of our thought and experience, even when they are empirical features of the real world, are not always things. In this respect it is healthy to compare values to the rate of inflation or to magnetic fields. Neither seems particularly furniturelike, and each is an interpretative construct related to (less conspicuously interpreted) underlying phenomena. Values, I have argued, also are interpretative constructs related to (less conspicuously interpreted) underlying phenomena. What is distinctive, beyond this, about values follows from the prescriptive normal function of ethical language: values are keyed, in the general run of cases (but not always), to motivational factors.

The motivational factors that are, in the general run of cases, associated with judgments of value are matters of degree. Some people are strongly committed to values they espouse and not easily tempted to behave in ways that run counter to their standing motivations; others can be less strongly committed and more wavering. There may be some rough correlation between degrees of confidence in value judgments and associated degrees of commitment. Bearing this in mind, we can say what the nugget of truth is in Plato's and Kierkegaard's insistence on the special nature of ethical knowledge.

Ethical judgments (including value judgments) have a motivational function that distinguishes them from scientific and mathematical judgments. The distinction is not sharp. On one hand, there are some scientific judgments (e.g., judgments in the medical sciences of what leads to death) that will normally have considerable motivational power; on the other hand, functions are not always fulfilled and sometimes ethical judgments lack significant motivational force. This is especially common among positive value judgments. It is tempting to make the basic distinction between ethical and non-ethical judgments look as sharp as possible, and this can be done in two ways. One is to treat the motivational power that scientific judgments sometimes have as a function of implicit ethical assumptions (e.g., that it is better to live than to die). The other is to separate cases in which ethical judgments fulfill their motivational function from cases in which they do not, and then to formulate a distinction between the former cases (only) and cases of scientific judgment. This can be accomplished by requiring that ethical *knowledge* satisfy a motivational requirement, a requirement that is especially plausible in that motivational commitment often correlates with confidence and it is customary to hold that only belief that is confident (and appropriately grounded) can qualify as knowledge. The crucial distinction then is drawn between ethical knowledge and scientific knowledge.

It should be clear that my own position is not very far from Plato's and Kierkegaard's on this point. I already have suggested that in order to be in a position to be confident of a judgment of value, one needs not only relevant experience but also an appropriate construal of what is experienced; and that this construal usually will be part of an appropriate emotional state. Further, the motivational and occurrent feeling elements of the emotional state typically contribute to commitment, which very often goes along with a high level of confidence. Nevertheless, there is no clear way to rule out cases in which someone has the relevant experiences, and the appropriate construal of them, that justify confidence in a judgment of value—and is confident of the judgment—without, however, having any corresponding motivation. It would seem doctrinaire to deny that this could constitute knowledge of the value (or lack of value) of something. The contrast between scientific knowledge and what might seem to qualify as ethical knowledge is significant in the general run of cases, but is less neat, as it were, around the edges than one might wish.

The overall contrast between ethical judgments and judgments in the sciences also is not neat, and this is especially the case when we compare value judgments with judgments in the sciences. Nevertheless, value judgments very often do have something to do with the personalities and styles of life of the people who make them. If we continue to say that they are about values, then the values that they are about seem peculiarly to have cultural and personal idiosyncracies projected on them. Does this mean that notions like "objective value" are misguided? Also, does it doom claims that judgments of value can be (in some sense) verified? It may seem a short step from (1) admitting that culture and personal idiosyncracies have a role in values to (2) regarding judgments of value as either purely personal or culture-bound, and hence as not capable of truth in any "objective" sense.

## Are Values Real?

Let us begin with the issue of the verifiability of judgments of value. Many philosophers have held that it makes no sense to speak of something as real unless a judgment that it exists or obtains can be verified, and this is a point that (in relation to what I will call tentative verification) I want to concede. It is now commonplace that verification in the sciences is not always as neat or as decisive as the logical positivists (including Ayer) had supposed. There are cases in which an experiment or an observation yields what looks like (within the context of widely accepted assumptions and ways of interpreting data) decisive refutation or confirmation of a hypothesis. But alongside these, there are other cases in which observational data are variously interpreted, debates between proponents of rival theories go on, and it becomes most implausible to equate the meaning of any of the theories with a set of observational data that would confirm it. Allan Franklin (1990, 195 and passim) has spoken of "the fallibility and corrigibility of both theory and experiment." The fallibility can contribute to continuing expert disagreement, even while the corrigibility gives some promise that there could be eventual resolution.

It can be argued that there is a similar variety of cases in ethics. We could verify that Anscombe owed money to her grocer by looking at a record of purchases and of money transactions, and perhaps as well taking testimony. Virtually everyone (within a context of widely accepted assumptions and ways of interpreting data) would regard this as decisive. No evidence seems to be decisive in a comparable way in long-running debates about the ways of life that are most desirable.

Even though the range of cases in philosophy and in the sciences is arguably similar, the distribution seems to be very different. It would be generally agreed that cases in which matters of real importance are settled by observation are more conspicuous in the sciences than in ethics, and that cases in which no observations seem to settle the issues are more conspicuous in ethics. Further, stubborn disagreements — in the face of a body of relevant evidence — among trained and thoughtful judges appear to go on much longer in ethics. No ongoing controversy in the sciences can compete with the more than two thousand years in which fundamental issues of axiology have been debated.

If it begins to look like a scientific controversy will not be settled in the foreseeable future by observations, there would be little inclination, I think, to regard it as meaningless. Something a little like what Ayer considered to be verification is possible; that is, there can be (and is) evidence that strengthens the case for one or another of the available hypotheses, even if cumulatively it does not confirm or definitively refute any of the major contenders. Let us call this tentative verification. It enables someone to adopt a view on the basis of evidence, but a reasonable person will keep her or his mind open and not assume that opposing views must be incorrect. Even someone who rejects a view still might be able to point to evidence that she or he will admit does strengthen the case for the rejected view. In short, scientific hypotheses are not insulated from observational evidence even if definitive confirmation or disconfirmation eludes us.

Much the same thing can be said about claims in axiology. If someone extols the value of a set of experiences, and you manage to have what it seems reasonable to think are pretty much the experiences praised, and if disappointing features emerge so that the experiences do not present the value that might have been expected, all of this puts you in a better position to be confident of a negative judgment (of experiences of that sort) than you otherwise would have been in. Furthermore, if people whose judgment you trust report the same experiences in relation to much the same evaluative judgments, you could reasonably feel in even a stronger position to be confident of your judgment. Because of these features of our ordinary discourse about values, and of our ordinary ways of arriving at or confirming judgments of value, it does look as if claims in axiology share with those in the sciences two features one associates with verification: experience is relevant to the strength of a case for a claim and to the degree to which one can reasonably be confident of it, and other people's reports of their experiences and consequent judgments also can have weight. Tentative verification is possible.

All of this is built into our normal practices of discussing and debating judgments of value. It is maintained even in the context of stubborn disagreement. We distinguish between cases in which, we would say, the person we disagree with "does not know what he (or she) is talking about," and cases in which it would be unreasonable to say this. We also recognize cases in which someone's testimony about experiences makes us think that our own value judgments might be wrong, that we might have missed something, and cases in which it would be clearly unreasonable to respond in that way. When our own value judgments change, sometimes there is no inclination to claim that we are now in a better position to judge than we had been: we merely see things differently, or "feel differently." But sometimes there is a strong sense, which others may confirm, that we really do know more, that thanks to our experiences or more judicious eye or reflection (or all of these) we are in a better position than we had been to make judgments.

Implicit in this is that many of the judgments we are in a position to make have been shaped by our personal and cultural orientation. First of all, many are *of* sorts of experience that people very different from us might be most unlikely to have. There is always a risk that the general language used to describe experiences can disguise this from us. But secondly, our take (so to speak) on these experiences is unlikely to be precisely the same as someone else's. What does this say about the value claims about which (I have been arguing) we are in a position to be confident? Let me submit that what we are, at best, in a position to maintain (in judgments of value) is that "something like this" is right, or correct, or acceptable.

A clear view of the role of interpretation in experience and in judgment dictates caution in our use of concepts like "objectivity" and "truth." It may well be that perfect objectivity, in the sense of experience and judgment that are untinged by personal and cultural factors and neutral among interpretative tendencies, is possible only for God. Nevertheless, "objective" in the sense of "reasonably objective" has a use in order to contrast what is balanced, fair-minded, and open to a range of views with what is biased or one-sided. In this sense there can be objective reporting and objective historical accounts even if not all the objective accounts will entirely coincide, and even if there is no single ideal of a definitive report or historical account that perfectly mirrors reality. In a sense parallel to this, some judgments of value can be said to be objectively right or pretty much right.

It probably would be best if the word "true" were not applied to judgments of value. It is not grossly inappropriate; but the word is at home in cases in which an interpretative element seems minimal, and in which the contextual importance of assumptions, ways of regarding data, and other beliefs also is easy to disregard. Thus, we can cheerfully agree that "the temperature outside my office at this moment is about eighteen degrees centigrade" is true; although, if we are very mindful of the ways in which future scientific revolutions might revise the framework within which we speak of warmth, or of possible differences with the outlooks on heat of intelligent non-humans, we might more cautiously say "something like this must be true." We are less likely to speak of scientific theories as true than as acceptable or correct, and complicated historical or sociological accounts that emerge as webs of belief also are not normally endorsed as "true." Both in the case of scientific theories and the historical and sociological accounts, empirical verification leads at best to a verdict of acceptability that often is presented as rough ("the account seems largely correct/pretty much right") and as not definitive. It seems reasonable to treat judgments of value in much the same way. Those that in a pronounced way are tinctured by personal and cultural orientation especially cannot be regarded as definitive; but that does not mean that they are worthless, or that all are equally justified. Experience, as I have argued (in the previous two chapters and in this one) can put someone in a better position to be confident that such a judgment is acceptable or pretty much right.

When someone has, or a group of people have, relevant experiences or reasons that support their claims, is this tentative verification really verification? It shares one feature with what Ayer had in mind: the claims in question are not insulated from the results of experience or more generally of inquiry, so that there are ways in which one can reasonably come to see whether they are warranted or not. There are two features of what Ayer had in mind though that are not in this picture. One is that Ayer seems to think of verification as not merely strengthening (or weakening) the case for a claim: it settles the issue. The second (which can underlie the first) is that Ayer's process of verification is thought of as impersonal and itself neutral, so that qualified observers whose initial points of view are different can yet get much the same results. It seems doctrinaire, especially in the light of ongoing controversies in the sciences (which we are sure are meaningful even though we are not sure if or when they will be resolved), to insist on verification that possesses the first of these features as a requirement for meaningfulness. There is no reason to assume that all meaningful issues, even in the sciences, can be settled. The second feature, though, is more problematic. Should the verification that we require for meaning be impersonal and neutral (or at least, if entire neutrality is impossible, highly impersonal and neutral)? I have already conceded that the ways in which we support many of our judgments of value lack this.

There is a great temptation to think, as Ayer himself thought, that to insist on the second feature of his (strong) conception of verification would be to disqualify all of ethics. This is simply incorrect. One counterexample is the claim that excruciating pain has negative value. Anyone who does not already know this can be subjected to excruciating pain, which serves to verify the correctness of the claim. Admittedly there are (as was earlier discussed) a few dissenters in this matter. But equally there can be observers in laboratories, now and then, who do not see what they are supposed to see, or interpret experiences in a bizarre way. In the real world the consensus of observers' reports is often merely near-consensus, as it is with regard to the value of extreme pain.

Some experiences relevant to value can seem impersonal and neutral in relation to a group or a culture. There can be groups (e.g., monastic communities) or cultures within which there can be shared experience supporting claims of the value of certain experiences or features of life. It is a contingent fact that the entire population of the world is not like that, as it is that there is not a wider range of observation reports (on any given occasion) in scientific laboratories. The case of the negative value of extreme pain, though, cannot be limited to the outlook and experience of a specific group or groups. Anscombe's case, in which her grocer's supplying her with potatoes on the promise of future payment constitutes the fact that she owes him money, although a more complicated counterexample (to Ayer's dismissal of all of ethics), also appeals to cross-cultural as well as impersonal experience. Indeed the point of her example is that certain moral visions can be so basic and widely shared that they seem built into experience (and can lead to a consensus rivaling the one that Ayer seems to have in mind as a feature of verification).

None of this is to deny the familiar point that no immediate experience is entirely neutral or free of preinterpretative structuring. Some immediate experiences seem neutral because their preinterpretative tendencies are so ingrained and widely shared that they can be taken for granted. The sorts of experiences that are appealed to in freshman science courses are like this, and these cases will be central to the vision that most non-scientists have of the sciences. But equally, Anscombe's experience of seeing that she owes money to her grocer is like this.

Such cases perhaps are not central to many people's vision of ethics. One reason is, of course, that we live in pluralistic societies. Another is that even non-ethicists are likely to arrive at (and then argue about) judgments that are more complicated and controversial than the observation that extreme pain is bad and that if you have bought potatoes on credit you owe the money. Thus, one of the differences between ethics and the sciences is that non-ethicists are much more familiar with debatable ethical issues (and the arguments they give rise to) than non-scientists are with debatable scientific issues.

To realize all these points promotes a sense that the differences between the sciences and ethics, in relation to verification, are neither as sharp nor as firm as they appeared to Ayer to be. Having said this, one has to come back to the point that very often the experiences and thought patterns relevant to ethical judgment are much more influenced by personality and by preexisting motivations than is usually the case in the sciences. The Christian fundamentalist and the freewheeling libertine may report pretty much the same observations in the laboratory, but they are likely not to see events and situations related to value judgments in similar ways. What do we make of this? Certainly there will be stubborn disagreement in judgments of value. Is there a principle of logic that tells us that stubborn disagreements on a point show that there is no view that actually can be right?

Our ordinary practices of discourse about values indicate the importance of caution: even if stubborn disagreement among intelligent people as to whether X does or does not have high value does not show that there is no view that can be right, it does indicate that very strong confidence in any opinion may be unwarranted. We can apply the words of Cromwell's famous letter (3 August 1650) to the General Assembly of the Church of Scotland: "I beseech you, in the bowels of Christ, think it possible you may be mistaken." We often take judgments of value to be appropriate (and possibly correct) in contexts in which we also take claims to *knowledge* of value to express excessive confidence and to be unwarranted. There are practical reasons for such a stance. It leaves ample room for second thoughts and wider experience, and it also facilitates the tolerance and willingness to compromise that are so important in pluralistic societies. Behind the practical reasons is the philosophical point that to say (1) that there is a view whose rightness is so luminous that one's opponents surely are mistaken is a much stronger claim than (2) that there is a view that is right. We often judge in ethical matters that 2 is justified and 1 is not.

We also often believe that some people are more reliable than others as judges of value. This leaves open the question of who the really reliable ones are; but, even if there typically is not widespread agreement on this point, there is considerable agreeement on *some* of the qualifications that a good judge of values should have. These include a broad range of experience, a continuing capacity to have experiences of a variety of sorts, a willingness to reflect upon and to have second thoughts about experiences related to values, and an openness to new kinds of experience and awareness of new values.

All of this helps to flesh out the concept of tentative verification, and to make clear that there are established and recognized ways in which people can put themselves in a better position to be modestly confident of a judgment of value. It does not prove (i.e., settle definitively) that tentative verification is the right requirement for meaningfulness and possible truth or rightness, and that Ayer's conception of verification is too strong. But it should, at the least, remove the burden of argument from the value realist who claims that judgments of value can be right.

This still does not tell us the form that a defensible value realism should take. Someone who accepts that there can be tentative verification in axiology, and also that this meets the requirement for meaningfulness and possible acceptability, still might wonder what role values — real values — are supposed to play in this picture. What is there to know in judgments of value?

To answer this question we need to look at alternative ways of formulating realistic claims in axiology. Here are four ways of saying pretty much the same thing, one of which seems less artificial and stilted than the others. Let us suppose that Smith and Bloggs both have been absorbed for months in attempting to arrive at a coherent solution to some problems of metaphysics. They both report their experiences and that they enjoyed them; in addition, we have the evidence of their work for what their thought processes must have been like during that period. Smith's were interesting and incisive, with a strong sense of flow from one part to another of her project. Bloggs's in contrast were consistently banal and turgid. On the basis of all this, we may judge (1) that Smith's experiences of arriving at a coherent solution to the problems of metaphysics really were of a high order of value (really were the sort that one should want in a life), and that Bloggs's (despite what he may think) really were not so wonderful. Or we might say (2) that there was real value in Smith's experiences, as far as we can judge, but not in Bloggs's. We also could say (3) that it was the case that Smith's experiences were of high value, more so (as far as we can judge) than Bloggs's. Finally, we might say (4) that it is a fact that Smith's experiences (as far as we can judge) were of a higher order of value than Bloggs's. All of these formulations draw a contrast between what Smith or Bloggs or a casual onlooker might take the value of some experiences to be, on one hand, and some more authoritative judgment, on the other.

The word "really" does much of this work in 1; "real," "it was the case that," and "it is a fact that" can serve the same function. The phrase "real value," though, invites associations, with spectral furniture of the universe, that "really of value" does not. (This is one reason for preferring the formulation that centers on "really," apart from the fact that it is more idiomatic.) This is also a difference between the boilerplate phrases "it is a fact that" and "it was the case that."

Such associations can influence even philosophers, but they scarcely should have argumentative weight. In sorting out the issues of value realism, we need to decide between two starting points. One is putative value facts, which (it might be said) we talk and think about but which may, after all, not be there. If this is our starting point, then we will need to train, as it were, our value telescopes to find out whether there was something we were talking about. The other is our talk and thought about values, including the standards of evidence and logical relations that are implicit in these practices. If this is our starting point, then we will need to inquire into justification of judgments of value, and in particular whether there is justification for claiming that some judgments are authoritative (telling us what really is of value). This line has been pursued in this and the preceeding chapter.

The first starting point has very little to be said for it beyond loose associations built into ways in which philosophical issues sometimes are presented. The notion of something like a value telescope is, of course, nonsense. Some might be influenced by the analogy between values and witches, especially the thought that we can tell whether so-and-so is a witch if there are any (and similarly our talk about values can be correct only if there are real values). But, in fact, the criteria for being a witch included the crucial requirement of special powers, a requirement to which we might be inattentive if we concentrate on what can be readily determined but that nevertheless is both essential and empirical. As far as we can tell, no one has ever met all of the requirements for really being a witch, although many people met some of the more obvious ones. It is far from clear that there is any comparable requirement for being really of value that has never been met.

Are there value facts? This is a less clear question than it might seem, in the absence of a clear and precise formulation of what counts as a fact. Until such a formulation appears, there seems no harm in speaking of value facts, as long as we bear in mind that to speak of the fact that X has high value is equivalent to saying that it is the case that X has high value, and that this is equivalent to saying that X really does have high value.

Are there values? Again, much depends on what we mean. We need to reject any images of spectral furniture of the universe. Sometimes an ethics is encased in a metaphysical theory, struggling to get out, as when Moore (1903, 110) said that goodness has being but not existence. To treat such a claim as one that can be straightforwardly settled by a test of correspondence with reality is exceptionally naive (what would one look for?), and a similar comment applies to the claim that there are values. There is no harm in saying it, as long as it is understood as equivalent to the claim that some things really do have high (or low, or negative) value. The evidence of the emotional awareness of value, discussed in the previous two chapters, strongly supports this claim.

## Conclusion

It is a general rule that what an X is depends on what we should count as an X; this in turn depends on the criteria for being an X. Similarly, if we are willing to say that there are values, what these values are must be understood in terms of the structure of our discourse about values. The argument of this chapter has been that this structure includes standards (for being in a position to be confident of judgments of value) that sometimes are met. Hence, we are in a position to say that it really is the case that some things have high value and that others have low or negative value. If to say that there are real values means pretty much the same thing as this, then there are real values.

This argument must be understood in the context of what I will call philosophical realism, which is the view that philosophies should not be seen as merely poetic-like frameworks for viewing the world but also have to be seen as attempts (which sometimes succeed and sometimes do not) to get the structures of the world and of our knowledge and experience pretty much right. My claim is that value realism, interpreted suitably, gets the world and our knowledge and experience pretty much right.

This is not, however, to claim that the acceptability of value realism is luminous, or that value anti-realists get everything wrong. Indeed, the context in which (I think) value realism is somewhat more acceptable than value anti-realism can be appreciated if we try to imagine two cases that would be more simple than the one we have actually confronted. In the first, value realism would be very clearly—luminously—right. In the second, value anti-realism might seem right.

(1) The universe might have been such that there were no significant variations among sentient beings in the motivational factors and other elements of emotion relevant to judgment of values. In addition, there might have been entire consensus among people of moderate maturity and intelligence, whenever the question arose, as to the circumstances in which someone was qualified to be confident of a judgment of value. (2) Conversely, the universe might have been such that the variations among sentient beings in motivational factors (and other factors of emotion relevant to judgment of values) were consistently as great as one might imagine, so what might have passed as experience of values was a blooming buzzing confusion. In addition, forms of discourse would not have developed that allowed for some degree of confidence in a judgment of value. Whether one could further stipulate, in this worst-case (for value realism) scenario, that such forms of discourse would not be *possible* is debatable. On one hand, arguably they simply could not, in fact, develop within the emotional chaos portrayed. On the other hand, it also can be said that there always would be logical room for them if the facts changed.

That value realism is a vexed topic is in large part tribute to the fact that the real world does not closely resemble either of these two cases. It resembles, though, the first more than the second, in particular in the ways in which structures of value discourse allow us sometimes to claim to be in a position to be confident of judgments of value. This is the heart of the case for value realism. It cannot too strongly be emphasized, however, that even though our world is less far from the one in which value realism is clearly true than the one in which it would be unthinkable, the distances in both directions are great. There are (in the sense outlined) real values, but we *know* far less about what they are than we would like.

# PART II

# AXIOLOGY AND CONDUCT

# 6

# Promoting What Is Good,
# Avoiding What Is Bad

It may seem intuitively that the judgment that something has value carries with it an implication that, other things being equal, it would be better to bring it about (or preserve it, or to have it) than not to bring it about (or preserve it, or to have it). Judgments of negative value may seem to have corresponding implications that are at least as imperative. Thus, there would seem to be a link between judgment of value, on one hand, and recommendation of—or commitment to—action, on the other. Certainly, if Bloggs says, "X has value," and has a clear opportunity to bring about (preserve, or promote) X, and does not, we normally expect that there is an explanation; and it seems odd indeed for Bloggs to say, "Yes, it would be good; I could bring it about, but I won't. There is no reason at all; I just won't." It is, if anything, odder for Bloggs to say, "Yes, it would be unfortunate; I could prevent it, but I won't. There is no reason at all; I just won't." In either case we wonder whether Bloggs really meant what he originally said about the value of X. Perhaps he was being hypocritical. Or perhaps he was mouthing a conventional sentiment that, as it turned out, was not his own at all.

On the other hand, it may not take much for Bloggs to convince us that he may well have meant his original statement about the value of X even though he is not taking steps to promote (or to prevent) it. "I don't feel like it" sometimes is an intelligible reason for not promoting what one claims to value. (I will argue later that in some cases it can function also as an intelligible reason for not preventing negative value; for the time being I will concentrate on positive value.) When Bloggs decides that he does not feel like promoting X, he also may not recommend to others that they do so. All of this may seem plausible if the value Bloggs assigned to X was not all that great, or if Bloggs and his friends have recently done a great deal to promote other values, some of them said to be greater than that of X. Someone can genuinely think that X has value and choose not to exert himself or herself to promote (or preserve, or to have) X or to recommend that others promote it. In a universe in which there are large numbers of values that we can promote, it is inevitable that this often happens. Finally, there is, of course, the extreme possibility of perversity, most dramatically found in satanism. To say, "I preferred that there not be more value in the world," may not represent an attitude that most of us would consider acceptable; but, given the right context, it can function as an explanation of behavior, making it understandable that someone really did believe in a value that he or she chose not to promote or recommend the promotion of.

An explanation in terms of perversity also can work in the case in which the value Bloggs assigned to X is very great, and Bloggs does not seem particularly short of time or energy, rendering it intelligible that Bloggs could have genuinely meant what he said about the high value of X and still not lift a finger to promote X. Perhaps, as an alternative, a policy of extreme indifference to value (even more rare than satanism) also could make this combination seem less hard to understand. Here, as in the preceding chapter, we need to avoid both an extreme prescriptivism, on one hand, and, on the other hand, the anti-prescriptivist view that holds that ethical judgments lack an implicature that gives logical support to statements of expectations about the conduct of the person who makes them. Instead, there is logical support that falls short of entailment, and can be defeated in various ways.

Our immediate concern, however, is not with the link between value judgment and conduct, but rather with the link (if there is one) between two kinds of ethical judgment: one of value, and the other of conduct to be recommended. The latter has to be formulated with an eye to the inexactitude of the terms available. We will ask in the next chapters about the link between judgments of value and judgments that one has a moral obligation to promote values. Not all obligations, of course, are moral. Some would hold, for example, that there is a general obligation to thank a gift-giver for a present. This would normally be considered one of etiquette rather than a moral obligation. Nevertheless, "Bloggs has an obligation to do X," even if the kind of obligation is not specified, constitutes a strong recommendation. A much weaker-sounding recommendation is "It would be best if Bloggs did X." Statements that Bloggs "should" or "ought to" do X may fall somewhere between, a great deal depending on context. Similarly, to say that Bloggs did not act in the best way is milder than the condemnation implicit in saying that what Bloggs did was immoral; to say that what Bloggs did was "wrong" could be at either extreme or somewhere in between. It was wrong of Bloggs to try to pound in a nail with the handle of a spoon; it also was wrong of him to beat up a hated rival. Words like "wrong," "should," or "ought" need either to be treated with great caution or avoided. For the most part I will avoid them. This chapter will be concerned with whether there is a logical link between judgments of value and judgments of what (all things being equal) it would be best to do.

## What It Is Best That One Do

We need to take a fresh look at putative relations among kinds of ethical judgment. In this we should be aware of pitfalls. It will help if some distinctions are borne in mind, including that between the position that I will develop and a somewhat similar one that is very familiar (and that, hence, some readers may expect).

A distinction that has already has been mentioned also needs to be underlined. To say that something is the best thing to do is much less pressing than to claim that there is an obligation of some sort to do it. This has been ignored by many philosophers who read works such as Mill's *Utilitarianism* simplistically as an account of moral obligation, despite the distinctions that Mill adumbrates in the fourteenth paragraph of chapter 5. In his view we call a choice that is not for the best "wrong" (by which he means I think "morally wrong") only if we think it worthy of punishment. This suggests that most of the things that we do that are not for the best do not qualify as "wrong" in the way in which failure to live up to moral obligations generally does. It is clear also that many of the things we do that are not for the best do not violate any sort of obligation, moral or otherwise.

A more subtle distinction is between what is for the best and what it is best to do. (In what follows I will use *optimific* as equivalent to "for the best.") If someone who is evil and powerful is murdered, it is possible for a morally conscientious person to think both that what happened was optimific (for the best) and that the murder was not the best thing to do (and indeed was morally wrong). This is like Leibniz's (1710/1951, 510) concept of *felix culpa*, a fortunate sin.

Because of this latter distinction, judgments of value can have different logical relations to statements of what it is best to do from those they have to statements of what is optimific. A familiar philosophical position, act consequentialism, tends to deny that the difference can be sustained, at least in cases in which we know what is or was optimific (assuming that there are such cases, or at least that they are imaginable). The label "consequentialism" is applied to a family of ethical theories that ground judgments of what it is best to do in assessments of the consequences of the actions or policies open to us. (This is an informal introduction of what will be discussed in much more detail in the final section of this chapter and in the next.) Any member of this family in which the relevant assessment is of the consequences of actions open to us counts as act consequentialism. The best thing to do, in the simplest version of this position, is what it is for the best to happen. Even if we do not know what this is, we might be able retrospectively to determine what would have been optimific (and therefore what was the best thing to do). If it turns out that we never really know what was optimific, in that there will always be further consequences of a choice, we still can hypothesize what an archangel would know to be best and hope that our choices meet this standard. In another version of the position (or alternatively, an element to be conjoined with the assertion of continued lack of complete assurance as to what is optimific), we should do what we have good reason to think will be optimific, weighing possible gains and their probabilities against risks. Reasons for thinking that none of these forms of act consequentialism is acceptable will become clear in what follows, and the position to be developed in this and the following chapter is not act consequentialist.

Let us begin with a truism. If X has positive value, then it will be better (other things being equal) that X be brought about or preserved than that it not be. If

Smith has a choice of whether or not to bring X about, should she? We need to distinguish at this point between the conditions under which it might be intelligible that Smith thinks X has positive value but nevertheless chooses (other things being equal) not to bring it about, and the conditions under which this would be justified. Perversity or systematic indifference to value could help to make such a choice intelligible, but they scarcely are justifications. To speak of what counts as a justification is, it should be clear, to make claims that are themselves normative but which also rest on an appeal to the common structure of normative discourse (a structure in which some normative positions fit comfortably while others require explanation or added justification).

One way of understanding this, and what follows, is to see the investigation as concerned with the logical connections between the present meanings of phrases like "for the best" and phrases like "the best thing to do." The logic is not one of straightforward entailment but rather has to do with the kinds of things that can justify exceptions, excuses, and the like. Further, it may turn out to be neither precise nor entirely fixed. Is it a problem that judgments that exemplify this logic also can be seen as normative? This may not bother those who are comfortable with attacks on the distinction between analytic and synthetic.

In any event, the normative element can be seen in the perspective of a long-standing problem of whether two areas of ethics, that concerned with value and that concerned with how we should behave (including morality), are connected. Kantians tend to treat the two areas as largely, although not entirely, disconnected. Act consequentialists, in contrast, treat the second area as entirely dependent on the first. My own (intermediate) view is that the second area should be viewed as semi-autonomous in relation to the first, which has a loose hegemony over the second. (This is, again, an informal introduction of what will be treated in much more detail as we progress.)

Our exploration of the relation between the two kinds of ethical judgments enters the territory of a pioneering symposium (Slote 1984, Pettit 1984) on satisficing consequentialism: that is, a consequentialism that sometimes yields recommendations that we do what is "good enough" but not optimific. A willingness to settle for what is not optimific can manifest itself on two levels. First, one simply may not consider in any detail whether A or B will have better consequences. Human beings, after all, live in a way that precludes constant reflection or calculation. Much of what we do comes spontaneously, perhaps as an expression of temperament and habits of mind. J. J. C. Smart (1977) has remarked that when he plays field hockey he never thinks about whether the consequences of his actions are good, and that it would spoil the experience if he did. To lose all spontaneity by making every action a result of calculation would be a form of mental illness.

Furthermore, the most supple mind cannot constantly adjust its policies. Much of the time we will simply stay more or less on course. Hence, given the costs (in loss of spontaneity, in effort and time, and also in risk of destabilizing the self) of frequent weighing of consequences, it is useful to have a trigger mechanism (a fairly quick and itself unreflective sense that major values of one sort or another may be at stake) for engaging in such consideration. If such major values are not at stake, the judgment may be that what we are inclined to do is good enough.

If major values do seem to be at stake, this can lead to a second level, at which one has considered whether A or B will have better consequences, and at which perhaps one will be able to have some degree of confidence as to what is optimific. Satisficing then takes the form of endorsing what is not optimific, and this is what the discussion that follows will explore. My account will be consistent with Pettit's claim (172 ff.) that reasonable satisficing itself needs a consequentialist motive (see Kupperman 1981 for related discussion). Such a motive can be as broad and simple, I think, as the undesirable effect on the quality of life of a tendency always to pursue small advantages.

Let us look at some putative justifications that Smith might use for choosing not to bring about something that (all things being equal) would be optimific. For the sake of simplicity, I will in this section of the chapter treat judgments of what is optimific as unproblematic, only later exploring complications that flow from our not in fact knowing with complete assurance what is for the best. I also will focus first on a single choice on a particular occasion. (The next section of the chapter will be concerned with the less simple choices of courses of action or of stances or policies maintained over a period of time.) Even someone who is convinced of the great importance of character, habit, and continuity in ethical choice can admit that there are cases in which, as it were, someone pauses and takes a fresh and decisive look at alternatives in a way that can lead to discontinuities in conduct. Even if there is no room for complete assurance, there can be a degree of clarity as to which alternative leads to greater value in the foreseeable future. Some may doubt this on the ground of the "incommensurability" of values: as it is commonly put, we may hesitate to compare apples to oranges. But in most contexts a ripe, clean orange is preferable to a moldy apple, as is someone's life being preserved to some flowers not being trampled. And a ripe, clean apple may be preferable to nothing, as is (normally) a friend's becoming happier at no cost to anyone else.

On an occasion on which she chooses not to do what is optimific, Smith may defend this with one of the following reasons.

J1. "It is difficult constantly to be making the world a better place; on this particular occasion I don't feel like it."

J2. "Others can bring about the better state of affairs. Why me?"

J3. "Taking the time and trouble to bring X about, even though the world would be a better place, fits very badly with my plan of life and sense of self."

J4. "Yes, the world would be a better place if X happened; but all the same it would run counter to my professional obligations, my relationships, or good manners for me to bring it about."

J5. "Yes, the world would be a better place if X happened; but all the same it would be immoral for me to bring it about."

This is by no means an exhaustive list; also, each of these five purported justifications is a short story that could be expanded in more than one way. Nevertheless, the list does capture, I think, the most pressing concerns that people have about the connection between what is optimific and what it is best that one do.

We need constantly to make distinctions if we are to gain a clear view of how these lines of justification work or fail to work. One crucial distinction is between what we think it better that someone do, on one hand, and what we would blame that person for not doing, on the other. It is arguable that even saints are not perfect, and that no one scores 100 percent in the advisability of her or his choices over a lifetime, or even during a given year or a given week. What we tend to blame in people's behavior are either (a) serious mistakes, especially those that could readily have been avoided and foreseeably bring harm or (b) a pattern of mistakes, especially if these are moderately serious. Hence, there may be cases in which it is obvious that we would not blame Smith for not bringing X about, would not even think less cf her, but in which nevertheless we agree it would be better if she did it.

Even the word "mistake" has to be treated with care. If it would be better that Smith do X than Y, we are not inclined to call her doing Y a mistake unless something significant is at stake, either for her or for others. Behavior that is mildly suboptimal is not normally a mistake. Indeed, to resist the view of the previous sentence is to flirt with mental illness by draining the spontaneity and expunging carefree moments from everyday life. In most cases, if X brings about slightly more value than Y, and if one does Y, no one should care.

Can J1 defeat whatever the link may be between a judgment of value and a judgment of what it is best that one do? In some cases it is hard to say. If what is at stake is some mild satisfaction or comfort or convenience, then it seems plausible to say that the link is very weak. That X has some slight positive value creates the mildest of presumptions that, other things being equal, it would be best if one brought about or preserved X. At the other extreme: if what is at stake is someone's life or happiness, to say, "I do not feel like doing X," scarcely defeats the link between judgment of value and judgment of what it would be best to do.

Let us look more closely at the murkier (and more commonly occurring) extreme, the one in which what is at stake is very slight. It is tempting here to say that the displeasure or very minor strain of being asked to do yet another optimific thing represents a slight negative value (so that, in a sense, "other things" are not equal) that must be placed on the scales opposite whatever slight value attaches to X. In concrete terms, deciding that it would be best if one wrote (yet again) to one's elected representatives in support of some worthy cause takes time, postage, and energy. This may in some cases offset the value brought about by writing; in those, J1 functions as an explanation of why there was no net value that was missed, rather than as an excuse for missing it.

To make this point can be part of a strategy to preserve the link between value and what it would be best to do. The general effectiveness of such a strategy for the cases now discussed is virtually impossible to judge, in that there usually is no precise or convincing way of weighing slight values against one another. Indeed the general imprecision of value assessments is such that often we are left merely thinking that the values on the two sides of an issue are comparable in importance (and impossible to adjudicate between). Even if many cases of what seems a slight surplus of value (that would result from what someone does not feel like doing) can change their valence of value on closer assessment, it seems dogmatic to maintain this of all cases.

What is clearest is that we normally do not blame people for not promoting or preserving slight values, when they simply do not feel like doing so; nor do we think that they have done something "wrong" or have made a mistake. Do we nevertheless think (mildly) that it would have been best for them to produce the slight value surplus at stake? Or do we regard what is advisable in such cases as simply what someone feels like doing?

Each of these verdicts seems plausible, nor is it possible to give a really compelling argument against either of them. Common sense may well tilt toward the second verdict. What it is best for Smith to do seems roughly to equate with what it would be best for a disinterested person to recommend to Smith to do. Our advice, in cases of this sort, often takes the form of "It doesn't matter; whatever you feel like doing is fine."

In all of this we need to bear in mind the nature of human beings, for whom our recommendations (including morality) must be tailored. As R. M. Hare (1981) has pointed out, archangels would be a different matter. Human beings cannot be expected to be continuously unselfish in even the smallest things, and any ethics whose pressure on them is relentless will be counterproductive.

Let us return now to cases in which only slight value is at stake, and look explicitly at ones in which the value is negative. It may be that the case in which Smith can prevent Z, which has some slight negative value, but does not feel like doing so, is much like the case of slight positive value just discussed. There is no reason to assume that judgments of positive and negative value are symmetrical in their logic, and many philosophers have held that the implicit imperative to avoid negative value is stronger than that to seek positive value. Something like that can be read into both Epicurean and Buddhist philosophy, and there is Anscombe's suggestion that accepting avoidable pain always requires a reason and that eschewing available pleasure sometimes does not. Nevertheless, it can be held that much of the apparent asymmetry can be explained by the fact that negative values frequently seem more serious than (i.e., outweigh) positive values. Perhaps the ordinary life that many of us have is, on any plausible chart of values, well above the halfway mark between the best imaginable and the worst imaginable. One might try the following thought experiment. Choose between two months of ordinary life as you now experience it, or one month of the best you can imagine and one month of the worst you can imagine. (The sequence may be reversed if you prefer.) At more modest levels of value, Anscombe's point can be met by pointing out that most of what we are willing to call pain simply is taken more seriously than most pleasures are, so that on the value scale the opposite of moderate and fleeting pleasure is moderate discomfort. We often think that no reason is called for when someone accepts moderate discomfort, and, indeed, many people choose habitually to be uncomfortable.

With this in mind, I think that the case in which Smith does not feel like preventing Z is much like that in which she does not feel like promoting X. She could bring her friend a pillow, but it has been a long day and she does not. Does the very slight strain of going to the trouble of bringing the pillow equal the discomfort of her friend's current posture, or is it not quite equal (but it scarcely matters)? It seems impossible to say.

Cases in which the value at stake in promoting X or preventing Z is significant look very different. In these more serious cases the first of our two verdicts is clearly justified. Surely it is better to produce or promote significant value (and to prevent significant negative value) than not to do so, and in such a case "I do not feel like it" does not defeat the general connection between judgment of value and judgment of what it is best to do. Of course it may obviate criticism. There are times when we think it best that someone bring about a value that we judge to be significant, but when the decision will be regarded as essentially up to that person. We are especially unlikely to think the choice open to criticism if the value at stake (while significant) was not nearly as great as that of a life or of someone's fulfilment or happiness, and if no recognized obligations or rights are violated, and if the same person has not been generally slack in promoting positive value where possible. If Smith says, "I have done a lot, and in this case I would rather not bother," this can disarm any tendency we might have either to criticize or to think that she might fault herself; all of this can be true even if we at the same time believe that it would have been best if she had promoted X (but under the circumstances that would have been asking too much).

It may be that we are more inclined to be critical if Smith did not bother to prevent significant negative value. We may simply have a higher standard for averting evils than for promoting goods; but this seems context-dependent, in that an asymmetry is most clearly evident in contexts in which there are many more opportunities to promote goods than to prevent evils. In the case in which Smith, who is very charitable, could have given even more to charities that help to prevent misfortunes that we judge to have significant but not great negative value, we would, I think, not be critical. Yes, it would have been best if she (and for that matter, we) had given even more; but past a certain point the $J_1$ defense disarms criticism.

$J_2$, the "Why me?" defense, also can disarm criticism in some cases in which significant (but not major) value is at stake, and can place in doubt any recommendation of action if the value at stake is slight. One complication is that "Why me?" raises issues of justice, and that it is arguable that negative value attaches to a social arrangement in which some are asked to do far more than their share. Philosophers in recent decades have written a great deal about the justice of distribution of resources such as money. Much less attention has been paid to subtle resources, such as those involved in the great division between people whose jobs are interesting and those whose work is numbing and thoroughly boring. There also can be a division, within an organization or in the society at large, between those who constantly think that they should be doing more (or are actually asked to take on more), and, on the other hand, those who take on less. It is often far from clear, in this division, that the advantages are all on one side. Indeed, a case can be made that it is far more gratifying, and better, to be useful and responsible than to be (to some degree) idle and irresponsible. Nevertheless, someone who is useful and responsible can have moments in which what is asked simply seems to add up to too much. At such moments the "Why me?" defense kicks in.

The gap between what we would recommend against and what we would criticize can be especially great when the "Why me?" defense applies. Very often our opinion of a person's behavior is strongly influenced by context, especially the context of other choices made by that person. A pattern of refusal to take responsibility is very different from an occasional refusal that can be seen against the background of a good deal of concerned involvement. Also, most of us are very aware of the risks of asking too much of others, or of ourselves. Saints and heroes can take on a very great deal, multiplying demands on themselves. Most of us are not up to that, although almost everyone could take on more than she or he does. One of the dangers is that a level of involvement may be accepted that cannot be sustained; another is that the person whom we urge to do more may become naturally resentful at the disparity between what she or he does and what others do, and in the end may do less rather than more. If we criticize Smith, who is an energetic, conscientious person, for not bringing about X (which she agrees would involve greater value in the world), she may come to see the efforts she does make to function as a good person as less rewarding than they had seemed. It may be unwise even to *say* to Smith, "It would be best if you brought about X (or prevented Z, which will carry negative value)," if she is very likely to feel that way.

Nevertheless, we think in general that if significant value is at stake in Smith's bringing about X or preventing Y, of course it would be best that she bring about X or prevent Y. To behave optimally (as a saint would) would be best; and the "Why me?" defense can be a way of saying, "I am not a saint (I am not trying to be perfect or near perfect), so please do not criticize me by those very high standards." In such cases, in which something significant is at stake, "Why me?" should be taken not as denying that a better choice is (or was) available, but rather as claiming immunity from negative responses.

So viewed, the "Why me?" defense can work well for Smith but seem ludicrous for Bloggs, who really does very little. Even for Smith, though, it has its limits. If someone is drowning, Smith is a good swimmer, and others in the area refuse to enter the water, we would blame Smith for not jumping in, even if she is tired and already has saved a number of drowning people.

Here both the immediacy of the result and the likelihood that the needs responded to will not be persistent and endless, as well as the seriousness of what is prevented, affect our response. It is very doubtful that we would criticize Smith in the same way for not sending even more money to Oxfam. Is this a moral slackness in contemporary common sense? The way in which we make demands on other people and on ourselves can itself be evaluated consequentially; and it is arguable that under current conditions the consequences of not treating these two kinds of cases (saving yet another drowning person and sending even more money to Oxfam) differently would be unfortunate. We do not want to discourage, by suggesting limitless demands, efforts to do what is for the best.

Saving the drowning (like some of the heroic things that people are called upon to do in response to catastrophes) does not involve demands likely to be endlessly repeated. It is unfair that Smith is called upon to save swimmer after swimmer; but the value of the human life, along with the other features of the case, outweighes everything else. We not only think that she best should save the drowning swimmer, but also would (sadly) criticize her for not doing so even if she has saved many others.

Let me summarize conclusions thusfar about defenses J1 and J2. They may be plausible in cases in which the value at stake is slight. They are not when it is significant or great: as a general rule, it is best that one create or preserve something of significant value (or prevent something of significant negative value), other things being equal. Someone who fails to do this can be criticized even if J1 applies, but sometimes J2 can give a person immunity from criticism for not having done what it would have been best to do. If the value at stake is significant but not great, we can judge that it would be best for Smith to produce or preserve it; but, considering all that she does, we would not criticize her for not doing this, nor would we criticize her for not sending even more money for famine relief. We would criticize Bloggs under the same circumstances, for the particular omission in the context of a general pattern of slackness.

Thus far we have considered cases in which someone is in roughly as good a position as others to do what would be for the best, and there are no strong reasons for that person specially to be called upon. Sometimes, though, the force of "Why me" depends very much on who utters it. An effective reply can be simply, "Because you are the child's father" or "Because it's your job." These two replies share an appeal to the notion that sometimes responsibility is not a matter of what one chooses at the moment to take on, or of who happens to be best placed to accomplish something. They are different, however, in the responses to entire failure that they can lead to. To do absolutely nothing even though you are the child's father can be inhuman, or at least reveal a lack of normal human feeling. To do absolutely nothing even though it is your job exposes one to a different kind of contempt, connected with ideas of laziness and vacuity.

J3 appeals to a sense of self that is very much connected with projects and activities, some of which can be engrossing or require single-minded attention. If what will result from Smith's writing to her elected representatives or volunteering at the local soup kitchen will be for the best, and she is trying to write a symphony (or her doctoral dissertation), is it best that she take time and attention temporarily away from her project in order to do these good things? If the value at stake (in what Smith may feel called upon to do) is slight, there is, of course, the complication that the negative value associated with the disruption to her life can outweigh it. This can remain a possibility even if the value at stake is significant, if the disruption to Smith's life also is significant or if Smith's symphony or academic work is likely to be very good.

Let us assume for the sake of argument that, all things considered, there will be some surplus of value (i.e., it would be for the best) if Smith disrupted her life. Would it be best if she did so? If we think the net surplus would be slight, my sense is that (as in relation to J1 and J2) we would find the issue not able to be resolved with confidence but would incline toward a negative verdict. If the value at stake is significant but not great, we would think it best that she disrupt her life but also would be likely to regard this as "too much to ask," and thus be disinclined to criticize her refusal. One reason for this reluctance to criticize has already been discussed: raising standards for people's behavior can be, past some point, counterproductive. Another is that interventions into people's lives, in the form of criticism, can be too intrusive; we may not want people, especially creative artists or scholars like Smith, to feel too much that there is social pressure (however high-minded) on the direction of their lives. If any action that Smith takes can be evaluated in relation to the values that it does or does not promote, then any criticism that we might be inclined to make also is itself (as an action) open to such evaluation.

If what is at stake in Smith's decision of whether to disrupt her life is of great value, say someone's life or happiness, this alters the case. Our sense that Smith ought to interrupt her work in order to bring about something of great value (or prevent something of great negative value) depends, of course, on such factors as whether the disruption will be great or minor, how important her work is to Smith, and how good it is likely to be. But if, after all of these factors are considered, the net value surplus at stake still seems great (and a great deal may have to be at stake for this to seem true), by and large there will be little hesitation in judging that it would be best that Smith interrupt what she is doing. If the disruption is significant or sustained, though, then Smith is in an ever-stronger position to ask, "Why me?" Here issues of gender become relevant, in that often women are asked unfairly to do what could be about as well done by men. Unless there is a very good answer to "Why me?" we would be, I think, reluctant to criticize Smith for not disrupting her work.

In some ways it would be very appealing to say that no one should ever be asked to disrupt projects important to him or her because of some greater good. But this simply goes against normative common sense. Serious emergencies of various kinds, in particular, are widely held to justify asking people to disrupt their lives.

What J3 brings to the fore is the possible conflict between the demands and needs of the world, on one hand, and, on the other hand, those of an individual life that has, to use Bernard Williams's term (Smart and Williams 1973) its own integrity. At one extreme is the view that the general good always should be decisive; at the other, that the individual plan of life always (subject perhaps to some qualifications, such as the requirement not directly to harm others) should be respected. Neither extreme is palatable. The first is counterproductive in draining from society the values that individualism makes possible. Something a little like it can be acceptable in emergencies of limited duration (such as wartime), but beyond this it is likely to be felt to be too confining. The other extreme seems egocentric, smacking of the romanticist cult of the genius (or would-be genius), and seeming likely not to be good for either the genius or for her or his work. Even a dedicated life is likely to have some slack, and some degree of flexibility, so that it is hard to regard most kinds of extraneous demands as damagingly intrusive; and the narcissism of insisting on an entire absence of disturbance is hardly appealing. It seems odd to regard the insertion of an unwanted incident, such as being required to help someone who needs help, as spoiling the unity and wholeness of the whole. Lives are not classical symphonies. Sustained demands can be a different matter; and that is why (as it seems to me) there can be some cases, even when the value at stake is great, in which J3 gives immunity to criticism of a refusal to do what is for the best.

J4 represents a disjunctive sampling of major constraints, that we can legitimately feel under, that may not amount to moral obligations. Codes of professional ethics require doctors, lawyers, morticians, teachers, and so forth, to behave in certain ways and not in others, and are likely to be internalized (in the form of strong inhibitions) by those they govern. In some cases it may be morally wrong not to follow the code: such may be our judgment of a doctor's refusal to save a life. But there are other cases in which violations will be criticized as serious, but not as serious in the same way as immorality. Is it always (regardless of circumstances and other things at stake) morally wrong for a lawyer to divulge confidential information? Sometimes (e.g., when what is involved is merely trivial gossip) unprofessional conduct can seem more sloppy than immoral. In short, role obligations are not always moral requirements (see Hardimon 1994, p. 334, for a somewhat different view). Also there can be cases, as when the life of an innocent potential victim is at stake, when we might argue that what is professionally wrong would be morally right.

Special relationships also can operate as constraints on what we think it best that we do. When a number of people's interests are at stake, it can be relevant that one of those people is our child, spouse, lover, or close friend. Social conventions (which can be argued to be useful in their general effect) govern when such considerations seem appropriate. We do not favor a loved one when we are deciding among candidates for a position (the boundaries of the socially permissible have evolved so as to exclude nepotism and kindred forms of favoritism); but it is considered normal to do so when we are giving presents, doing favors, or deciding whom to help.

Finally, there can be constraints of etiquette, which can have a greater hold over some people than over others, and also can seem more pressing in some circumstances (e.g., the ordinary formal occasion) than in others (e.g., when someone's life may be at stake). Sometimes rudeness should be the least of our worries. But it can be argued that it is socially useful, especially in reducing unnecessary abrasions, if many people sometimes are guided by recognized forms of etiquette. To be "well brought up" can be to internalize these, so that it would seem difficult (and indeed unnatural) to behave in a way that goes against ordinary good manners.

Nevertheless, there can be occasions when (even giving due weight to factors such as discomfort and embarrassment) it can be for the best if someone goes against ordinary good manners. What violates good manners can be instrumental in making some things of value more possible, or some things of negative value easier to prevent. The very fact of rudeness, like a sudden musical discord, can be useful in jarring people out of their accustomed patterns of thought in a situation that calls for a fresh look. If significant value (all things considered) can be gained, we would think it best that Smith, who always has been kind and considerate, act in an unkind and inconsiderate way if this is what is required. If she does not do what is best, our criticism of her inflexibility would be softened by respect for her habits of mind; but there still would be room for criticism, especially if the value missed was great and apparent. What if, on the other hand, her unkind and inconsiderate behavior would lead to a slight surplus of value? My sense is that, as in the cases of J1, J2, and J3, there is no luminously clear resolution but that we might tilt in the direction of recommending that (in that what is at stake is slight) Smith act in her accustomed way.

The case looks different if what is required to achieve the slight surplus of value is that Smith let down her friends or loved ones, or that Smith violate the ethical code of her profession. It is difficult to assess such cases, in that the consequences of damaging important personal relationships or of undermining loyalty (one's own and that of colleagues who may be influenced) to professional ethics normally will be a good deal more serious than those of bad manners; and because of this, much more must be at stake in order to produce what would be (all things considered) the slight surplus of value. Nevertheless, it is also true that recommendations typically carry force beyond the particular cases for which they may be tailored. It is dangerous to recommend at all lightly that someone set aside a generally useful code of professional ethics or override what is normally expected of love or friendship. Because of this, I think it clear that we would recommend that Smith follow the code of her profession or the dictates of love or friendship even if not doing so would result in a slight surplus of value.

The recommendation here may amount in some cases to what has been called an agent-centered restriction rather than (as in relation to J1, J2, J3) an agent-centered prerogative (see Scheffler 1982). That is, we might in some cases blame Smith if she violated the code of her profession or the dictates of love or friendship for the sake of a slight surplus of value.

If her going against these accustomed constraints would result in a significant surplus of value, our recommendation might depend on how significant it is, and also how singular (and unlikely to be repeated) the case is that might inspire the violation. These questions would need to be answered on a case-by-case basis. Clearly there are times when we would recommend that Smith, for a much greater good, violate the ethics of her profession or let down friends or loved ones. In some of these cases, when the importance of what is to be gained or prevented is both great and clear, we also would criticize Smith for not doing what was needed, although the criticism might be softened by our respect for some of the habits of mind that led to Smith's mistake.

Some readers may think that, if Smith's concern for loved ones and friends deserves special attention, so too (in a different way) should her attitude toward complete strangers or toward people whose desert points in the direction of negative value. Suppose that Smith's doing X rather than Y will result in a significant surplus of value, but that all this benefit will go to Bloggs (whom she does not know) or to Blumpf (a reprobate who deserves discomfort or worse rather than good fortune)? The temptation may be to say that none of what happens to Bloggs or Blumpf is Smith's business or concern.

In the case in which Smith can do a significant favor for Bloggs, a complete stranger, the natural question is "Why not?" A nice person normally would. We have seen, though, that there are circumstances in which even a very nice person would not: even very nice people sometimes do not feel like it, and then there is the "Why me?" defense along with J3 and J4. The "Why me?" defense is the one most likely to be invoked in relation to complete strangers, and unless there is a very good answer (e.g., you are the only one who can help) it can earn immunity from criticism for not doing what (in fact) it would have been best to do. We certainly do not blame Smith, who is, in general, an energetic and conscientious person, for not doing a significant favor for Bloggs when others could do it about as well. If it is a matter of saving Bloggs from drowning, that, of course, is a different thing. Even in the case in which what is at stake is significant but not great, we would, I think, criticize someone who did nothing to be helpful if that person had a general record of doing little or nothing to be helpful to others. A better person would go out of her or his way sometimes to help others.

The case of helping Blumpf is more thorny. One might recall the holistic insistence in the first part of this book that the value of a world is not necessarily the sum of the values pertaining to the elements of that world (and also that the value of such elements is affected by context). Unjust distributions of benefits certainly adversely affect the overall value within a society, and in assessing a drastically undeserved significant benefit for Blumpf one must take account also of side effects (including envy, resentment, and loss of moral confidence on the part of those who have behaved better than Blumpf). What looks at first like a significant gain in overall value may not be one at all. On the other hand, there is the complication that, arguably, the greatest benefit one could confer on Blumpf is to make him a better person. Why not, one might ask? What Blumpf and the average sensual person will see as a considerable benefit may well be, seen against the background of his present poor character, really not worth very much.

Bearing all of this in mind, one can see the connection between "It would be for the best, all things considered, if Smith benefited Blumpf in way X" and "It would be best for Smith to benefit Blumpf in way X" as not departing too sharply from the patterns thus far established. It is not at all clear that it would be best for Smith to benefit Blumpf if, all things considered, the surplus of value would be slight. If it would be significant, then something great must be in store for (or some great evil must be prevented for) Blumpf in order so significantly to outweigh the side effects. A good person normally would do this to benefit Blumpf, just as a good person normally would save Blumpf (knowing who he was) from drowning. But, given Blumpf's record, we would not blame Smith for inaction if the value at stake was significant rather than great, especially if she has other demands on her.

Finally, a reason for thinking it not best to do what would be optimific is J5, that it would be immoral. This reason, if it is compelling, can generate agent-centered restrictions; and the case for regarding it (when the moral judgment on which it rests seems correct) as always or almost always compelling will be a case for such restrictions. The strength and nature of this reason will be examined more fully in the next chapter. But we may now take a preliminary look at it, as a way of seeing how it could function.

An act consequentialist of the most straightforward kind would deny, of course, that J5 counts as a reason at all, and would insist instead that what it is best to do is always what is optimific. But even such a consequentialist would be very likely to concede that this is not how the matter presents itself to most people. Most of us work with some pre-reflective sense of what is morally impermissible, before we begin the detailed reckoning of (likely) consequences required for a judgment of what is optimific. For someone who is well brought up, this prereflective moral sense is both deeply rooted and stubborn, and will not be readily reversed by analyses of likely consequences. Sometimes consequences that are both clear and grave will convince someone that what is at hand is a "special case," but even here there usually was a burden of demonstration that had to be shouldered.

Related to this is a tendency to respect the views of someone whose morality seems approximately right even in areas in which there is moral disagreement. Should such a person go against her or his morality? There may be times at which a great deal is at stake, or the moral judgment in question seems a sheer misjudgment, when a case can be made for an answer of "Yes." But there is no doubt that we often give weight to a person's sincere moral conviction in recommending what she or he do, even if we think that the conviction may be a mistake. What complicates the matter is that even a mistaken sincere conviction can play an important role in someone's finely tuned system of motives and inhbitions, which in turn will have a great deal to do with that person's sense of self. To risk disruption of a system that, in general, works pretty well counts as a (possible) negative side effect, one that may weigh as heavily as anything to be gained by a person's going against her or his conscience. But there can be cases in which, even weighing the psychological risks to Smith of her going against her conscience, we think it would be (on balance) for the best if she do so; even in these cases, respect for Smith may condition what we would recommend, along with any willingness we might have to criticize her if she does act on her conscience.

In short, there is some initial plausibility, even when we do not agree with the moral judgment it expresses, in treating "It would be morally wrong" as a reason of some strength (but not necessarily unlimited strength) for thinking that the person who gives it would be advised not to do what (she or he agrees) would be for the best. We may regard it (assuming that it is sincere and not totally preposterous) as a good reason except in cases in which great value is at stake, and even then it may give us pause. In part this is a result of social attitudes of respect for conscience, which themselves can be argued to have considerable utility. At a deeper level, this reflects the fact that both people's choices and our practices in judging these choices and in making recommendations have to be seen as embedded in networks of habits, inhibitions, and long-standing attitudes. Occasionally they can be wrenched from these contexts and held up in isolation for evaluation. But to do this repeatedly or systematically is to do violence to the nature of ethical life for human beings. I will turn now to an examination of what it is best that one do as viewed in this context.

## Living for the Best

A question conscientious people sometimes ask when deciding what to do is "What kind of person would this make me?" This can express anxiety about aspects (that may have been submerged) of one's present character; it also is, on the face of it, yet another query about consequences. All of this rests on assumptions about actions and personhood. Actions affect the kind of person we are; but, of course, the relation is reciprocal, in that the kind of person we are affects the way in which we structure our sense of the situation about which we have to decide, along with what the alternatives are. It also has a major effect on our immediate inclinations, which may well be decisive (especially if we have to act quickly). One of the striking features of "What kind of person would this make me?" is that even conscientious people ask it only occasionally. This infrequency suggests that a choice in which this is an explicit consideration is very likely to condition a whole series of further choices in which it is not, and further that the occasional review of the kind of person we want to be is itself conditioned by the results of previous reviews. Normally people do not constantly reinvent themselves, and even the occasional reinvention will be more thoroughly constrained by what has gone before than may at first seem to be the case.

Because of this, the device (shared by act consequentialists and by philosophers such as Kant) of treating choices, especially moral choices, as if they can be understood and assessed independently of other choices made by the same individual and of the general character and habits of mind that individual has established, represents a drastic oversimplification. The distortion is least serious in those cases in which someone pauses and attempts to take a fresh look at a situation that may be novel or could represent a turning point. It is most serious in relation to everyday decisions in which deliberation is either perfunctory or absent, and in which a prereflective structuring of the case represents at least nine-tenths of the process of decision.

In life one thing leads to another. Let us suppose that Bloggs now works in the Mergers and Acquisitions department of a major brokerage, and cheerfully bends a few rules that it would seem naive to follow to the letter. No one is harmed, he reasonably may think; it is only a device to expedite matters. Further on, though, some much more dubious things may be expected of Bloggs because of this initial choice. Or he may find it necessary to commit perjury in order to avoid a good deal of trouble that, in some sense, he does not deserve.

This journey through gray areas in which the landscape may get progressively darker (but may not) is an increasing phenomenon of modern life. Sometimes, arguably, there is no harm in bending rules. Much depends on the rule, the circumstances, and the pattern of likely involvement. The immediate point is this. Bloggs's initial decision of whether to bend the rules or not is more complicated, and less discrete, than it may seem to him. On one hand, what is at stake amounts to a pattern of involvement that includes commitments that may be difficult (although not absolutely impossible) to avoid, so that in making the initial decision Bloggs is more than half of the way toward making a variety of future decisions about whose nature he now cannot be entirely sure. When these future choices do present themselves, Bloggs may well have a sense that he has already to a considerable degree decided about them, even though he was not fully aware of having done so. On the other hand, the Bloggs who decides to bend the rules is the same person who as a college student took up a certain attitude toward authority and toward preexisting rules; decisions taken then may flow smoothly into the one about bending the brokerage rules.

All of this suggests that a person's most important choices may be of the attitudes taken to other people, toward social demands, toward the difficulties that present themselves in one's own life, all of which goes under the heading of character. A very large number of major choices, then, are, to a degree, predetermined by the character of the person who makes them. So also is the likely quality of that person's life. But it is relatively rare that someone asks, "What kind of character would I like to have?" and embarks on a course of action that is directed in a sustained way toward the goal indicated by the answer. Furthermore, even if someone does ask this question in a serious spirit, this will occur when such a person is already old enough to have a character, whose habits of mind will be somewhat resistant to change. It is unusual for someone to be able to change her or his character in major respects within a short period of time by an act (or acts) of will. Major changes in the longer run are another matter, but often they take place as a side effect of changes in the circumstances of someone's life.

Let us return to Smith, who is asking whether it is best for her to do what is optimific. There are two ways in which the kinds of consideration we have been discussing can change the question. First, it is natural to regard what is optimific in terms of a balance of consequences (especially ones that are foreseeable) such as loss of life or money, gains or losses of happiness or of gratifying personal relationships, and so forth. But one set of consequences of whatever Smith decides to do will include the further choices that will confront her later on, and the effects on the kind of person Smith is both of her present decision and of the further choices that this will lead to. Sometimes these consequences will be a minor factor in relation to the balance that determines what is optimific; sometimes they will be a major factor. But in the great majority of cases of both sorts, they will be incalculable. This makes the judgment of what is optimific, in many cases, much less a rational matter than might be hoped. The instinct, almost a sense of personal destiny, that an intelligent and sensitive person may have cannot always be discounted. It also needs to be said that, if there is drastic uncertainty about consequences, sometimes an attitude of "Here I stand; I can do no other" is simply the most reasonable one to take. What is foolish and stubborn in many cases can count in others as reasonable steadiness of purpose.

Second, Smith can place alongside the question of what is optimific on this particular occasion another: "What life can I lead that would be, all things (in the world that might be affected) considered, for the best (optimific)?" Her answer to this much broader question can inform, and in some cases change, her answer to the first. But it also is going to be difficult to arrive at an answer to the broader question that either is at all definite or inspires strong confidence. In the real world, "What kind of life would be optimific?" typically operates as a constraining worry, affecting responses to "What in this case is optimific?" rather than as a way of getting specific advice.

This leaves open the question of whether, if some kinds of answer to "What kind of life would be optimific?" (i.e., all values, whatever and whosoever they may be, considered) do look highly plausible to Smith, it would be best for her to choose a life that would be optimific. The linkage between what is optimific and what it is best that one choose may well look weaker here than when the issue concerned a single choice on a particular occasion. That is because demands that focus on an entire way of life generally look more serious than those that focus on a single choice. It may not be too much to ask Smith to drop what she is doing, on some specific occasion, in order to do something for the general good. It is asking a great deal to recommend that she change her entire way of life.

Much depends on whether what might be asked of Smith is merely a change in aspects of her way of life, which could be changed in a way that did not damage the general character (or personal satisfactoriness) of the life, and further whether such aspects were intimately connected with harming others or weakening personal relationships. If Smith frequently breaks promises or insults her friends, there would be little hesitation, I think, in recommending that she adjust her policies in these areas. We might also be willing to recommend that she be more helpful in various ways, especially if this would have little effect on the aspects of her life that are most important to her. But this might seem more intrusive (because less strongly justified) than the recommendation that she start keeping her promises.

Suppose, though, that what is at stake is not some policy of Smith's that involves harming others or weakening personal relationships, or that ignores other people's needs for help, that is not near the center of any reasonable sense of what her life is about. Suppose instead that the problem is that Smith's central projects turn out not to be as useful as they might be. For example: it is important to her that she has chosen to be an artist rather than an engineer, but she would do a lot more good for her society as an engineer. My sense is that we would be strongly inclined not to make a recommendation of this sort if the anticipated value surplus (weighing both social gains and personal costs) were not great. Again, bear in mind that the consequences of making a recommendation can themselves be evaluated as part of judgment of whether the recommendation is appropriate or justified. Also, just as a single choice of Smith's can both express an entire way of life and affect the development of that way of life, so also a single recommendation concerning another person's life can both express a whole set of social attitudes or policies and affect their development. Something like Mill's central argument in *On Liberty* seems to hold generally for modern societies: there are more happy and fulfilled lives if there is a general policy of not putting pressure on people's choices of life as long as these do not involve harm to others.

Mill's further recommendation not to apply such pressure in cases in which the harm to others was only indirect can be challenged, at least in cases in which choices made by a number of people contribute to considerable indirect harm. This thorny issue in social philosophy is relevant to our present concern. If we accept Mill's central argument, we would not recommend that Smith become an engineer instead of an artist (which is what she really wants) if her society could not be said to be harmed by her choice to be an artist. Suppose, though, that her society were in dire straits because of the acute shortage of engineers. My own judgment is that this could justify the recommendation, although even here the strength of Smith's disinclination would certainly matter, along with whether she would be a good engineer and not a good artist. Also, even if we said, "Look, they really do need engineers very badly, and she would be good at it; it really would be best if she chose that life," this could be consistent with our refusal to criticize her if she chooses anyway to be an artist. The need has to be great and glaring indeed for us to be willing to blame someone for refusing to change his or her whole life in order to help to meet it. The best examples of cases in which this condition is met are of wartime or other emergency conditions, although no doubt there can be cases spanning generations in which a whole culture struggles for survival.

## A Defensible Consequentialism

The argument of this chapter has been kept untechnical, despite an early reference to the unacceptability of act consequentialism. But I should now explore some of the ramifications. I will begin by characterizing the status of consequentialism, and then (in preparation for the next chapter's examination of morality) give an interim account of the most plausible form it can take.

Occasional attempts to argue for consequentialism (cf. Kupperman 1981, 1983, chapters 7–9) can be seen against the background of singular lack of direct argument on the part of the leading early consequentialists. Mill, for example, in *Utilitarianism* offers to give a "sort of proof" of his theory; but what he provides, in chapter 4, at best supports only the hedonistic component, and has no bearing on the (separable) conseqentialist component. G. E. Moore (1903, 25, 146–48) suggested that what is right is by definition what has the best consequences. But clearly, even if consequentialism in some form is acceptable, it is not true by definition. This chapter, on the other hand, has argued that there are some logical relations weaker than entailment between judgments of what is for the best and judgments of what it is best to do, that are embedded in the current structure of normative discourse.

A fuller account of consequentialism may seem to require deciding what counts (for consequentialist purposes) as consequences. There are a number of issues here, not all of which can be addressed in detail. (I am indebted to Bennett, unpub., for a disturbing and very useful discussion of some of these.) One concerns whether consequences must be subsequent to what they are consequences of, or can be simultaneous with it or perhaps even in some cases temporally prior. Could someone's actions — to take an Aristotelian example — change the eudaemonia of the life of a dead parent? (For relevant discussion, see Ni 1992.) In what follows I will be assuming that anything that becomes true or the case as a result of an action can be included as a consequence. This gives a temporally unrestricted view of what might count.

It also sidesteps a second major issue, that of drawing the line between an act and its consequences. It has been pointed out (see Oldenquist 1966, Bennett unpub.) that something (e.g., the killing of a rival) could be regarded equally as the consequence of an action (say, pulling a trigger) or as part of the nature of the action in the sense of what is done. When a philosopher (e.g., Kant) insists that consequences do not matter to morality, it may be hard to be sure whether the philosopher is including what might be thought of as foreseeable and intended consequences in the nature of what is judged. The consequences excluded, in other words, may be merely those that are unintended or unforeseeable. Or it may be that certain familiar categorizations of action (e.g., "telling the truth") in some contexts will strongly suggest themselves as descriptions of what was done or is considered, and at the same time will imply a particular way of drawing the line between act and consquences (see Sidgwick 1907, 97). Be that as it may, I am not assuming that the act itself (whatever that may include) is excluded from what is made the case by performing the act. Hence, it can count as part of its own consequences in the very broad sense I am accepting.

This approach to what can count as consequences may seem so latitudinarian as to be toothless. However, the latitudinarianism stops in relation to the issue of how consequences can be given weight. In particular, we need to be aware of a way in which those whose views would be thought of as drastically anti-consequentialist might try to accommodate these views to a consequentialist frame-work. They may claim that the very fact that Bloggs did X (something particularly offensive) outweighs any positive consequences that X could have had. Hence, regardless of (these) consequences we can know that by its nature X was wrong. How can they know in advance that X will outweigh all positive consequences? The answer will be either that X is infinitely bad (which guarantees greater weight than any aggregation of finite goodness of consequences) or simply that the bad-ness of X has "lexical" priority over any goodness of consequences.

We should respond to this kind of move in two ways. One is to say that the kind of position normally regarded as "consequentialist" rules out assignment of weight to any consequences that cannot be regarded as either (a) psychological states, (b) states of society, or (c) states of the natural world (e.g.. the majesty of a mountain range). Further, no consequence will have an infinite weight or lexical priority over consequences of other kinds. This is to insist that "consequentialism" does have meaning as a polemical range of positions in philosophy, and does not include everything. Other facets of what counts as consequentialism will be dis-cussed shortly.

The second response is keyed to the way in which anti-consequentialism mas-querading as consequentialism will need to be defended. If someone claims that the mere fact that Bloggs did X outweighs (as a negative consequence) all imag-inable positive consequences, he or she will need to explain why. The pattern of normative discourse imposes a burden here. Let me hasten to point out that what is at issue is *not* whether something can be morally wrong (because of the kind of action it is) even though it has lots of positive consequences. Chapters 7 and 8 will acknowledge this possibility and also that morality generally overrides positive assessments of the consequences of a particular action. The present issue is whether the generally overriding character of morality can be translated, on a case-by-case basis, into a special sort of overriding bad "consequence." It is here that argument is needed.

For one thing, the move from "morally wrong" to "consequentially bad" looks ad hoc. The anti-consequentialist philosopher looks ready to come up with what-ever numbers or weights are needed to make the picture acceptably neat, and this seems arbitrary. At a deeper level, we should ask what the evidence is that Bloggs's doing X in itself has a badness that is infinite (or lexically prior to any goodness that results). No one should deny that actions typically include psychological states, and also aspects of social relations, that can have considerable negative value.

Bloggs's torturing a prisoner, for example, by itself (even apart from what the prisoner experiences) is horrible and disgusting and easily outweighs the good consequences that in many cases would be urged as justification. However, it does seem plausible to say that we always could imagine consequences that, qua consequences, outweigh the nature of what goes on in Bloggs's activity. The consequences might include, for example, that several comparable acts of torture are prevented. How can this be ruled out in some blanket way in advance? It should be said again that even if there are (a highly unlikely possibility) major good consequences that outweigh the badness of what goes on in Bloggs's activity, it does not follow from this that torture is morally acceptable. The argument just given is not against anti-consequentialism per se; it is against any attempt to present anti-consequentialism as a fringe form of consequentialism.

There is more to consequentialism, of course, than a conception of what counts as a consequence, of what kinds of consequence be given weight, and of limits to the weight that reasonably can be assigned. Consequentialism is, first and foremost, an account of the relation between judgments of value and judgments of conduct. Certain kinds of claims are characteristic of it as such.

Here are four consequentialist claims that I accept.

1. The structure of morality is justified in terms of consequences.
2. The content of any acceptable morality is justified in terms of consequences.
3. Catastrophic consequences may provide exceptions to generally valid moral rules.
4. There are occasions on which what one should do is what is likely to have the best consequences.

These claims together play a part in a consequentialism that is far from simple. The simplest form of consequentialism, act consequentialism, in contrast, centers on a stronger version of 4 that claims that on all occasions one should do what will have (or is likely to have) the best consequences. Anti-consequentialism, like consequentialism, has many varieties; and there are doubtless some anti-consequentialists who could accept 3 and 4. Anyone who accepted all four of these claims, though, would be well over the line into consequentialist territory.

In the next chapter I will explore what is meant by the structure and by the content of morality. Clearly morality is the major battleground between consequentialism and its opponents. Clearly also, the consequentialism of my four claims gives an account of morality far less reductive than that supplied by act consequentialism.

# 7

# Morality

The last chapter left us with two questions about morality: (1) in what kinds of case does the claim that it would be immoral constitute a good reason for not doing what would be optimific, and (2) are there indeed cases in which what is optimific is immoral. (Can there be, to repeat Leibniz's phrase, a *felix culpa*?) These questions point toward the nature and authority of morality. We can begin by asking how moral judgments are to be distinguished from other judgments that recommend that we do or not do certain things. This is, among other things, to investigate the structure and also the typical content of morality. Following this we can ask how moral considerations are to be related to other factors in our decisions. The answers to the two questions will be completed then in the next chapter.

It can be argued that the concept of morality is largely an invention of modern western culture, in that in the work of ancient philosophers (such as Aristotle or Confucius) there is nothing like a sharp line between what we would term moral and non-moral choices. The good life is a seamless web. The modern concept of morality presupposes a division within life, perhaps between an area that should be treated as private or personal and one that is subject to various forms of social control. Thus Mill, in paragraph 14 of chapter 5 of *Utilitarianism*, links what is "wrong" (as opposed to what falls short of "expediency") to what we think a person ought to be punished for doing "if not by law, by the opinion of his fellow creatures; if not by opinion, by the reproaches of his own conscience." *On Liberty* can be read as arguing that what are nowadays called "lifestyle choices" should not be subject to this kind of pressure, presumably belonging instead in the realm of "expediency" (and inexpediency). We can have negative views, Mill allows (1859/1978, 75), of such things as "depravation of taste"; but he seems to assume that these will not carry the pressure that moral censure does.

It may be that Kant did not have a very different division in mind as one result of the distinction between the categorical imperative (which tests the moral acceptability of maxims) and the hypothetical imperatives (which advise on how to reach various goals, including happiness, and which clearly provide non-moral judgments). Presumably there often are occasions on which two or more of our alternatives pass the test of the categorical imperative. Deciding which one to adopt, then, is hardly a moral matter, and, indeed, would seem to belong in a realm very like Mill's "expediency."

The maps of life, with their central dividing lines, that Kant and Mill give us, then, do not seem all that different. The principles of division are another matter. For Kant the crucial tests are in relation to an ideal of universal principle, to the ideal of a world whose agents follow universal principles, and to the constitutive importance that is implicit in all of this of respect for persons. For Mill, in contrast, the dividing line has to be seen in relation to social policy: what kinds of things should the society (either legally, or socially through the pressure that when inappropriate becomes the "tyranny of the majority," or by childhood training in guilt) come down hard on? This leads to a revisionist argument, that in modern societies people would be on the whole happier if certain matters traditionally treated as moral were instead viewed as personal choices.

The principles of division begin to look less and less clear if one takes seriously areas in which the philosophers' positions have seemed most vulnerable to attack. Mill's view reflects a wonderful optimism as to the ways most people will orient their lives if pressure on their choices is lessened. This optimism enables him to take a cavalier view of the British aggression against China in the Opium War, the assumption apparently being that (as the British government in effect insisted) ordinary Chinese should be allowed to decide without restriction from their government whether or not they will take the drug (see Mill 1959/1978, 94–95, also Waley 1950). He also ignores the possibility that choices that arguably are not a threat to society if they are made only by a small minority assume a different character when the numbers making them become significant. Drug taking again provides an example: one's response to proposals that it be legalized would be affected by estimates of the percentage of the population that would be addicts. A "liberal" view would be much more appealing if the estimate were 1 or 2 percent than if it were 10 or 15: the social (as well as personal) costs of the latter would be enormous. Finally, Mill's revisionism seems plausible to many of us in relation to a number of traditional sexual taboos, which (although many "cultural conservatives" will protest) are now widely thought to pertain to the realm of the private and personal. But there are other kinds of taboo that may be more resistant. Some concern treatment of the dead, as nicely captured in a Monty Python sketch about a young man who is told by a funeral director of a really cheap way of disposing of the body of his mother. It is hard to shake a sense that there are some things that are—and will remain—socially unacceptable (in the way traditionally associated with what is morally unacceptable) even though there is no obvious respect in which they cause harm. Perhaps there is a form of subtle (psychological and social) harm that comes from the violation of taboos like those governing treatment of the dead. Mill himself seemed to stumble over some taboos, as evidenced by his unargued acceptance of prohibitions of public offenses against "decency" (1859/1978, 97).

Kant also may have known more than he said. At first glance the realm of the moral is distinguished simply by the considerations developed in the three formulations of the categorical imperative. However, the role of the categorical imperative presupposes the formulation of maxims to be tested, which itself requires judgment (and perhaps other capacities). In the *Metaphysical Principles of Virtue* Kant discusses issues of maxim formulation and speaks of casuistry as the art that is brought into play. There are many different ways to describe what one is doing at any given moment, and arguably the moral acceptability of an action can depend heavily on what counts as its maxim. Thus, a great deal depends on whether Frederick the Great's carrying poison into battle (Kant 1797/1964, 84), for use if he were captured and held for ransom (a case that Kant presents but does not analyze), is viewed in relation to a willlingness to commit suicide or in other terms. Also, if someone contemplates promise-breaking or lying because of extraordinary circumstances, much arguably depends on whether a description of these circumstances is included in the maxim of what is contemplated. If we look at the actual examples of maxims that Kant provides in the *Grounding for the Metaphysics of Morals*, it is striking that they are broad and that they (especially the first two) are drawn from the traditional moral rules that most of us learned as children (and that are central to the prephilosophical sense of what morality is).

This may be linked to a tacit assumption that traditional moral categories largely set the agenda of what needs to be evaluated morally. It is inconceivable that Kant or anyone else believes that the categorical imperative needs to be explicitly employed in relation to even the tiniest of actions of everyday life. Preselection of the occasions of its employment is required; here the prephilosophical sense of what counts as a moral choice plays a role. There may be maxims, for example those affirming celibacy, that would not pass the test of universal law but would not be put to the test.

Part of what I am trying to suggest is that both Mill and Kant present a division between moral and non-moral choices that is somewhat less neat than it first appears. This leads to the further point that (especially if we take seriously the difficulties for their accounts) our division may involve multiple criteria and contestable areas. Virtually everyone would agree that choices traditionally central to morality, such as when homicide, rape, torture, or theft is contemplated, are moral choices, and that the great majority of choices of, say, what to do on one's vacation are not. Many societies, including ours, lack consensus about how to classify other choices: for example, those that concern premarital or extramarital sex or homosexuality, where the first question can be not "Does one approve or disapprove?" but rather "Is this a personal matter or is it subject to moral judgment?" The categorization of some choices (e.g., to eat meat) that traditionally had not been included within morality also has become contested.

One criterion that has considerable weight is the one Mill appealed to in *On Liberty*: if an action would cause harm to someone, especially if the harm is direct, we tend to regard it as subject to moral judgment. Clearly any such action (at least if its victim qualifies as a rational being) is subject to moral judgment in Kant's view also. In that people generally do not want to be harmed, its maxim (arguably) cannot be willed to be a universal law; it also violates the requirement of respect for persons. These Kantian criteria independently carry weight in most people's sense of what counts as a moral issue. If a decision can be viewed as one of principle that one must be able to will to be universal law, especially, we are that much more likely to view it as subject to moral judgment. This is linked to the widespread image of a virtuous agent as a woman or man of (universalizable) principle. In the classic central cases of morality the criteria of harm, universalizable principle, and respect for persons point in the same direction. Torture, for example, involves harm, cannot be willed to be a universal law, and violates respect for the victims.

There are occasions, though, on which these criteria do not pull in the same direction. Inflicting gratuitous pain on animals, which Kant regards as inhumane (but not as immoral), is such a case. There is harm. But it is far from clear that a human could not will the inhumanity to animals to be a universal law; and, insofar as the victims do not count as persons, respect for persons is not violated. My sense is that most people nowadays would hold that inflicting gratuitous pain on animals is morally wrong, but there is room for a view that it is seriously wrong in some other way (i.e., is wrong but not immoral). Perhaps inhumanity should be a separate category from immorality? Kant's criteria also seem questionable to many people in relation to very trivial ("white") lies or broken promises when hardly anything is at stake and no one cares. Even though such cases can be subsumed under important universal law, and arguably involve a slightly cavalier attitude toward the persons lied to (or to whom the promises had been made), these very trivial lapses may seem not to raise moral issues. Neither does a failure to return two pennies of incorrectly given change. Some kinds of harm, conversely, may seem so subtle and so hard to deal with in terms of (universalizable) principles, that (even when we are appalled) we may hesitate to treat them as straightforwardly subject to moral judgment. My sense is that often the most serious harm that befalls people in life is psychological damage (e.g., becoming demoralized or severely conflicted) that occurs within a family or close personal relationships. We do condemn this morally if the abuse is exceptionally clear, especially if it can be viewed as the result of a very small number of decisions. The more subtle cases, though, in which there is a slow and undramatic pattern of psychological damage, tend not to be viewed as in the realm of morality. To the extent that we are aware, we do not like the pattern of behavior; but that is different from viewing it as immoral or morally wrong. No doubt the guardedness of our negative attitudes has something to do with the risks of social intrusion into personal relationships. Mill (at least on my reading of him), it has to be said, also would emphasize the fact that psychological harm in its nature is "indirect," which prevents it from justifying intervention in the way in which direct harm does. But this consideration does not prevent us from regarding exceptionally clear-cut psychological abuse, especially of children, as immoral. Let me suggest that our hesitation in regarding subtle and sustained psychological harm as immoral has a great deal to do with our difficulty in arriving at a clear and sharp formulation of the kind of behavior (comparable to categories like "torture" and "rape") that we can say simply is wrong as a matter of universalizable principle.

It may be also that cases like those of subtle abuse are too far from the cultural roots of our concept of morality. These are to be found in the mixture of law and divine command presented in the Old Testament, centering on the Ten Commandments. It does not equal (especially in the lack of distinction between social and legal norms) our modern concept of morality, but there are strong resemblances. And there is nothing very like it in ancient Chinese or classical Greek culture. This starting point provided paradigmatic cases of immorality. Some that chiefly violated religious or cultural taboos may have dropped out of many people's image of what is morally wrong. The remaining ones, by and large, center on dramatic and readily identifiable harm (e.g., murder, theft). "Thou shalt not make the people close to you depressed" would hardly qualify. What is forbidden violates general rules of conduct that can be enforced both in law and through social pressure. It is arguable that something like an appeal to universal law is implicit in this early on. Current conceptions of morality are not necessarily very near this starting point, but even those that are not may bear the marks of it: that is, there is some general tendency to think of morality as linked to universalizable principles, and to regard at least some of the activities condemned in the Ten Commandments as paradigmatic of the morally wrong. Departures from the starting point proceed, by and large, either by including within morality matters that have some family resemblence to the paradigmatic cases or by marshaling (as Mill did) normative arguments to exclude matters traditionally included.

Here, as so often, the reality of our thought and language is less neat than most of us would like. The discussion thus far does not give us a clear and precise meaning for "morality" or for "It would be immoral." Furthermore, there are many cases whose classification is contestable.

## Function and Structure

The nature of morality may be somewhat clearer if we look at function. In chapter 5 it was noted that a major function is to coordinate social behavior. Morality can be personal in the sense that a moral view can be held only by one person or a small group; but any morality qua morality is implicitly designed for an entire society or in a few cases for a subculture (e.g., a monastic order), and to be acceptable must be viable for that society (or subculture). To say all of this leaves open the possibility that the same central elements will be found in all acceptable moralities anywhere in the world; but it also leaves open the possibility that there could be some legitimate local variations, especially in such matters as property rights or rules governing forms of family life. It counts heavily against a morality if its general acceptance (within the society or subculture) would be disastrous. It also counts heavily if it is not one that we should want generally taught (see Steven Kuhn 1996). In these respects, morality differs from axiology: judgments of what is valuable or has negative value need not be designed for general use, and it does not count against them if they were best pursued by only a few people.

One implication of this is that the acceptability of moral judgments is a more complicated matter than the acceptability of value judgments. In the latter, there can be a straightforward testing of the judgment against what really seems the case. If the claim is that, say, a certain kind of experience has very high value, one may be able to have the experience and see whether it does. There can be difficulties, but these will center on whether one really had the kind of experience that was praised and whether one took it in (and appreciated it) properly. The testing of a moral judgment involves much broader considerations. The case or practice judged must be considered in relation to a network of other cases or practices. What might intuitively seem right could be very undesirable within a social matrix. The sort of action that, this time, foreseeably made everyone happy could as a general practice be disastrous. This could be understood by analogy with the way soldiers sometimes are court-martialed for decisions that foreseeably worked very well but are such that it would be most unfortunate if others generally emulated them. To say "the decision worked" is far from the whole story.

This is a pretheoretical point about special characteristics of morality. Clearly it is at the heart of much in Kant's ethics, including Kant's apparent leaning toward selection of broad moral maxims rather than ones that are extremely specific of the case at hand. There is no reason, though, that a consequentialist could not take the same pretheoretical point to heart, rejecting what Marxist consequentialists used to call "opportunism." Mill rejects opportunism in relation to rights such as free speech: he does not allow the relevance of questions such as "Would the general happiness be promoted if on *this* occasion we denied so-and-so free speech?" Moral and social decisions spread beyond individual cases, and in this respect we need to look at general policies rather than particular cases.

We have seen that the function of morality has a great deal to do with the coordination of behavior within a society or a subculture. The emphasis is on prevention of harm, and also on the predictability of behavior in areas of life that really matter, a predictability that is made possible when a small number of relatively simple rules are followed with some consistency by most people. The importance of not undermining this structure is a constraint on moral choice.

It should be added that due recognition of all of this need not commit anyone to "rigorism" about moral rules, nor is rule consequentialism the only immediate competitor of act consequentialism. There can be moments when it makes sense to pause and reconsider a policy or to make an exception. Due recognition of the ways in which moral judgments point toward social practices should ensure that this is not done lightly in relation to morality, and in practice it may be that moral and social policies are workable only if we treat only cases of very serious negative consequences as exceptions.

The structure of morality is determined by its function. At its core is logical universalizability: the requirement, common to all sorts of normative claims, that very similar cases be judged in very similar ways (see Hare 1963). There also is the crucial role of general rules (often broad general rules) as determining most commonplace moral decisions. It includes also the general relationships between judgments of what is morally required, on one hand, and judgments, on the other hand, of what we expect of people and of blame and guilt. It is part of the nature of morality that its dictates are often, if not always, taken seriously, and that they often are reflected in strong motivations (and either then in corresponding conduct or in feelings of guilt on the part of those who failed to do what they thought was right). The seriousness with which morality often is taken is reflected not only in the phenomena of guilt, but also in the anger and desire to see punished that are often directed against those who are seen as transgressors. The structure of morality, in short, includes both the way in which claims are shaped and justified (i.e., the preference for broad general rules) and the typical connections of moral judgment with motivation and with community pressures.

This is a heterogeneous set of elements. One can certainly imagine something that we would term morality that did not center on broad general rules. But, as a consequentialist can insist, this would yield a much less useful structure for human beings than the kind of morality we are familiar with. Ours is suitable, at least in its core elements, for teaching even to young children and in general to people of subnormal intelligence. To the extent that the core content of what is taught has a great deal to do with forbidding harmful actions, the utility of seeing that the central message is simple enough to get across and to be remembered is very great indeed. Furthermore, reliance on broad general rules has the useful function of helping to block the tendency, that perhaps all of us have, to rationalize what we would really like to do so that it seems somehow acceptable. A morality that as much as possible avoids intricacies and weighing of subtle features of particular cases, and instead on a variety of topics insists "Just say 'no,' " can have sometimes the disadvantages of rigidity; but it can be argued that these are more than balanced by the advantages of keeping people off of moral slippery slopes.

The connections of morality to motivation and communal pressure look not only useful but also essential. That is, if some alien culture had a system of norms that in some respects resembled our morality, but that was largely disconnected both from motivation and from any general tendency to respond negatively to people who violated them, we would be unlikely to think of this as a morality. Furthermore, such a system of norms could not be useful in the way in which a morality is. If the central content of morality concerns prevention of harm, then of course it is highly desirable that it be taken seriously both by agents and by those who interact with them. Human beings will often have angry or greedy impulses or other kinds of feelings of temptation. These sometimes strong impulses cannot be counteracted by merely, as it were, carrying around a moral code book. Strong inhibitions are needed, along with a vulnerability to feelings of guilt and to social pressure (which may make us think twice about yielding to our impulses).

Implicit in this structure is that in particular cases consequences do not always rule. If moral norms are to work usefully, they must be internalized. And this means that we cannot always be open to the thought that, in this case, it might be best to violate the norm. Inhibitions do not allow us to approach each separate decision of our lives with a completely open mind.

Arguably, in a useful social morality rules can have exceptions; but the apparatus of inhibition, guilt, and social pressure requires that they not be claimed at all lightly, and that they be pursued only reluctantly. As we will see, it is not an acceptable reason for violating a generally useful norm that on this occasion the violation would have slightly better consequences than following it. That moral norms have this power itself has very good consequences. The point is analogous to Mill's insistence, in *On Liberty*, that it promotes the general happiness to recognize rights like that of free speech, and that this forbids asking, on a case-by-case basis, whether on this occasion suppressing so-and-so's free speech might have good consequences.

All of this adds up to an argument that consequentialism (of a type more sophisticated than act consequentialism) is in a strong position to explain and justify all of the structural features of morality, with the exception of logical universalizability (for which the explanation, I think, is logical). It is useful to have a system that coordinates behavior that can have a serious negative impact on people. This enables people to get on with their lives without constantly feeling extremely anxious and insecure. If human nature were extremely benevolent and selfless, pressures would not need to be part of this system. As it is, the social pressures of strong disapproval and the psychic pressures of inhibition and guilt play a necessary role. Broad general rules contribute to simplicity and speed of decision, both of which can be important especially if large numbers of people (many of whom are not very thoughtful) must be relied upon to make up their own minds on how they will behave.

In short, a sophisticated consequentialism can provide both arguments that justify morality's having the structure with which we are familiar, and also in this an explanation of how this structure would have developed. Much of the content also can be justified and explained. We do need to recognize that the content of morality is very contestable around the edges. This is true in relation to whether what is widely taken to be a moral question should be answered positively or negatively. The permissibility of abortion is currently such an issue: it is debated in a way in which central moral claims such as, say, that torture is wrong are not. The content also is contestable, as has been noted, in relation to what is regarded as a moral issue at all. There is considerable disagreement as to whether, for example, morality includes norms governing sexual behavior, or whether (alternatively) any such judgments we might care to make lie outside of morality. The status of judgments of eating meat also has been debated.

It is clear, though, that the core of morality, as manifested in the elements that are emphasized to children and become prominent in the general consciousness, concerns visible and dramatic forms of harm to others (murder, rape, torture, theft, etc.) and also that there is considerable consensus among civilized people in these areas. Why are visible and dramatic forms of harm (as opposed, say, to gradually being made depressed and demoralized) so central to morality? Maybe they are what we fear most, partly because they are the kinds of harm over whose effect on us we have the least control (which is why the harm is "direct"). But there is also the fact that morality works, as we have seen, through guilt and community pressure. It is very difficult to focus guilt or organize community pressure if harm is far from obvious to everyone, or if what actually was done is highly subject to interpretation. When subtle and not dramatic harm has been brought about, the agent can convince himself or herself that "it is really nothing; why are they so upset?"; others in the community may have difficulty in seeing that something of serious importance has happened. If what happened was murder or torture, this is far less likely. Thus, in terms of the way in which morality actually functions in a society, that it tends to focus narrowly on dramatic and visible forms of harm has good consequences. Arguably, it enables morality to do the most good.

Conversely, a morality that has broad scope, in that it governs a large variety of everyday decisions, will have major negative consequences in inhibiting the spontaneity that is a normal part of human life. To make people continuously anxious and self-critical is, for that matter, not altogether a good consequence. Hence, to have a morality of somewhat narrow scope, as opposed to one that is broad and in this respect relentless, has good consequences.

## Morality as a Factor in Decision

Let us look at morality from a less theory-oriented angle, coming closer to the questions with which this chapter began. We can examine the way a claim that "X would be immoral" works in deliberation about whether or not it is best that one do X. Part of what the claim typically does is to appeal to a constraint that is thought of either as (1) always overriding all others (in that it is widely assumed that, whatever the advantages of X, to say that it would be immoral is to say that it is not to be done), or as (2) often but not always overriding all others (in that there must be compelling non-moral reasons for X to outweigh the moral objections), or as (3) comprehensive and conclusive (in that ideally advantages and disadvantages of all sorts have been given due weight in a moral judgment, so that there is nothing not already taken account of that could outweigh the moral judgment).

   The first two of these possibilities are most likely to occur to those who think of what morality is largely in terms of core categories of wrongdoing or of appeal to principles. This sets up an opposition between what is a matter of principle and what seems not to be (but may be important all the same), or between what pertains to the traditional core of morality and considerations that do not but yet might influence a reasonable person. Once this is constructed, it may not be clear that one side always wins (see Scheffler 1992, 60). The third possibility will be most congenial to those who view morality (as consequentialists traditionally have) in terms of a balance of social benefits and harms. This view may seem to imply that a moral judgment tells us about what is right (in an especially pressing way), all things considered (and given the due weight they deserve in a decision). So of course there is no further consideration that can be legitimately opposed to the moral judgment.

   The possibilities just outlined represent alternative ways of thinking (in common sense or in philosophy) about the relation between moral considerations and other factors in deciding what it is best to do. We need to look more closely at all three. Each may turn out, on closer inspection, to have vulnerable points or to be difficult to defend.

   (1) It is appealing to think of morality as a trump card that always wins. Perhaps morality always wins because, when it loses it turns out that what had seemed to be morality really is not? The moral imperative to return two pennies of incorrectly given change may be an example. On some occasions it is arguably silly: punctilious to a fault and embarrassing. If we allow our embarrassment to overrule our principle of honesty, it may seem as if morality loses. But it can be claimed that the familiar principles of honesty apply only when something significant is at stake. Their implicit meaning is such that they do not actually require returning the two pennies. Hence, morality has not lost.

This argument rests on a point about language. Statements, requests, and recommendations can contain implicit conditions even if these are not consciously "in the mind of" the person who makes them. Wittgenstein's example (1953, 33) is of someone who says, "Shew the children a game," and then is dismayed when the children are shown how to gamble with dice. This exclusion was not in the mind of the person who made the request, but all the same she is right to insist that the gambling with dice was not part of what was meant. Similarly, Alan Donagan (1977, 93) has suggested, a general rule that one should keep promises contains as part of its (culturally understood) implicit meaning that there are certain kinds of occasions (e.g., serious emergencies) on which one simply is not expected to keep a promise of a less serious nature. If one follows this line of thought, traditional moral general rules should not be taken too very literally. The cases in which it would seem most preposterous to follow them are just those in which, arguably, they are not meant to apply.

This is a very satisfactory way of upholding 1 in relation to cases like that of a seeming requirement to return two pennies of incorrectly given change, or in which someone because of an urgent need must break a promise to meet a friend for coffee. There may be more difficult cases, however. Suppose that what is contemplated involves real harm, and also violation of respect for persons, but the need to do it is very urgent indeed?

There are imaginable cases in which refusal to violate traditional moral norms and respect for all persons affected by one's actions could have disastrous consequences. Discussion of these is complicated by the fact that, in the reality we are familiar with, such cases are exceedingly rare: by and large respect for persons and refusal to violate traditional moral norms work well, and their general tendency to coincide with what is for the best may not be a coincidence at all. Furthermore, moments when respect for morality might seem not to lead to what is for the best are typically marked by deep uncertainty about consequences, so that a consequentialist like G. E. Moore (1903, 154 ff.) is able to recommend that one follow established moral rules even on these occasions as a reasonable "play safe" strategy.

Hence, cases in which it is clear that refusal to violate traditional moral norms and respect for persons would have very bad consequences tend to be fantastic. They may provide the only clear instances in which consequentialists and anti-consequentialists would give opposed recommendations, but there are at least two reasons that consequentialists would be ambivalent about discussing them. The first is that, from the consequentialist point of view, the morality we actually have is tailored to the kinds of cases we actually tend to encounter. Central to this morality are a number of prereflective safeguards, including strong inhibitions about behavior of the sorts that generally have serious bad consequences, and a tendency to treat options along those lines as literally unthinkable. These are protections against the general human tendency to slide down moral slippery slopes, making exceptions in one's own favor or viewing difficult cases in a light that is conducive to what one wants to do anyway. But inspection of fantastic cases often makes the unthinkable look thinkable. Hence, from a consequentialist point of view, it is a philosophical activity that can be harmful.

Second, it has been noted that moral judgments point over their shoulders, as it were, toward general moral and social policies, and have to be evaluated in that light. We have to ask, "How would it be if this were generally emulated?" Related to this is the fact that moral judgments, even in recondite philosophical writing, themselves do have consequences. Hence, a consequentialist can have good reasons for *not* making a recommendation (in relation to a fantasy case) that runs counter to the general pattern of how we want people to behave.

What kinds of cases do I have in mind? Let me give (reluctantly) two classic examples. In one, some evil and very predictable power (Nazis or extraterrestials can take this role) declares that large numbers of people will die or suffer horribly unless we offer someone (who would not be among those who would die or suffer horribly) as an innocent (and unwilling) victim. In the second, terrorists are about to explode a nuclear device that assuredly will kill millions, and the only way (predictably) that we can prevent this is by torturing an innocent relative of one of the terrorists (thus eliciting the information needed to prevent the explosion). These are exceedingly unpleasant cases, and one of the most fantastic elements in them is the assumption that we would be able to predict with considerable assurance what the major consequences of our alternatives would be. Nevertheless, we cannot rule out with complete certainty that we might at some point have that kind of assurance about consequences.

Cases like these elicit two contradictory responses in many people. On one hand, there can be a response like Kant's "Do right even though the heavens fall." If morality means anything, it may be felt, it must be decisive even when things are very difficult.

On the other hand, some people (including some of the same people) will say that surely what would amount to a catastrophe justifies making an exception to any moral rule. It might be claimed that this escape clause is implicit generally in moral rules. But this seems not to be the case. If we break a not-very-important promise because of a serious emergency, our sense typically is that no one (including the person to whom the promise had been made) would expect us to keep it under these circumstances; the exception was understood. There would be no comparable understanding of the case in which the terrorist's relative was tortured, whether or not one thought that the torture was justified.

So we are left with the question of whether extreme and extraordinary consequences justify violating an exceptionally important rule of morality. I leave the answer to readers, who almost certainly will be divided. Let me point out, though, one ironic complication. Anyone's response to cases of this sort will imply a moral stance, which itself can be judged in terms of usefulness and appropriateness. In the real world in which we live, there is a great deal to be said for a stance of unswerving loyalty, come what may, to important central rules of morality. In a world in which awful fantastic cases actually begin to come up, there might be something less to be said for this stance. Hence, it can be argued that it is entirely legitimate to have different responses to the cases under discussion depending on whether they are fantastic or real.

A further point is that someone who judges that, in a really extreme case, one would be justified in violating an important central rule of morality is likely also to hold that the justification is itself moral. The moral rights or well-being of those who will be saved or protected if the rule is violated can be appealed to. Indeed, it may be asked, what other kind of justification for violating the rule can there be? Hence, although the fantasy cases pose difficulties for conceptions of morality as entirely rule-governed, they do not look promising for those who would like to attack 1.

Point 1 may be most vulnerable in relation to cases in which what is contemplated can be argued genuinely to violate morality in a significant way (unlike the failure to return the two pennies) but in which what is at stake does not have the very urgent social importance found in our fantasy cases. Bloggs lies about the improperly witnessed will of a relative, from which he and a number of people he cares about (and whom the deceased relative cared about) derive significant financial gain. One of the witnesses, let us say, actually had entered the room a minute or two after the will was signed. Had Bloggs not lied, the will through a technicality would have been disallowed; and the benefits would have gone to some wealthy and (in most obvious respects) undeserving people. (This example was loosely suggested by an incident in Sean O'Casey's *Juno and the Paycock*.) A cleaner (but more fantastic) example is Smart's (1956, 350) case of a desert island promise to a dying man, to dispose of his estate in ways that do little good for anyone; the utilitarian promiser then chooses to bring significant benefits to a number of people (thus promoting the general good) rather than to keep the promise. Smart's case is cleaner, not only because no personal benefit is involved in the choice to break the promise, but also because the action clearly violates not only the generally understood moral requirements of honesty but also respect for persons (i.e., respect for the wishes of the dying man). Perhaps Bloggs's lie violates respect for persons (those who might be held to be entitled to the truth), but the violation is somewhat less dramatic and clear-cut.

Again, these are cases about which many of us will feel conflicted. One complication is that it is possible both to hold that the best thing to do would be to tell the lie or break the promise, and at the same time to judge that one would not be able to bring oneself to do so. Smart (1956, 351) indicates this in relation to another case, when he speaks of the "tensions" that would be set up in him if—for altruistic purposes—he surreptitiously violated a generally useful rule.

Someone who believes that it would be best to break the desert island promise to the dying man, because it would be better to benefit numbers of people than to waste the money, is very likely to hold that it would be morally right to do so. Hence, this case may count (again) against a view of morality as entirely rule governed, but it seems unlikely to count against 1. Bloggs's case though may be more difficult for 1, in that someone who holds that it would be best for Bloggs to lie might well hesitate to say that would be morally right. One relevant difference between this case and Smart's is that we may be reluctant to label a justification of Bloggs's lie as moral because some of the benefit will accrue to Bloggs himself. That the justification is not exactly moral can be counterbalanced by the fact that the traditional moral norm that is violated might be felt to have lost—in this case—some of its usual authority if we are uneasy about the role of legal technicalities.

My inclination here is to take the view that in the end one should tell the truth, come what may. But the phrase "in the end" needs to be emphasized. It is possible to feel more divided about such cases than about the general run of violations of traditional moral rules, and to believe that many basically decent people might have more latitudinarian views. This is especially true if the gain at stake for Bloggs is not really significant, and if, on the other hand, those others who would benefit from his lie badly need the money (and if the person who made the improperly witnessed will really cared about their getting it). Furthermore, our normal tendency to allow no middle ground between what is morally acceptable, on one hand, and what is immoral, on the other, may be rather weak here. Someone could hold that Bloggs should tell the truth, and that it is not quite morally permissible for him to lie, without being willing to regard the lie as immoral.

It is uncomfortable to discuss all of this, both because of the moral ambiguities and because what is to be adjudicated looks both vague and messy. But the immediate point is that cases of this general character seem to be in people's minds when they express doubts about 1. The thought is that moral requirements sometimes can be overriden — not because they are trivial (in which case they could be argued not to hold at all), and probably not if something really major is at stake — but rather in cases in which they make a demand that would generally be reasonable, but in this instance something non-moral that is of greater importance is opposed to them.

Thus far we have seen that there is a gray area that may pose difficulties — but perhaps not very great difficulties — for 1. Cases like that of Bloggs and the will are such that basically decent people may divide over whether non-moral considerations override moral considerations. This suggests that there is something, but perhaps not a great deal, to be said for 2. Are there cases in which non-moral considerations clearly triumph over moral ones? Our discussion here, it should be emphasized, is preliminary. A more assured determination will be reserved for the next chapter.

If there are cases that make 2 clearly the correct view, they must be ones in which whatever overrides moral considerations should not be viewed as itself a moral consideration. This implies a circumscribed account of what counts as a moral consideration (as opposed to some views in which anything that matters can qualify as a moral consideration). Perhaps the best thing to do is such that there are reasons keyed to traditional moral categories against it, but there are even stronger reasons for it that are not keyed to these categories. Or perhaps the moral is a species of the other-regarding, and what are mainly self-regarding reasons can override other-regarding ones. Or perhaps moral considerations are all derivable from a group of general rules, and some reasons that override them cannot be expressed in terms of an appeal to general rules of this sort.

It is easier to draw this portrait (of the triumph of the non-moral over the moral) in general terms than it is to defend it more specifically or to create clear cases. Suppose that Bloggs can advance his own happiness by depriving Smith of some money that we would judge to be rightfully hers, or by breaking a promise to her. If Bloggs's action is justified, in short, this would represent the triumph of the self-regarding over the other-regarding, and also the triumph of something outside of traditional moral categories over something within. Could the action be justified? Unless the gain for Bloggs would be huge and the harm (or disappointment of legitimate expectation) for Smith would be exceedingly slight, we would simply advise Bloggs (on moral grounds) not to do it. To the extent that the harm or disappointment is slight, we are inclined to move away from the position that what Bloggs is about to do is morally wrong or that the considerations that are overriden are moral ones. If the money that was rightfully Smith's consists of two pennies, or the promise was to meet her for coffee, we might be inclined (depending on other details of the case) to advise Bloggs to go ahead; but we would be equally disinclined to view what he is about to do as morally questionable. The trick, for someone who wishes to defend 2, is to find a middle ground at which we retain an inclination to regard Bloggs's action as overriding moral considerations with non-moral ones but are willing to recommend it. Such a case is not easy to construct.

Suppose (alternatively) that Bloggs is willing to violate generally valid moral rules (such as those that forbid stealing and promise breaking) because of positive considerations that cannot themselves be viewed as derivable from general moral rules. Earlier I suggested that there are forms of harm so subtle and so hard to deal with in terms of universalizable principles, in part because of the difficulty in arriving at a clear and sharp formulation of the kind of behavior involved, that we tend to place choices involved in inflicting them outside of the realm of morality. We may abhor them, but we tend not to speak of them as immoral (instead speaking negatively of them in different terms). A good deal of incremental psychological harm is like this. Suppose that Bloggs is willing to break promises in order to prevent subtle harm of this sort from befalling, say, some children. If we are convinced indeed that his promise breaking will prevent genuine harm, we might well recommend it. Is this a triumph of the non-moral over the moral?

Cases of this sort are difficult to talk about, in large part because their nature is such that some of the traditional broad categories that are used in moral justification are not readily available. Even if the subtle, incremental harm to be prevented does not readily fit such a category (it is not exactly abuse, but the children do seem less confident and more nervous and depressed), this does not mean that preventing it cannot have moral weight. In particular, our unwillingness to label the causing of the harm as "immoral" does not imply a similar unwillingness to allow that preventing it could be a moral consideration for someone who recognizes the harm.

Bloggs may have trouble in convincing others that the results of his action justify breaking promises: what does not readily fit traditional categories is often difficult to see. But, to the extent that we see what he is talking about, and to the extent that we think it important, we can be convinced that there are strong moral considerations that justify his breaking promises. Perhaps then the case becomes one that is more like a conflict between moral rules than a triumph of the non-moral over the moral?

None of this leads us to a clear decision between 1 and 2. We can find disputable cases, like that of Bloggs and the will, which might make us think that

2 cannot be entirely dismissed out of hand. Part of the difficulty for 2 is that, even if not all considerations important to a decision are moral, there is a tendency for morality to absorb or take account of important considerations, especially, of course, if they are other-regarding.

Why not then go the whole distance, agree that anything that matters can be the subject of moral consideration, and opt for 3? There is something appealing about an "all things considered" view of morality. But it is to ignore the specificity of the concept of morality. Not every consideration that legitimately pulls us counts as a moral consideration. What is reasonably excluded from consideration depends on the case. If we are thinking of killing someone, the fact that it would please some of our friends normally would not be an acceptable consideration. On many occasions of moral choice self-regarding factors are either excluded from consideration or discounted. Thus, 3 is untenable, given the nature of morality.

This may seem a surprising result, in that 3 is associated with some forms of consequentialism and I am a consequentialist. But it is possible for a consequentialist to hold about morality (roughly as Mill did about rights such as free speech) that it limits the factors we need to consider and that, generally speaking, it trumps whatever lies outside of it; the consequentialist can hold that this dominant role is itself justified by good consequences.

Some considerations that have special importance in morality can be grouped under the heading of "respect for persons as ends-in-themselves." A consequentialist can agree (with qualifications indicated earlier in this chapter) with philosophers who claim (see Kamm 1992) a decisive role for this. Human life is greatly improved if respect for persons suffuses our social relations, not only in relation to moral choice but also in non-moral areas.

Earlier I remarked that consequentialists traditionally have viewed morality in terms of a balance of benefits and harms. A consequentialist of my stripe, though, will view this balance as important chiefly in relation to how we set up and formulate a moral system. It determines how we decide or adjust our general policies or social norms. If we have arrived at what seems an optimal policy or social norm, then by and large we will simply follow it.

There can be moments, however (as when extraordinary circumstances lead us to waive or reconsider our general policies), when particular actions should be governed by consideration of consequences. There are public policy decisions also, when obvious moral considerations or relevant moral rules pull approximately equally in opposite directions, that reasonably can be made by assessing which alternative seems likely to have the best consequences. For example, the Federal Reserve Board can drastically cut interest rates, which perhaps would stimulate growth in the economy, thus creating jobs for some people, but also negatively affecting retired people who depend largely on income from bank deposits and perhaps having other unfortunate consequences after a while. Cases like these fit the worldview of act consequentialists very well. In the real world of moral choice (or choice when there are morally relevant considerations), they are the exception rather than the rule.

# 8

# Moral Obligations to Do What Is Not for the Best

The last two chapters have left us with a complicated image of what it is best to do. We sometimes could recommend that Smith not do what is optimific if she does not feel like it, or if she reasonably on this occasion can ask, "Why me?" or complain about disruption of projects central to her life. Much depends on what is at stake, both for Smith and for the people affected by her choice. Morality complicates the picture still further. The previous chapter has developed an image of morality as relying on stances and policies that normally will not be constantly adjusted, so that often a moral person will decide what it is best to do without the reckoning of consequences required to determine what is for the best.

We now may address the question of how "It would be immoral" can justify not doing what is for the best. First, we will look more closely at obligations, a broad class that includes not only moral obligations but also those arising from membership in a profession along with family obligations, obligations of friendship, and so forth. Obligations, as I noted in chapter 6, involve constraints on action. To feel obligated to do X is normally (i.e., in the absence of compelling factors apart from the obligation) to feel that there is no choice as to what it is best to do: in this sense obligations can create "agent-centered restrictions" (see Scheffler 1982). Of course, people sometimes in the end, even if they lack a compelling reason, fail to do what is required. But, if they genuinely felt obligated, this comes under the heading of *akrasia* as an instance of failing to do what one thinks is right. There then will normally be a sense of regret or of something owed.

In everyday life most of what we do is not the result of any deliberation or calculation. We simply do what feels appropriate, or (on occasions on which we lack any strong sense of one option as appropriate) what we feel like doing or what comes naturally. The occasions on which we consider reasons of any sort for and against doing something are fairly rare. Felt obligations create a sense that fulfilling the obligation (barring special countervailing factors) is appropriate, is the thing to be done. This interrupts the spontaneity of ordinary life, and also (more often than not) steers our behavior along the lines of the obligations.

The obligations may not be very precise. Professional ones usually are, especially if they are derivable from a code of professional ethics; and requirements of etiquette frequently also are codified. But family obligations and those of friendship usually seem much harder to specify. To be genuinely someone's friend implies the possibility of moments at which the friend needs comfort, help, and so forth, and one ought to provide whatever is needed, even if it is inconvenient and one is not in the mood. Something similar can be said about family obligations. Cases vary, as do the strength and character both of friendships and of family connections; so that the form and urgency of these obligations will be difficult to generalize about. Even within a particular friendship or family, there can be considerable leeway in fulfilling whatever the obligations are. One telephones and visits parents not too infrequently, although, as Confucius (II. 8, 89) points out, it is demeanor that matters most. One makes a point to be with friends sometimes when it really matters, and to appreciate their concerns. As loose as these obligations are, the great majority of people are familiar with them as factors in their lives. Part of their role is that they make the answer to "What is for the best (in terms of the value in the world)?" not necessarily the last word in determining what it is best to do, and they usually make asking the question inappropriate.

The relation between other kinds of obligation and moral obligations does not always involve sharp difference. Some professional obligations that normally would be thought of as distinct from moral obligations can begin to look like them when a great deal is at stake. For a lawyer or a psychologist to break confidentiality may look merely sloppy if what is involved is trivial gossip among friends. If instead it is foreseeable that someone's life will be ruined, or that the general tendency to trust lawyers or psychologists with confidential information will be seriously undermined, the professional obligation begins (in that case) to look like a moral one.

Whether family obligations or ones of friendship can amount, in really serious cases, to moral obligations is a more difficult matter. Certainly there are occasions on which we take them very seriously indeed, and failures are viewed in highly negative terms. Even on those occasions, though, "immoral" is usually not the negative term that seems most appropriate. As remarks in the last chapter indicated, it is almost as if there is a shadow category of seriously deficient behavior running alongside of immorality, in which the deficiency is something like inhumanity or lack of what we would consider to be normal human connectedness. Here our conceptual arrangements for praising and blaming people may not be as clear-cut as one might like, and the haziness is augmented by the absurdity of even attempting to codify what we would expect of normal human connectedness.

In any event, there is room for doubt as to whether the general run of family obligations or ones of friendship qualify as moral obligations, even in cases in which we take them very seriously indeed. Of course, there are occasions on which people harm family members or friends, or violate commitments (including some that can be viewed as quasi-contractual) to them, in visible and dramatic ways; and we do condemn this behavior as immoral. But what is in play here is in large part the traditional array of moral categories, and special relations of family and friendship then serve mainly to make behavior look worse that in any case would have seemed immoral.

These are unusual cases. We need to bear in mind that in the great majority of cases family obligations and those of friendship are loose, and do not involve issues of immorality. Moral obligations, in contrast, are very often not loose at all. Arguably sometimes they are: the traditional view that we all have an "imperfect" duty to help others implies that we should on some occasions give to charity and provide other forms of help, while it leaves considerable leeway as to which these occasions should be. But most moral obligations do not offer much leeway. We are obligated to keep a specific promise, perhaps at a specific time and in a specific way. We are obligated not to remove Bloggs's cash from his wallet without his permission: typically the sense of obligation is activated at a specific moment when we might think that we could get away with it. And so on.

In what follows I will examine more closely moral obligations that represent "perfect" rather than "imperfect" duties. One reason for excluding imperfect duties from the discussion is that they seem very unlikely to provide cases in which moral obligation justifies doing what is not optimific. Given leeway as to when we should give to charity (with the assumption that not even a saint could help everyone who needs help), and given the fact also that helping those who need help implies significant positive value in the vast majority of cases, we may think it implausible that it be best to be charitable on one of the relatively rare occasions on which it would not be for the best. There would be so many better occasions for this kind of behavior.

Paradigmatic perfect duties fall out from generally valid moral rules or policies: for example, duties not to murder, steal, torture, and not to fail (without very good reason) to do what one had promised to do in a matter of some importance. "Moral obligation" and "immoral," at least in relation to such cases, are correlative terms. That is, to fail (without good excuse) in relation to a moral obligation of this sort is to be immoral. Conversely, if we are convinced that some behavior is immoral we can generally either point to an established (and we think generally valid) moral rule or policy that is violated or we can formulate a moral rule or policy that we think generally valid that forbids the behavior.

The case whose possibility most needs to be discussed is that of a clear-cut violation of a central moral rule (e.g., someone is murdered, stolen from, or tortured) in which it is foreseeable that the overall consequences, all things considered, of the violation are positive. This would be the classic *felix culpa*. The first question is whether there actually are such cases (real or imaginable). If the answer is "Yes," then the second question is whether in some of them it would be best not to do what is optimific because it would be immoral. The answers to these two questions will have implications for the role of "It would be immoral (or morally wrong)" as a reason for not doing what is optimific. This role may be more complicated, though, than it might first appear to be. In examining it we can move from cases in which (by and large) moral fallibility is not a significant factor to ones in which it is.

## Immorality and Consequences

It can be argued that immoral acts never foreseeably have overall consequences that are good on the whole. This can be argued on three grounds: (1) that we are never in a position to be confident of such an assessment of consequences, or (2) that the immorality itself must be given considerable weight in the assessment of consequences, thus yielding a negative outcome, or, conversely, (3) that if the consequences foreseeably are on the whole good, then the act is not really immoral. None of these arguments seems to me to be valid, although each appeals to some grains of truth.

It is true that our ability to predict the future is far weaker than we would like. This can be seen in the fate of economic or political forecasts that extend more than a few years into the future. Furthermore, there is no way in which we can be highly confident about even limited aspects of the remote future. Relevant to this is the way in which very insignificant events sometimes can have major, unforeseeable ramifications at a much later time.

This inability to predict the future can be taken as an argument of some strength for what might be termed moral conservatism, loyalty to traditional central moral rules (which can be regarded as generally having worked well in the past) in the face of uncertainty. But is it true that we can never have *some* degree of confidence in our assessment of the consequences of actions? A denial that we can ever have any degree of confidence actually would undermine the argument for moral conservatism, by suggesting that the reason for expecting traditional moral behavior to have generally good consequences is not really stronger than reasons for expecting the reverse. Furthermore, even though sometimes an action can have surprising major consequences at some point in the remote future, to say this does not imply that in most cases actions do. Often we can reasonably assume that remote consequences are more likely than not to even out, so that the consequences we have to take most seriously are the relatively immediate and foreseeable ones.

There are some cases that offer abundant reasons for uncertainty even about relatively short-term consequences. When a major political leader is assassinated, it is usually impossible to predict with any confidence how this will affect the social order or the dead leader's movement. Actions in the public sphere sometimes seem to have equal and opposite reactions, but there is no reason to regard this as a general rule. The consequences of actions that directly affect social, political, or economic structures in a significant way are notoriously difficult to predict.

A quiet little murder of a private citizen may be a different matter. The consequences include the fact that the victim misses out on a period of continued life that may well have been important to him or her; there can be reactions of shock and grief from those close to the victim, and perhaps increased edginess on the part of those who know about the crime and see themselves as being in a position similar to the victim's. There also can be gains for various people, including the murderer; there also can be losses. The murderer may suffer from inner conflicts and guilt. This last factor is significant in the case that Dostoevsky created in *Crime and Punishment*. The murder of the money lender might have seemed to Raskolnikov likely to have predominantly good consequences, but given more self-knowledge he would have *known* that there would be major bad consequences that extended beyond the victim's loss. The word "known" deserves emphasis. Sometimes we can know the future. On the other hand, Dostoevsky's novel is a more complicated example than it might first be taken to be, in that someone who reads to the end of the story of spiritual redemption might well be in doubt as to whether the overall consequences of that particular murder were good or bad.

The immediate point, though, is that sometimes we are in a position to be reasonably confident (even if not entirely sure) about the goodness or badness of the consequences of an action. Perhaps virtually all murders, robberies, and so forth, have bad consequences. That still leaves open the possibility that there are some that foreseeably do not.

Plainly it matters how we assess consequences. The idea of referring to a precise-sounding standard (e.g. pleasure minus pain) may have appeal, but the investigation of value in part I makes the inadequacy of such standards clear. Raskolnikov's spiritual redemption arguably counts as a very good consequence of his crime, in a way that cannot be captured by measurement of units of pleasure and the like. Might the immorality of the murder count directly as a bad consequence, in that it creates a future in which there is one more very bad deed on the record? Might this bad consequence then outweigh everything else? I have already stipulated that a genuine consequentialist cannot accept this claim, but might it be true all the same?

This can be a strategy for making act consequentialism converge with commonsense morality, which otherwise would be a hopeless task. There is something to be said for it, but not much. The element of truth is that the moral character of an action or of a policy can have subtle effects as important in their way as the obvious and dramatic effects.

Imagine a zealous police chief who realizes that in one or two cases torturing criminals will have some highly beneficial consequences, say by yielding information that reduces the crime rate. There will be the risk, if word gets out, of the negative consequence of public shock and revulsion, and resultant distrust of the criminal justice system. But suppose that the police chief renders this unlikely by resorting to torture only in one or two cases, firmly resolving not to make it a general practice.

This is a textbook example of limited moral corruption. The obvious point is that there are likely consequences for the character and future behavior of the agent. It is notorious that people who say, "Only this once," rarely confine themselves to one instance of whatever it is. Even apart from this, the police chief will have (as we say) "to live with" what she or he has done, and in that respect will become a different person. There can be effects also on the practices of subordinates and colleagues. The exact nature of all of this may be difficult to predict, but one can say in general that there are foreseeable serious risks. These can be placed under the heading of "fruits of immorality," and in this sense the likely bad consequences of the immorality (of the torture) can be said to outweigh the good consequences. In much the same way, even if Stalin's policies that included the deaths of millions of (previously prosperous) peasants had made sense as economic policy, and in that respect had in the end produced a positive balance of prosperity and human happiness, they still (by poisoning political and social life) would have had on the whole bad consequences.

This is larger than a grain of truth. But notice that it points toward what will be in the end specifiable social and psychological consequences of actions, and not toward some mysterious moral stain that can be assigned any weight one wishes. If it is a general truth about the world that violations of central moral rules are likely to have serious negative social and psychological consequences, this leaves open both the possibility that these negative consequences will be more serious in some cases than in others, and also that there may be cases in which the positive consequences outweigh them. Compare the case discussed, of the police chief who tortures one or two criminals to get information, with one from the last chapter: the torture of an innocent relative of a terrorist in order to elicit information that predictably will save millions of lives. In one respect the latter case is even more distressing than the former, in that the victim is innocent. But there are two other differences that matter. One is that, it could be argued, an action taken in a dramatically unusual case is less likely to function (psychologically and socially) as a precedent for similar actions in the vast run of cases than is one taken in a case that is not so very extraordinary. The other is that the harm prevented in the case of the terrorist's relative was specified as being extraordinarily great. If the torture still is wrong, most people would regard it in that instance as a *felix culpa*.

Viewed against the range of possible cases, the insistence that immorality (either in itself or in its subtle social and moral results) always counts as a negative consequence that outweighs all positive consequences looks dogmatic. It has no clear justification other than that it can save a tidy worldview. If the weight is shifted to the subtle social and moral results, the insistence seems an a priori judgment that may well not accord with all empirical evidence. We can condemn immorality without distorting our sense of the variety of ways in which the world works.

Someone who wishes to preserve a general connection between morality and good consequences might say that, in the unusual case in which the consequences of the violation of a central moral rule foreseeably are on the whole good, the violation does not count as immoral. As we have seen, that claim can be advanced in cases in which adhering to a central moral rule predictably will have catastrophic consequences (such as the case of the terrorist's relative). If someone says, "Do right though the heavens fall," the response can be "If the heavens predictably will fall, then whatever it is cannot be right." My suggestion in the last chapter was that the cases in which adherence to a central moral rule would have catastrophic consequences are contestable. Neither side of the argument here can regard its position as very obviously or by definition correct.

Let us turn instead to a case that is simpler, less dramatic, and (while imaginary) perhaps less highly fantastic. Suppose that Raskolnikov Mark-2 is contemplating the murder of a rather grim, malicious elderly person who predictably would not be missed by anyone; indeed, a number of worthy people predictably would have their lives changed much for the better by not being under the victim's thumb. Let us suppose also that the predictable negative social and psychological consequences of the murder will be slight. The victim's death will hardly get much attention. Raskolnikov Mark-2 knows that he (unlike the original Raskolnikov) will not be consumed by guilt. Perhaps he has committed a number of rather ordinary murders over the years, and this unusually selfless crime seems to him a step up?

It needs to be emphasized that it is not at all easy to construct a case in which the consequences of a serious crime are predictably good, and this difficulty is itself significant. But—even if more details would need to be filled in—the reader ought to be able to see that there are imaginable cases in which foreseeably the good consequences of a serious crime will outweigh bad ones. It never is possible to be sure; but we can be in a position to assume that more remote consequences are likely to even out, and to be reasonably confident that the balance of immediate consequences will be favorable. Cases in which this will be true are very rare, but that does not mean that they are non-existent.

What can we say of such a case? As I have presented it, it is different from the catastrophic cases (e.g., the terrorist's relative) in that very few people would be inclined to deny that the violation of the central moral rule was morally wrong. Thus, that the consequences on the whole in such a case are foreseeably good does not disarm our negative moral judgment. Indeed, we would strongly recommend, in moral terms, that Raskolnikov Mark-2 not commit the murder. Here we have a *felix culpa*.

Let me summarize some results of the argument thus far. There can be cases in which we would morally condemn an action that nevertheless foreseeably has good consequences. In some or all of these we would judge, then, that it is best to do what is not for the best: for example, it is best that Raskolnikov Mark-2 not commit his useful little murder. There are cases (those involving catastrophic consequences of traditional moral behavior) in which the desirability of violating central moral rules is especially contestable. But even in these, those who endorse violating the central moral rule are likely to contend that, in the case at hand, it would not be morally wrong. Thus, we have not seen any clear case in which it looks highly plausible to hold both that conduct is morally wrong and that nevertheless it is to be recommended. There may be a few cases, such as that of Bloggs and the will (in the last chapter), in which this conjunction (morally wrong and recommended) cannot be rejected out of hand. But in these the recommendation looks highly contestable, and the judgment of moral wrongness is very likely to be softened by those who would recommend the violation of usual morality. All of this leaves us with a general tendency—clear in the great majority of cases but fuzzy around the edges—to connect a judgment that something would be morally wrong with one that it is best not to do it, even if what is contemplated would be for the best.

This leaves us also with a sense that "It would be immoral (or morally wrong)," generally speaking, trumps non-moral considerations. But it would be a mistake to accept this conclusion too quickly. Thus far our discussion has concentrated not only on cases in which we can have some reasonable degree of confidence about consequences, but also on ones in which either we can have some reasonable degree of confidence in our moral judgments or about which decent people might well divide (with some plausibility to both sides' views). It is important to keep in mind that thoughtful people sometimes are not all that confident in their moral judgments. But beyond this, there is the serious problem of what to make of the practical reasoning of people whose moral judgments one distrusts. Do we allow highly fallible moral convictions a role in justification?

Suppose that Bloggs says, "Perhaps such and such would have on the whole good consequences, but it would be morally wrong." Our general tendency is to believe that, if what is discussed is some action that Bloggs might or might not take, and if he thinks that it would be morally wrong, then he should not do it. But a great deal depends on how good the consequences seem likely to be, and how plausible or preposterous Bloggs's moral opinions are. If several lives are at stake, and Bloggs's "moral" objection is that mixing of races (or public nudity) would be required to save them, then we would surely judge it best that he over-come his scruples (which we would regard as preposterous) and do whatever is required to save the lives.

Many readers will be inclined to think that cases of genuine moral mistakes or of moral uncertainty are marginal, and that usually most of us know right from wrong. I myself am inclined to agree in relation to the central, traditional moral cat-egories. But, all the same, many may underestimate the areas open to moral doubt. Not so long ago a great many who in most respects seem to have been normal, de-cent people participated in practices (e.g., slavery, exploitation of women, mistreat-ment of the very poor, imprisonment of debtors) that now horrify us, although in fact some of these practices have not entirely disappeared. Might there be behavior that seems to most of us to be entirely normal and permissible that will similarly horrify our descendents? There is no guarantee against moral blind spots. John Stuart Mill, an extraordinarily thoughtful and liberal thinker whose views on the equality of the sexes were far ahead of his time, had a blind spot in relation to imperialist exploita-tion (see 1859/1978, 94–95). It is possible to share some of the moral blind spots of one's time even if one does not share all of them.

Furthermore, in the account thus far given, determination of what is morally acceptable is ultimately more complicated than it looks, requiring evaluation of social practices and of the moral stances that correspond to them. In relation to some very fundamental social protections, such as that against murder and rape, this still looks pretty easy, given the wealth of relevant experience in cultures around the world and the obvious fear and misery when things go wrong. But not all moral practices will be that easy to evaluate; and even ones that centrally seem clearly right (e.g., the prohibition of theft) may have cases around the edges that raise difficulties (as to what, exactly, counts as theft or as unjustified taking of another person's property, or whether extreme need is ever a justification).

The consequences of someone's doing what she or he doubts is morally per-missible also can be difficult to assess. Plainly guilt, lack of confidence, and a sense of personal dividedness are risks. Even if Bloggs compromises a moral opin-ion that the rest of us think preposterous, there is the further risk that he may be encouraged to be careless also in relation to moral requirements that we all would agree are clearly justified. If we factor in possible consequences of these sorts, we will be encouraged in our general tendency to believe that it is for the best if people follow the dictates of their own consciences. But this general tendency leaves room for occasions, as when the misery of innocent people or lives are at stake, on which it clearly would be for the best if Bloggs violated his conscience.

The issue here concerns what we would recommend (or recommend against), and it is important to realize that it is distinct from that of what we would blame.

(For a recent discussion of moral error and blameworthiness, see Fields 1994.) My own view is that moral ignorance sometimes mitigates behavior that we would recommend against, and sometimes does not. Much depends on how grossly wrong the behavior is or was. Also we are much more reluctant to take moral ignorance as mitigating lack of what Hume called natural virtues (as when someone behaves cruelly) than lack of artificial virtues.

On some of the occasions on which we think Bloggs's moral view is wrong, we still would advise Bloggs (if he wants our advice) to follow his conscience. One reason for this is that (as was noted in chapter 6) the social attitudes of respect for conscience themselves have utility, and we ourselves would be advised to maintain these attitudes in our treatment of (and comments to) others. This general respect, however, does allow for exceptions, especially in cases like that in which Bloggs needs to be persuaded to do what is required to save lives (which would go against his absurd moral opinion about race-mixing, or would require his being nude in public). Both the seriousness of what is at stake and the preposterousness of the moral opinion justify our rejection of "It would be immoral" as a reason (in such a case) for not doing what would be for the best. But it has to be granted that there are many cases, when nothing very serious is at stake and when a moral opinion we reject is not preposterous, when we would regard "It would be immoral" as a good reason for not doing what is optimific, even if we thought that the agent's moral judgment was wrong.

But it remains true that there are clear cases in which "It would be immoral" is *not* a reason for refusing to do what is optimific. The failure in these cases is a compound of the implausibility of the moral opinion and the seriousness of what is at stake. There are, on the other hand, no clear cases in which a judgment "It would be immoral" that we are inclined to regard as correct would not be regarded as a good reason for refusing to do what is optimific.

To say that there are no clear cases is not to assert that there cannot be cases (in which consequences justify what would be immoral). It is just that the candidates are all highly contestable. Let us review cases in which it might be thought best (because of consequences) to go against moral reasons that are generally sound. In some, like that of Bloggs and the will, it can be argued that some morally shady behavior would be so beneficial as to be justified. Others involve catastrophic consequences, so that someone might hold both that it was morally wrong to violate a generally valid moral rule *and* that the violation nevertheless was justified by the disastrous consequences (in the case at hand) of following the rule. Are these cases in which it is best to do what is morally wrong? Arguably they are not. It can be argued that the prevention of catastrophic consequences itself provides a moral reason that overrides others, and which can morally justify violation of generally valid rules, and that Bloggs's lie (which brings many benefits and only slight harm) belongs (to the extent to which it is justified) in a gray or shady area between the morally permissible and the morally wrong. All of this leaves "It would be morally wrong" as a reason that (when we think the moral judgment justified) either always or almost always wins.

Some readers may feel that one issue has been totally ignored. Philosophers in recent decades have sometimes spoken of "moral holidays." This appeals to a general human need not to be always on one's best behavior. Are there occasions on which, because of this, "It would be morally wrong" does not count as a reason against doing something, whether or not it is for the best? If Bloggs has been kind, conscientious, and so forth, in a sustained way, might he deserve one or two moral lapses?

Perhaps very few of us will have a perfect record in all decisions that are moral or verge on the territory of morality: we may have hurt others or failed to keep promises when something serious was at stake. Imperfection is acceptable. But to say this is hardly to endorse any specific poor choice.

Nor is it to defend the notion of "moral holidays." Its basic confusion is a conflation of the general practical conduct of life with morality. It is abundantly clear that the vast majority of decisions we make, for good or ill, in our treatment of others or in our own pursuit of happiness, do not involve moral issues. Eating or drinking too much on occasion, or sometimes speaking abruptly to people or neglecting to reply to letters, can be open to criticism (its seriousness depending on the circumstances) without being even slightly near to being immoral. Sometimes, arguably, it is beneficial. Perhaps all of us need periods of time when we are not concerned with doing what is best (see Swanton 1993). Arguably also the exhilaration of real self-indulgence has its psychological uses. We criticize it when it is habitual, but, conversely, we also are suspicious of extremely austere people (wondering when and how whatever is repressed might break out).

Hence there is a great deal to be said for what might be termed "practical holidays," moments when we actively go against what is generally required in the realm of what Mill termed "expediency." The term "moral holiday," on the other hand, suggests that a generally decent person might go in for a spot of murder, torture, or rape as a psychological release or reward—or at the least deliberately hurt people and break serious promises. The most charitable view is that this represents a serious philosophical confusion.

# PART III

# AXIOLOGY AND SOCIAL CHOICE

# 9

# Do Perfectionism and Liberalism Conflict?

It has been widely taken in the last quarter of a century that the answer to the question in this chapter's title is "Yes." Perfectionism has been defined by John Rawls as a teleological doctrine (governing what social policy should be) that advocates "the realization of human excellence in the various forms of culture" (Rawls 1971, 25). The promotion of excellence presupposes a set of ideas as to what constitutes excellence. To be guided by such ideas in the allocation of resources is not to be neutral about values or about what count as important goals. Liberalism, on the other hand, increasingly has been thought of in terms of the balance within a pluralistic society, in which people who by any normal standards count as good citizens do disagree about values. Fairness to various groups and individuals may seem to require that the society not favor the values of any group or individual over others. Liberalism, in short, it is thought, requires neutrality; perfectionism violates it.

This is a simple presentation of what in fact is a complicated social and political issue. Liberalism comes in many varieties. It may be tempting to take John Rawls's version as canonical; and much of the subsequent discussion will be keyed to his formulation of, and argument for, liberalism. But we need not assume that an authentic liberalism must coincide with Rawls's. Perfectionism, also, comes in many varieties. Much depends both on the values that are supposed to be promoted, and also the degree of preference that they are supposed to get. Much of the anti-perfectionist literature has sought to score points without much argument by focusing on the most extreme and least plausible forms of perfectionism (e.g., on some fairly wild sayings of Nietzsche). This is part of a wider picture in which, increasingly, political arguments between Left and Right have taken this form, on both sides. But philosophers have a responsibility not to focus on the least plausible versions of views they wish to criticize.

The view that liberalism and perfectionism conflict can be seen as a very strong claim, in relation to the possibility of milder forms of difficulty in combining the two. Clearly it is true that some forms of liberalism are, as Rawls contended, incompatible with any form of perfectionism; and some forms of perfectionism (e.g., Nietzsche's) are incompatible with any form of liberalism. But this leaves open the possibility that the most reasonable forms of liberalism can be combined with reasonable forms of perfectionism.

Perhaps (even if this is so) there will be, we might say, a tension. But designing a good society and political order may well involve a variety of desiderata that pull in different directions and strain against one another, so that compromises and limited satisfaction of some of our goals may have to be expected. This part of political and social philosophy, then, will be more like engineering than like mathematics or physics, in that we have to think in terms of tolerances rather than ideal requirements. Perhaps an even better analogy is with architecture (in which engineering problems play a significant role). There is a great deal to be said for thinking of a social order as a creative product that must carry various loads and work to the satisfaction of those who use it.

Let me give an example from another region of social and political philosophy of how genuine desiderata can conflict. The word "justice" is used in relation to many different aspects of the process of deciding which persons get (or are given chances to get) various things that many desire. Admirers of Rawls will immediately think of equal liberties and of pressure to promote the financial well-being and opportunities of the worst-off members of a society. Others will think of the sense in which it is arguably just that people who, through effort and self-discipline, do good work get some of the rewards that are commonly thought of as tending to go with achievement; and an admirer of Rawls can also care about justice in this sense. The likelihood that good work will be rewarded is a social desideratum. Many would say that a corollary of justice in this sense will be high social and economic mobility, so that people will not be, say, condemned to a certain role in society because of who their parents were, or on the basis of an examination taken at the age of eleven. This social mobility is also a desideratum. A third is a possibility of reasonable security: people should be able not to worry continuously or repeatedly about what their future status will be or what kind of work, if any, they will be doing in a year. A fourth is that decent hardworking people who in one way or other have low status or do low status jobs should not be made to feel like failures. Besides endorsing these four social goals, I want to suggest that they are not (at least at present) very controversial, and also that they would be relevant and important even within a society that would meet Rawls's requirements.

However there is a tension among these desiderata, and it would be impossible to combine the four of them in their ideal forms. Ideally, it should always be possible, through effort and self-discipline, to achieve great rewards; but, insofar as these rewards consist of scarce resources or of a limited number of highly desirable positions, this ideal conflicts with the desideratum of reasonable security. A world in which people always have fair chances of the rewards that are generally craved will be one in which many people will be worrying constantly about holding on to what they have, and some of them may have to compete again and again for their jobs. It should be emphasized that this point is quite separate from economic competition. Even in a society in which everyone is paid the same amount for the same number of hours worked, some positions will be more attractive and prestigious than others.

The point in a nutshell is this. What if I had done some things in the past that made me deserve the job I have, but Bloggs has been doing some marvellous work lately (and my job is the only one that would suit him that is more attractive than the one he currently has)? In terms of current work he deserves my job more than I do. It may well seem that the demands of justice and of the possibility of reasonable security pull in opposite directions.

Most of us would agree that social and economic mobility is highly desirable. But the possibility of real success entails that of real failure: a society in which there actually is, or is thought to be, considerable mobility is vulnerable to the self-blaming attitudes of ordinary workers (who have not moved upwards) that are described in Sennett's and Cobb's *The Hidden Injuries of Class*. We may think it good that most people be reasonably satisfied with their lives. But a high degree of what most of us think of as justice (in the sense under discussion) undermines this possibility, by giving very many people a sense that they could and should have more.

In these respects there is not, and cannot be, an ideal social order. A great deal can be said for a degree of social mobility, and for the possibility (extending through most of a lifetime) of greater rewards; but movement up whatever scale is held to matter should not be frictionless or necessarily quick, and we need to build in a degree of security for people who have positions they are satisfied with.

It is also desirable that people think less about status and rewards than both the competitive winners and losers in our culture tend to do. Arguably, though, a widespread attitude of entire indifference would carry its own risks, making various forms of innovation less likely. For people to care less about status and rewards would lessen the tension among our desiderata, but it could not be eliminated as long as they care at all.

A shrewd reader can already glimpse the outline of the position with regard to liberalism and perfectionism for which I will argue. They too represent desiderata that pull in different directions. There is a tension between them. But there are ways of lessening (although not eliminating) this tension.

First, though, we need to look at the basis for Rawls's rejection of perfectionism, and then at the different forms that liberalism and perfectionism might take. Rawls's construction of a liberal social order is rooted in what he calls the original position, a hypothetical setting in which self-interested individuals must agree on social arrangements even though they do not know what their positions will be in the society whose contract they are formulating. This hypothetical ignorance is an ingenious device to ensure that social arrangements are designed to be acceptable to those in every social position. It has a strong affinity to the Kantian insistence that we act only on maxims that we could will to be a universal law, which includes the requirement that we reasonably could will them even if we were in the positions of people who might be affected by our actions.

The elegant thought experiment of the original position is less simple than it looks. Ignorance of social position is, in effect, a requirement of fairness. Global ignorance, on the other hand, would prevent the thought experiment from yielding any results at all. That is, people in the original position who not only did not know what their social positions would be but also lacked knowledge of the general character of human life would be unable to formulate and agree upon a desirable social framework. Clearly one of the design problems (in Rawls's original position) is in drawing the line between what people will be presumed to know and what they will be presumed not to know.

Suppose that Rawls's social contractors know a little about human life, but lack knowledge about what people generally value (beyond food and drinkable liquids) or about the means by which people get what they value. If the original position were to have this form, then the only possible results for distributive justice would be extremely abstract and schematic: there might be agreement that there should be some degree of equality of . . . whatever. At the other extreme, we might stipulate knowledge of various forms of human fulfilment, including happiness and including also what some people claim to be the superior and enduring satisfaction of the flow of creative and demanding activities (cf. Csikszentmihalyi 1990). This extreme would have a number of drawbacks from a Rawlsian point of view. Insofar as the values of various forms of satisfaction are contentious, it would severely undermine the possibility of the social contractors' reaching unanimous agreeement; it also would open the door to what might be termed elitist views.

Furthermore, how would a society that aimed for distributive justice go about trying to equalize various forms of satisfaction? Would there be some built-in form of compensation for people who had been feeling depressed? When people have awful diseases, it may be a straightforward matter to pay for their medical care, but it is far less clear how a society could go about trying to achieve distributive justice in relation to suffering. What about sex? People in the original position who know about sex might be inclined to give some priority to the desires of the least well off: the old and ugly. Aristophanes has presented such a social policy amusingly in his *Ecclesiazusae* (see Aristophanes 4th c. B.C.E./1962, 457 ff.).

There is, in my view, no ideal answer to these questions. Perhaps it is desirable for a theory of social justice to avoid trying to answer them. Rawls's solution to the problem of what the original contractors are supposed to know does avoid some of the worst difficulties. We are to assume basic knowledge of the structure of human practical life, and of the ways in which liberties function as opportunities. On one hand, Rawls stipulates that people in the original position do not know what their idea of the good is. On the other hand, they know that money (as well as liberties) functions to open opportunities to do or get various things that one might turn out to want. This enables Rawls to have it, so to speak, both ways in relation to the role of values in the social design. Values are in a way excluded by the requirement that people in the original position not know their views of the good. But a core of values appears, and is usable, in that liberties and money are important in their role of providing opportunities. A just distribution then includes both equal liberty and a distribution of money that is optimal for the worst-off members of society.

It should be emphasized that what is at work here are the structural demands of a theory, and clearly not the philosopher's own idea of the good or for that matter any of the kinds of evidence of value that were discussed in the first part of this book. Nevertheless, the result is that Rawls's theory of justice privileges money. What presents itself as a rigorous and precise line of thought in the end seems to give us a claim about value (insofar as it has weight in social design); and, furthermore, the claim (in some form) may seem to most of us to be pretty plausible, enough so that we may not be disturbed by the truncated axiology in which it plays a part.

Why is the privileging of money so appealing? One good reason is the one that is operative in the construction of Rawls's theory. There is a sort of bland neutrality to money, so that in a sense to want it or to take it is (by itself) not to take sides in the issues of what is important in life. Money can be used in all sorts of ways. Conversely, there are many things that one might want that are impossible without money. Some of these may be very high-minded and unselfish. A critic might be tempted to point out that there are people who place no value on money: religious people, for example, who have taken vows of poverty. But even these might like to be able to give money away to those in need.

Second, if we want to arrive at a social design whose implementation is clear-cut, the public and countable nature of money is ideal. Perhaps in the end what most people think is most important in life is happiness, or joy, or a legitimate sense of achievement; and most of us might say that money is, in itself (apart from its uses) worth nothing. But it is not so easy to assess in any clear and precise way how much happiness or joy someone has, and any attempt to do so would be intrusive. Anyway, we are not exactly going to take some happiness away from a lucky person in order to give it to someone less fortunate! Money is much more convenient for the theoretician of social justice. We can measure it, tell how much someone has without being terribly intrusive, and it can be redistributed.

On the other hand, money is not unique in its role of providing opportunity to pursue whatever ends one has, and in its suitability to precise measurement. The amount of free time that someone has also has these features. The opportunities that a person has, given a moderate amount of money, can depend very heavily on time; and there are some goals that require more time than money. Why could Rawls's social contractors not think of free time as a good to be distributed? Perhaps, to arrive at a reasonable distribution, they would need to know yet more than Rawls allows? After all, some people can really use their time, much more effectively and to greater good than other people.

Rawls in fact has expressed willingness to include leisure time on his list of primary goods (Rawls 1993, 180). But what he goes on to say about it (pp. 181–82n) seems unhelpful. Thomas Hurka has argued (Hurka 1993, 174), on perfectionist grounds, that there is a weaker case against inequalities in leisure time than against economic inequalities. The point is well taken, although "free time" is a better phrase than "leisure time" for what a perfectionist should be concerned with: time to think, read, and look about in ways not closely related to any immediate work project.

It could be argued that Rawls's privileging money amounts to the benevolent face of a pervasive money-mindedness, in our society, that itself is a social problem. Rawls, for his own reasons, resolutely refuses to distinguish between money needed to raise the worst off members of society to the level of a basically decent life and money needed to raise them to a yet higher level. In this, the emphasis is heavily on the money and the relative economic position it represents, and not on reasons apart from this why it might be important.

Rawls's rejection of perfectionism has a great deal to do both with his truncated axiology and with the importance he gives (at any level of well-being) to money. Perfectionism is the social promotion of values other than liberty (and ancillary political virtues) and economic equality. There is no warrant for this in the social contract that will be arrived at by Rawlsian people who do not know their own view of the good. This by itself perhaps would not make perfectionism unacceptable: a great many things may happen in a society for which there is no warrant in the social contract, but which do not violate the social contract and are acceptable. What seems to ensure the unacceptability of perfectionism, in Rawls's view, is that it demands things from people (especially bits of tax money) in the name of values that they may not share.

Rawls's objection to perfectionism, put this baldly, does have a certain degree of plausibility, appealing as it does to ideas of fairness. There are perfectionist replies that also have a certain degree of plausibility, and that, indeed, I think should be convincing. I will explore these in the next chapter. What I need to do first is explore some of the varieties of liberalism, of which Rawls's is only one, and also some of the varieties of perfectionism.

## Liberalism

The term "liberalism" has a range of meanings that are exhibited both in political philosophy and in ordinary political discourse. Thus, it is not always easy to be sure of the meaning of a passing reference to liberalism. Some might argue that Rawls has attempted to hijack the term for the purposes of his brand of egalitarianism. An additional source of confusion is that a familiar form of nineteenth-century liberalism, with its emphasis on individual rights, is at the core of one strain of twentieth-century conservatism and also finds its way into right-wing libertarianism. Because of this, one might say that there now is liberalism of the left and liberalism of the right. But, of course, there are many more than two varieties.

Nineteenth century liberalism also was hardly monolithic. Larry Seidentop has usefully contrasted the English liberalism of people like John Stuart Mill with contemporary French liberal thought, of which Alexis de Tocqueville is an important representative (see Siedentop 1979). One difference is the greater emphasis placed in French liberalism on "positive liberty," a pervasive sense of social responsibility and civic duty within a liberal culture. This has roots in the civic humanism of the Renaissance (see Skinner 1984). This element is not totally absent from such English liberal texts as *On Liberty*, although readers sometimes ignore it.

John Stuart Mill's liberal vision famously centers on individual rights, on the ability of individuals to develop their thinking and their styles of life without interference either from the law or from the "tyranny of the majority" (as long as they were not doing direct harm to others). There are other elements that are less congenial to those contemporary conservatives that think of themselves as descendents of Mill. He clearly was uncomfortable with the concentration of wealth and privilege in the hands of a small percentage of the population. The utilitarian calculus, conjoined with the assumption that money and privileges have diminishing marginal utilities, points in the direction of much greater economic and social equality than existed in Mill's day (and probably than exists in ours). Egalitarianism does not have the primary role in utilitarian theory that might satisfy Rawls's requirements, but there is no doubt that nineteenth-century utilitarian liberalism resembles Rawls's liberalism in containing egalitarian tendencies.

Another (largely implicit) feature of Mill's liberalism is relevant to our present topic and deserves comment. The non-interference that is at the center of Mill's *On Liberty* does not imply neutrality, in relation either to ideas or to styles of life. Mill's remarks in the same work (p. 75) about "depravation of taste" to which we cannot help responding negatively make this clear, as does the famous discussion in *Utilitarianism* of the higher and lower pleasures. Mill may well have thought that one of the undesirable consequences of extreme social and economic inequality was that many people were prevented, by inadequate education and excessive work, from experiencing the "higher" pleasures for themselves. *On Liberty* argues that the justification in a modern society of the liberties discussed is that they enable as many people as possible to fulfill themselves and to be happy, and *Utilitarianism* makes it clear that (in his view) the most desirable kind of fulfillment involves the pleasures of culture and the intellect.

It may be also that Mill was taking for granted that the liberties he advocated, all of which explicitly are liberties of adults, will be exercised against the background of education in restraint and self-discipline. This is one way of making sense of Mill's optimism about the choices that most people will make, and would explain why he might have thought it unnecessary to dwell on civic responsibility. It sometimes is suggested (cf. Walzer 1965, 300–306) that modern liberalism was made possible by the habits of mind produced by puritanism, but that it then over time has the unfortunate tendency to undermine these habits of mind. Mill's reply to such a challenge very likely would have been in terms of a fortifying role of a certain kind of education, which also should have the function of enabling as many people as possible to enter into cultural and intellectual pursuits.

This can be viewed as speculation about what Mill did not think it necessary to say or to dwell on. He does make it clear that, in his view, schooling for the very young should center on "moral culture" (Mill 1834/1984, 70–71), and quotes with approval the thought that it should awaken children to "a life of love and intelligence." In any event, my suggestion is that Mill's liberalism should be seen as including four significant elements: a strong emphasis on individual liberty, some insistence (albeit less than in French liberalism) on civic responsibility, a push toward greater social and economic equality, and a desire to enable numbers of people to experience the pleasures of culture and the intellect. This is not a random assortment of desiderata, and it can be argued that there are positive connections among the four. Individual liberty of some general and abstract sort is not going to mean very much to people so poor that they have to spend all of their time just struggling to stay alive. We have already seen that there is an argument that the continuation of such liberty in a society presupposes some correlative sense of social responsibility. It also is questionable whether the liberty can be used effectively, either in personal life or in political choice, by people who lack all ability to pursue a coherent train of thought or to evaluate options at all critically. Thus, at least a modest level of intellectual development may be required for liberty that is to be meaningful. It also may be required for workable democracy, which scarcely can flourish if most voters have very short attention spans and are easily captured by slogans.

If we turn from such general considerations, and from philosophy, to politics at the end of the twentieth century, we become keenly aware that these elements, which fit together so well in Mill's thought (and in the abstract), can begin to pull in different directions. Does our emphasis on individual liberty temper our demands on people who seem to lack a sense of civic responsibility, and could there be (as a result) a cumulative widespread loss of such a sense? Some theorists (cf. Glendon 1991) have contended that we in America overemphasize rights at the expense of responsibilities. Conversely, might a really effective push toward social and economic equality require restrictions on some that, they might argue, limit their personal liberty? What if many people come not only to disdain the pleasures of culture and the intellect, but also to think that programs that promote them smack of the old-fashioned elitism of times when there was great social inequality?

Hence, there can be a liberalism that is concerned first and foremost with individual liberties, and not so much with the social and intellectual conditions that (in the long run) promote these as with the case-by-case defense of them in the present. One might regard such a liberalism as shortsighted; but long views have become less common in political thought, and they lead to considerations that can complicate one's vision. There also can be liberalisms, such as Rawls's, that heavily emphasize social and economic equalization. Some of these may gravitate naturally to governmental action as the chief means of achieving this desirable goal. There also can be liberalisms that strongly emphasize civic responsibility. The temptation then may be to limit the liberties or the further opportunities of those who fail to exercise their civic responsibilities. Finally, there can be liberalisms that heavily emphasize culture and the intellect. Some of these may severely limit the options of those who entirely reject anything that smacks of culture and the intellect.

A contemporary liberal who endorses all of the elements of the original agenda might come to think of them not as parts of a single ideal, but rather as goals that must be balanced, with some calculation of tolerances in cases in which they come in conflict with one another. Thus, there can be a liberalism that refuses to set lexical priorities among key liberal desiderata. Such a liberalism can emphasize individual liberty while insisting that encouragement of civic responsibility and education in the higher pleasures are vital in preserving it, and that sometimes individual rights and the social importance of these goods will need to be balanced; it also can balance the advantages of social and economic equalization against possible costs to a society (including what might be argued to be limitations of individual liberty).

## Perfectionism

Perfectionism also need not set lexical priorities among desiderata. No doubt there have been some who maintained that peaks of human achievement justified any costs in human suffering, including especially the suffering of people thought to be inferior. This variety of perfectionism is a soft target for the anti-perfectionist, in that it seems doctrinaire, callous, and potentially cruel. It is far from clear that the choice envisaged, between enormous human suffering, on one hand, and the elimination of peaks of human achievement, on the other, occurs at all often. It is not as if Beethoven required heaps of human skulls before he could write his string quartets. If an artist did require something of this sort for her or his best work, we might well wonder whether some spirit of extreme callousness or cruelty infused the work, and what difference that made to its quality.

On the other side, it might be maintained that no cultural achievements justify extreme human suffering. As a slogan this is much more appealing than the extreme perfectionist slogan that is its opposite. There are two respects in which it is, I think, clearly right. First, most of us would agree that it is morally wrong to inflict grievous suffering on people in order to make possible cultural achievements. Having agreed, one may have difficulty in thinking of an actual case in which the infliction of such suffering was required. Perhaps work crews were badly mistreated in order to create some of the most beautiful ancient Egyptian monuments. But is this to say that their creation would not have been feasible if the workers had been treated better?

Secondly, there clearly are some cases in which the relief of suffering imperatively takes precedence over the promotion of cultural pursuits. When there is famine in Ethopia, it would be grossly inappropriate to send money to establish a symphony orchestra in Adis Ababa. Even here though we might pause. Suppose that some of the very beautiful early examples of architecture in Ethiopia had been at the same time threatened with ruin, and that funds had been needed to protect them? Might it have made sense, in that case, to have divided one's contributions into famine relief and cultural landmark preservation, especially given the importance to Ethiopian culture of the early churches?

Such choices are not easy. Most of us could do more, both to relieve suffering and for purposes such as cultural preservation; but needs are very great and resources will be limited. It is tempting to think that the relief of suffering can have lexical priority over support of cultural activities (including the kind of scientific research that is unlikely to have practical applications in the foreseeable future), without serious impairment of the latter. Let us relieve the suffering, it will be said, and then we will turn our attention to culture. There are two things wrong with that. One is that sometimes the needs of various cultural activities or preservation cannot wait. But the other is that, even if we have limited our concern to the kinds of suffering on which social policy or individual goodwill can have a direct impact, the magical time at which we can turn our attention away from suffering will not come. This is especially true as long as world population continues to increase while many resources are depleted.

Lexical priority gives us two implausible forms of perfectionism. One is the extreme variety sometimes associated with Nietzsche, in which the promotion of human excellence (or allowing it free play) always takes priority. At the other end is what might be termed feeble perfectionism, in which the promotion of human excellence is allowed some weight as long as pressing needs (including the relief of human suffering) are met. In a society (e.g., that of Kant's Königsberg) in which the only suffering one realistically could relieve was local (and thereby was limited), such a perfectionism might have had some weight. In today's world it has virtually none.

In between these two extremes, there are many possible forms of perfectionism, all of which will seek to balance the promotion of human excellence in its various forms with other desiderata. One of the variables will be how much weight the promotion of human excellence is given in this balancing. There can be variation also in the kinds of intellectual and artistic activities that are most zealously promoted. Any plausible perfectionism will be directed toward some combination of three elements: (1) education that increases some people's likelihood of being able to do significant artistic or intellectual work, and increases many people's intellectual abilities and sensitivity (including the ability to appreciate such work); (2) preservation and dissemination of cultural achievements of the past; and (3) support for new artistic work or research of high quality. Each of these is important and needs to be discussed separately. Such a discussion will bring out, also, the importance of achieving some kind of balance among them.

Education that strengthens intellectual abilities and cultural knowledge and sensitivity has a great deal to be said for it. Inevitably there will be practical (e.g., technological) as well as theoretical advances that will result from the intellectual training, and the advantages for a democracy in having numbers of citizens who can actually think through an argument have been noted. The practical advantages of cultural knowledge and sensitivity are more indirect. But insofar as much of what we think of as culture is located in the past, education that promotes cultural knowledge and sensitivity also strengthens an awareness of (and a sense of connectedness to) cultural traditions. There may be some political benefits in this, in that a citizenry that has very little sense of the past may be less rooted, lack a sense of direction and of the ways in which events and movements develop, and thereby be more easily swept away. There is an opposite danger if sensitivity to the past is very heavily emphasized to the detriment of openness to the new. There then would be real risks of stagnation and complacency. There is room for debate about what the balance should be, in cultural education, between interest in the past and in innovation. But some balance is desirable.

Clearly there is a case for holding it desirable that education provide the intellectual resources and necessary experience for those people who might turn out to do interesting research in "pure" science or in other areas, or might turn out to be creative artists. What is most controversial in this follows from the apparent fact that classroom and curriculum arrangements that most benefit superior students do not necessarily benefit average students (and indeed might be experienced by them as discouraging), and vice versa. This is a complex and difficult issue. A great deal could be said about the risks to morale of average (and especially of below average) students in schools that give superior preparation to able students, and of the boredom and alienation of bright students in the more usual sort of school. At the least, it could be argued that there is a tug between what works best for average or below average students and what works best for very bright students.

There also is a special problem for any liberalism that includes something like Rawls's brand of egalitarianism. Schools that adapt at least as well to the needs of bright students as to those of below average students may, in effect, increase the eventual social and economic distance between the two groups. Rawls is very aware of this, and suggests that "greater resources might be spent on the less rather than the more intelligent, at least over a certain time of life, say the earlier years of school" (Rawls 1971, 101). Many people who are broadly sympathetic to Rawls's egalitarianism might recoil from this suggestion. But this creates a tension between broadly egalitarian positions and the anti-egalitarian tendencies of perfectionist education (cf. Nagel 1991, 135–36). Even apart from this, the difficulty of the issue, and the fact that any policy has its own educational risks for some, should not be overlooked.

I will not pursue this point, except to remark on a related social policy issue. Let us assume (for the sake of argument) that demanding schools, with curricula that are enriched intellectually and aesthetically, work well for above average students, and lead by and large to greater achievements on the part of these students. Let us assume also (again for the sake of argument) that less demanding schools can work somewhat better for average and below average students, who at least are happier in them. In a democratic society, there will be a strong tendency, then, for local tax-supported schools to be of the latter sort. But what of affluent parents of bright children, who can afford to send their offspring to more demanding private schools? The liberal dilemma is this. We are left with a social choice among three alternatives, all of which are unpalatable on some liberal grounds. One is to overrule the wishes (and perhaps the needs) of the majority of students and their parents and to make local tax-supported schools more demanding. This would be undemocratic, and also arguably would be such that most of those affected would lose a little more than they gained. A second alternative is what is (by and large) present policy in the United States: we keep local schools (at least most local schools) fairly undemanding, but allow the private option to those who can afford it. One objection to this is that it drastically separates the level of opportunity available to bright children whose parents are affluent from that available to bright children whose parents are not. Third, we might (because of this objection) ban or severely restrict private education. This has been suggested by some on the left in Britain. But it would seem to run counter to the liberal emphasis on individual (and family) liberty.

Here, yet again, there is a real problem and no ideal solution. A variety of attempts at balancing can be found here and there, such as special classes or programs for bright students within local schools, or scholarships at private schools for bright children from poor families. To the extent that there are very many different accommodations that could be included in a perfectionist social philosophy, there are myriad forms of perfectionism.

Any perfectionism will have to place some emphasis on what amounts to elite education, as preparing the way for intellectual and artistic achievements. It also is very likely to emphasize preservation and dissemination of cultural elements from the past. This emphasis will facilitate some kinds of what Mill considered to be "higher pleasures." It also will, at least in the arts, underlie new achievements. Many of the early twentieth-century artists thought to be most revolutionary (e.g., Stravinsky, Picasso) have dwelt upon the relation between their own inspiration and their awareness of a set of forms and models embodied in past work. Traditions often are very important to those who wish to challenge or go beyond them.

Finally, it is arguable that the vitality of people's sense of cultural traditions will be manifested in the emergence of work that is interesting and new, and in the ability of such work to gain an audience. There is a huge difference between traditions that are ongoing and evolving and cases in which one might speak of the "dead hand" of the past. There is not very much to be said for the cultural experiences of any society in which there is a widespread sense that all of the good music has been written, all of the good paintings have been painted, all important scientific knowledge has been gathered, and so on. We need to encourage and support the liveliness of the new.

Any plausible perfectionism will give weight to all three of these elements in a society, and will claim that we should evaluate societies in terms of their possession of these as well as such liberal desiderata as individual liberties and a reasonable degree of economic and social equality. The importance of all of this can be appreciated if we reflect on what a society would be like that lost the intellectual and artistic vitality necessary to produce good new work, and also lost touch with the meaning and importance of its own past achievements. Aldous Huxley's *Brave New World* is a clever thought experiment of such a society, one that seems distinctly unsatisfactory to most readers. It may be that Huxley intended his novel as a refutation of hedonistic utilitarianism. In the dystopia he depicts there is no suffering and much pleasure. But if Huxley had made the design egalitarian, it would have been able to meet Rawlsian standards; and in this respect it can be adapted for use against Rawls. Even if it were entirely egalitarian, such a society—lacking in the production or appreciation of intellectual and artistic excellence—is unacceptable. This leads us in the direction of some form of perfectionism apart from the feeble kind.

Let us return to the question of this chapter. Do perfectionism and liberalism conflict? Much depends on the form of liberalism and that of perfectionism under consideration. Nietzschean perfectionism conflicts with any plausible kind of liberalism; Rawlsian liberalism conflicts with any perfectionism, apart perhaps from the feeblest varieties. This leaves open the possibility that there are forms of liberalism and forms of pefectionism that are very compatible. Even here, though, compatibility may require adjustments and a willingness to accept what might seem to fall short of the ideal. It is possible, for example, to have educational policies that would satisfy many liberals and many perfectionists (and, for that matter, many liberal perfectionists); but compromises are required. The case for a limited perfectionism, that would be compatible with most forms of liberalism, will be developed in the next chapter.

# 10

# The Case for a Limited Perfectionism

In this chapter I will argue that a perfectionism with certain broad characteristics represents good social policy. There will be no attempt to specify the nature of the perfectionism in detail. One reason for not doing so is that, as I argued in the previous chapter, social policy in many cases should not aim at ideal solutions but at reasonable balances among desiderata. If there is any one good version of perfectionism, there undoubtedly will be many. Relative advantages among very similar versions could fluctuate from year to year depending on changes in circumstances. Part of what all good versions of perfectionism share, I will argue, is that the weight in social policy that they assign to perfectionist considerations is relatively modest.

The argument for a limited perfectionism will have two parts. The first will defend against Rawls's objections to perfectionism. The second will be positive, establishing the claim that perfectionist elements in social policy contribute to social well-being.

## Rawls's Dismissal of Perfectionism

Three sorts of objections to perfectionism can be gathered from what Rawls says in *A Theory of Justice*. They are (1) that perfectionist policies in effect are coercive of those who do not share the values they promote, (2) such policies also represent a failure in the neutrality that the society should maintain among the competing values of individuals or groups within it, and (3) that perfectionist policies are in effect ruled out by the conditions of the original position. The third objection is most fundamental; but, on the other hand, it also can be viewed as a report of ad hoc devices, in constructing the original position, to rule out what the first two objections show is unacceptable.

The charge of coercion can be appreciated if one realizes that Rawls's specific discussion of perfectionist policies is always in the context of taxpayer-supported programs. Rawls's liberalism of the Left is at this point ironically close to a good deal of current liberalism of the Right. A great many people will complain about the percentage of the taxes they pay that goes to causes or projects that they do not support, or to activities thought of as outside a narrow range of essential governmental functions. Government aid to the poor and unfortunate especially is a target of this criticism; but support for cultural activities and for projects in pure science, although involving much smaller amounts of money, also is considered objectionable.

The idea behind libertarian protests seems to be something like this. The protestor thinks of himself or herself as an autonomous individual, drawn (without anything like explicit consent) into arrangements that involve forced contributions to a variety of activities support for which ought to be entirely voluntary. Very probably the protestor would agree, if asked, to subscribe to government services such as police and fire protection, state highways, and the like. But the government does so much more, as reflected in the tax bill, without the explicit consent of the individuals who protest.

The right-wing form of this protest is frequently linked to a sense that the money one earns is deserved, in a strongly realistic sense in which this desert is a normative fact about the universe. This ignores the large premium that is awarded to those lucky enough to be born American (and the less large premium for those born in other advanced industrialized societies) in earnings, above those in third world countries for people doing similar jobs and working just as hard. It also ignores the way in which a variety of social and cooperative arrangements make us the people we are, and contribute to personal opportunities. Be that as it may, Rawls shares — in relation to government activities that are important to perfectionists — this sense that money is required of taxpayers that should be contributed, if at all, voluntarily (cf. Rawls 1971, 329). He presumably differs, for obvious reasons, with regard to the much larger amounts taken for programs to aid the poor and unfortunate; but his view of government-supported culture is not very different from that held by many on the far Right.

Is it coercion if the government extracts tax money without one's consent? To the extent that "coercion" implies no real choice in the matter, there are grounds for an answer of "Yes." If, however, one takes "coercion" to imply unreasonable constraint, then the issue of reasonableness becomes crucial. Our real choices are limited, without our explicit consent, in a wide variety of ways: by speed limits on highways, pedestrian walk lights, a host of other measures to facilitate social coordination, and measures also to promote the interests of this or that group or individual. (A benign example in the United States of the latter is government-supported rural electrification early in the twentieth century, made palatable in part by the fact that the beneficiaries did not thereby become enviable.) The notion that personal explicit consent should be required, for all of these, may be appealing to someone who takes seriously Huey Long's slogan that every man should be a king. But its social disadvantages include the radical dwindling of social cooperation, and increasing psychological isolation of individuals from one another. Because of these, it seems most implausible to insist, as a general principle, that no taxation is justified without the explicit consent of each taxpayer to the expenditure of public money for which it is designed.

To make this statement leaves open the possibility that there could be legitimate protests against some forms of taxation or against expenditures for which we are taxed. The precursors of anti-tax libertarians include those who, during the Vietnam War, withheld part of their tax as a protest. Their case, however, was different from that of most current tax protestors: the complaint was not that the taxation ipso facto was coercive, but rather that the activities it supported were immoral. There is room for argument here. Similarly, someone who convinces us that taxes support activities not in the public interest, thus making the taxation to that extent unjustified and unfair, has at least a case for claiming that they are coercive in a sense that includes unreasonableness. There was a strong case for saying that rural electrification was in the public interest. Can a similar case be made for the parts of taxation that support cultural activities and research of the sort that is most unlikely to have immediate practical benefits? If this element of taxation is unjustified or unfair, then there is a strong case for regarding it as coercive in the sense that implies unreasonableness.

The issue of whether public expenditure for perfectionist purposes is unjustified ultimately hangs on the general merits of perfectionism as public policy or on the issue of unfairness. We need to compare perfectionist expenditures with others that are unjustified either because they are pointless or because of what amounts to favoritism.

It is against the public interest to tax people in order to build expensive desalination facilities, if in fact there is plenty of drinkable water already and no need for desalinized sea water. The pointlessness of the project would make this element of taxation unreasonable. If it is useless and unnecessary to give public support to cultural activities and research, then taxation for this purpose is unjustified in much the same way. This kind of objection will be dealt with at some length in the latter part of this chapter, which will create a positive case for perfectionism. On the face of it, it is not very plausible.

It also is against the public interest to tax people in general in order to enrich honey producers or horse breeders. In this case the issue of fairness comes to the fore. It might be said that it is important to society to have suitable quantities of good honey and of fine horses, but this is highly contentious. It could be argued that it is similarly unfair to tax people in general in order to support cultural activities and research, thus subsidizing (it will be said) museum goers, opera lovers, and intellectuals. Again, the justification in terms of cultural values is contentious. This charge of unfairness on the face of it is plausible, much more indeed than the charge that it is useless and unnecessary to spend money for perfectionist purposes. I will examine this argument now.

There are two elements to the charge. There is, first of all, possible unfairness in government-supported policies that benefit some individuals and not others. Virtually all government policies in one way or another will make some people's lives better or worse. If military pay is raised, to further the goal of having an effective professional armed services, this will make the lives of ordinary soldiers and officers and their families better. Resultant spending in areas around military bases will benefit the local economy and merchants. Plainly it would be unreasonable to insist that government policies never benefit individuals directly or indirectly. Nevertheless, unfairness of this sort is a worry. Much depends on the general justification of the policies, but also it is highly relevant how enviable the lives of the individuals who are benefited become. A rise in military pay could be seen as, in many respects (given current conditions), relief of hardship rather than a windfall. The rural poor who benefited from government-sponsored electrification also pass the test of enviability. So do the disabled people who, thanks to tax-supported programs, achieve a minimally decent life, although this would not be the case if they were showered with luxuries. Similarly, government support for scientific research and the arts would be objectionable if the physicist or composer given a fellowship by the National Science Foundation or the National Endowment for the Arts thereby were raised to great affluence. On a much more banal level, subsidies for the arts could be seen reasonably as unfair if opera tickets became positively cheap. Any reasonable perfectionism will avoid this kind of unfairness, and a perfectionism that does not benefit individuals in highly enviable ways can be defended against it.

It may be said that this is to make an unwarranted concession to the politics of envy. Envy, though, however ugly it can be, is a normal (and widespread) human emotion. If the design of a good society is, as I argued in the last chapter, more like engineering or architecture than physics, then we must be concerned with all of the factors that can make a variety of individuals dissatisfied with the society as a representation of their needs and interests. The structural tolerances for perceived enviable benefits to individuals may not be very great.

The charge of unfairness, alternatively, can focus on general policy goals rather than on benefits for individuals. Taxation for perfectionist purposes is coercive, it may be said, because it is unfair to those who do not support these purposes; it is unfair because it takes sides on issues of values. In this form, the claim of unfairness rests objection 1 to perfectionism on objection 2. Perfectionism might make sense, it will be said, if such things as preservation of famous works of art, performances of classic operas, and support of new art and research in the "pure" sciences had an objective and entirely uncontentious social importance. But the importance of these things *is* contentious. Some of us hardly care about them at all, and would not think it mattered if they were eliminated. Thus, a society that uses public money to support cultural activities is in effect taking sides with those to whom these things matter, against those to whom they do not, and (to add injury to insult) is extracting money from those in the latter group, in order to support activities in which they do not believe. It is a breach of societal neutrality that amounts to unfairness, which in turn makes these elements of taxation not genuinely in the public interest, unreasonable, and in a related sense coercive.

The first thing that needs to be said is that even a thoroughly convinced perfectionist should remain mindful of such complaints. They can be much more telling against some perfectionist policies than against others. What is relevant is not only how much public money is spent for perfectionist purposes, but also how it is spent. If perfectionist policies are to be supported by something approaching an overlapping consensus (to borrow a term of Rawls's), then they must appeal to a broad range of cultural emphases. A good example of a perfectionist policy that counts as unacceptable by this standard (as well as, perhaps, because of general considerations of fairness) would be that of giving considerable support to opera while an established company that specializes in Gilbert and Sullivan is allowed to fail.

Should government policy be neutral among competing value systems? A first response is that entire neutrality is impossible, in that policies inevitably will have beneficial consequences (some of them unintended but foreseeable) for some and negative consequences for others. If cities plant trees in parks and states plant shrubs along highways, this favors some people's values over others. This lack of neutrality is tolerable as long as the amounts of money involved are relatively small, and some attempt is made to accommodate one way or another the values and interests of virtually everyone. Similarly, it is not a violation of reasonable neutrality if public libraries spend a percentage of their budget on classics greater than what would correspond to readership, as long as they do also acquire current best-sellers that represent a variety of tastes. Is it coercion if drivers find that their sideways glances encounter shrubs instead of bare grass, or if library users have to pass by Proust in order to get to a Harold Robbins novel? To say "Yes" would be very implausible in that what is involved is rather small, and there is plenty of room for people to pursue their own tastes and interests. It arguably *would* be coercive (or at least objectionable in a form resembling coercion), on the other hand, if public libraries stocked no best-sellers or if homeowners were required to plant flowering shrubs.

Reasonable neutrality should be seen not as a straightforward corollary of social theorems but rather as a complex stance that admits of degree, can vary from issue to issue, and may require occasional acts of leaning over backward. I will argue that in one respect a society simply should not be neutral: in the general choice between assigning importance to knowledge of cultural traditions and support of innovations (along with education that facilitates this), on one hand, and being indifferent to these things, on the other, it should take the positive side. A degree of neutrality is then desirable within the space that this basic choice creates. A sense of unfairness will be created if social policy is seen as slighting some cultural traditions, or drastically favoring some styles over others. Judgments inevitably must be made about what possibly has enduring value and needs public support. Very popular forms of art will not meet the second of these qualifications. Among those cultural activities that do meet both qualifications, it will be desirable to aid as wide a variety as possible.

What this advocates will seem to many people to be a limited kind of fairness, within an elitist framework. It is time to meet the general charge of unfairness head-on. Consider this analogy. It is unfair, some people contend, for schools not to give the doctrines of creationism equal time to that devoted to evolutionary biology. One reason that this complaint seems preposterous to most educated people is that we do commonly distinguish between knowledge, on one hand, which relies on strong arguments or evidence, and mere opinion, on the other. It seems absurd to assign what is merely opinion the same status as knowledge, especially within an educational context.

It would be unfortunate, nevertheless, if creationists came to think of themselves as drastically scorned or ignored by the society at large. How public institutions should treat this doctrine is, in my view, a complicated issue. It would be absurd if the National Science Foundation began leaning over backward in order to fund ill-conceived research projects designed to further the creationist agenda. On the other hand, it is imaginable that some projects motivated by creationist assumptions would deserve support. Even if it is agreed that creationism is counter to scientific knowledge, there might be highly intelligent creationist research projects with the prospective virtue of exposing gaps or weak points in current evolutionary theory. Biology courses should deny equal time to creationism; but that does not mean that it should be dismissed without supporting argument or not mentioned, or that all ideas advanced by intelligent creationists should be treated with something less than respect. (I speak as someone who once taught a philosophy of religion class in which the best students, who got the only grades of A, were fundamentalist creationists.) In the end anything like entire neutrality would be unreasonable, but civility (including a reasonable degree of willingness to listen) is not.

The argument of the first part of this book was that there are cases in which people have real knowledge that certain things have high (or low, or negative) value. These can be as banal as the knowledge of how awful it is to suffer excruciating pain over a long period of time, or can involve the value of unusual experiences or states of being. Much of the argument of this part of the book, in fact, tended in the direction of skepticism: there are very many kinds of value judgments, especially about experiences and forms of life different from our own, in which our confidence should be limited. Along the same line, let me say that many of the judgments required by perfectionist social policy (e.g., which young composer's work merits support) similarly will leave room for a high degree of doubt. Nevertheless, I will argue that there are some values directly connected with social policy that we can know. One of these is the value of a society's having some living sense of cultural traditions and innovation as opposed to having none. If this argument is correct, then to oppose any form of perfectionism on the ground of unfairness is comparable to opposing preference for teaching of evolutionary biology rather than creationism on similar grounds.

With this in mind we can review the fundamental objection, that perfectionist policies are ruled out by the conditions of the original position that decides the features of a just society. It is important to be clear just what the issue is. Even the most ardent perfectionist will be likely to concede that a society that is in touch with its cultural traditions and also features lively and innovative work in the arts and sciences is not thereby more just than one that is both stagnant and also not in touch with its cultural traditions. If the issue concerns the qualities that a society must have in order to be just, then perfectionism is irrelevant.

(As an aside: if the issue concerned the qualities that a society must have in order to *become,* or *remain,* just, it might be a different matter. Perfectionist considerations, especially in relation to education, arguably would be important. One of the distinctive features of Rawls's theory of justice is its static, outside-of-time quality.)

The perfectionist must argue that, even if perfectionist policies are not dictated by what counts toward the justice of a society, all the same they are not ruled out.

The perfectionist also can argue that, as important as justice is, a society that is both just and culturally alive is better than one that is just but mediocre. It is when we ask what counts as a very good society (not restricting our purview to justice) that perfectionism comes into its own.

Rawls's original position represents an ingenious rationalist strategy for eliminating irrelevant considerations (that rest on accidental variations in position in society and in social orientation) from our judgments of what kind of society should be preferred. This can be viewed as a way of concentrating our minds on what is essential to justice. But there is also an implicit appeal to what might unite us rather than divide us. So far, one might say, so good.

Problems begin when (as sometimes happens in rationalist philosophies) the search for good solutions becomes a search for the perfect solution. An example of this is Descartes' important, and (up to a point) very useful, argument in *Meditation 6*, about ways of eliminating risks of error. Relying on more than one sense and on multiple sources of testimony clearly are good strategies; and, if the risks of error in each source are independent, one is in effect multiplying a small probability of error by another small probability, and another . . . , the product progressively becoming more and more minute. This is a process, Descartes suggests, whose ultimate result will be zero chance of error. Rawls makes, to my mind, a similar move when, relying on the intuitive idea that what is fair ought to appeal to unbiased judges, he assumes that the original position must yield a result that would be accepted by everyone.

This emphasis on unanimity may be one of the reasons that Rawls stipulates (1971, 137, 142) that people in the original position "do not know their conception of the good." Or it may be that Rawls assumes that there is no knowledge of values. The arguments of the first part of this book stand as a rebuttal of this view. In any case, there is no clear and compelling reason that some knowledge of values could not be available to those in the original position. Rawls allows them to know various social facts, including the usefulness of money. Why can they not know that there is reason to think that a society in which the arts and sciences are very much alive is, all things being equal, a better place to be than one that is culturally stagnant? There is no clear line of argument in Rawls's work that answers this question.

Hence, the reply to Rawls's objection to perfectionism at its most fundamental level is that the original position is rigged. There is no clear reason that those who are imagined in it should be denied knowledge of values. If they had such knowledge, the results of their deliberations of course would be messier and would be most unlikely to attract (even in the virtual-world of theory) unanimous support. But perhaps political theory that takes account of everything that is relevant needs to be messy and contentious?

All of this adds up to a defense of a limited (modest) form of perfectionism against the most powerful set of criticisms. It is not a complete defense, though. To complete it we need positive argument that shows that there is a strong basis for the claims about value that underlie perfectionism, and that (in the context of the real world as it is at present) some kinds of perfectionist policies can be justified by what they are likely to accomplish. This argument follows.

## The Positive Argument for Perfectionism

The first element needs to be an assessment of claims about the goodness of social settings and arrangements. It is important not simply to present highly general propositions with an air of bland satisfaction. "Clear your mind of cant," Dr. Johnson once said to Boswell. We should not assume that something must be true merely because it is a lovely statement that all right-thinking people want to be true.

With this in mind, let us look at the difficulties of becoming confident about value judgments related to social settings and arrangements. One such judgment that seems to most people (including me) to be true is that a free society is better, generally speaking, than one that is not free. A closely related claim is that life in a free society is better, generally speaking, than life in one that is not.

How do we know these things? They seem very plausible, but might they be regarded as (for many of us) articles of faith or as shrewd guesses rather than real knowledge? There are more complicated possibilities, intermediate between faith and guessing, on one hand, and genuine knowledge, on the other. Perhaps we have good reasons to expect that life in a society that is not free would be inferior, generally speaking, to life in one that is, but our grounds for confidence are not as good as they would be if we had actual experience of life in both kinds of society?

A further complication is that, of course, not all free societies are very much alike, nor are all societies that are not free very much like. We would expect life in societies as lacking in freedom as Hitler's Germany and those in eastern Europe dominated by Russian communism to be fairly horrendous. It should be added, though, that those of us who thought all along that life in communist countries was generally unenviable gained stronger grounds for confidence with increased contact with people who had grown up in such societies, or when a better sense of the lives of people like the composer Shostakovich became available. Societies that have been lacking (but perhaps not as drastically lacking) in freedom like Tito's Yugoslavia and Franco's Spain may represent more complicated stories, in that the effects of the lack of freedom on the quality of life may depend more greatly on circumstance, and especially on the degree of political involvement. Generalizations about value within these social settings may have a wider range of exceptions and qualifications.

Nevertheless, the basic point remains. To have lived within a certain kind of society, or to know and be able to rely on people who have, is to be in a position to make judgments about value related to that kind of society. The judgments will be of two sorts: one of the likely value of individual lives in such a society, and the other of the overall value (insofar as the value found within any social system cannot be assumed to be merely the sum of individual values) in the society. It cannot too strongly be emphasized that a judgment of the first will be very imprecise, allowing for individual exceptions and variations and for ranges of cases, and that a judgment of the second is likely to seem both vague and tenuous. Nevertheless, we can say that to have lived in a society that is highly unfree is to have a sense that the values possible within individual lives tend to be lower than is generally the case in free societies, and that the overall value tends to be lower.

The lack of precision and of definiteness of these judgments may well seem embarrassing. But what are the alternatives? They are either to present judgments that are more precise and definite (which, given the quality of the evidence, would be dishonest), or to say that we are in no position to make judgments of value in these cases. Insofar as there is genuine evidence of value, so that some people know from experience what they are talking about, to deny that we can make judgments of value in these cases would amount to fastidiousness of the most unreasonable sort.

My suggestion is that we are in a somewhat similar position to make value judgments that involve a comparison between societies that are culturally and intellectually alive and ones that are not. Again, any judgments that we are in a position to make will be neither precise nor definite. We can say that the overall value within a society that is not culturally and intellectually alive seems likely to be less than that within one that is, and that some individual lives (especially those of intelligent people) seem likely also to be somewhat impoverished.

There are differences between this and the comparison between free and unfree societies. One is that the comparison involving cultural vitality draws somewhat less on direct experience, at least of different societies. The direct experience that some of us might draw on is likely to concern localities (as opposed to entire societies) that seemed culturally stagnant as opposed to those that are culturally vibrant. More generally there can be the experience of spending a considerable amount of time in a setting in which one never hears (or otherwise encounters) ideas that are not very familiar. We also can readily imagine societies, like that of *Brave New World*, that are entirely culturally stagnant. Our sense that value is lacking in such societies should be taken seriously (and should be assigned some weight); but, all the same, thought experiments are not real experiments, and this kind of evidence probably should not be assigned all of the weight that we give to real-life experience.

Some people's experiences of localities or of more limited milieus in which there is a low level of awareness of cultural traditions, and also very little awareness of anything that is intellectually or artistically new and vital, on the other hand, should be given considerable weight. Not everyone minds cultural impoverishment, of course. For that matter, many people appreciate the orderliness and predictability of life in societies that lack freedom. Life may well be genuinely better for some people in societies that lack freedom, or in societies that have become culturally impoverished. If what one most cares about is that the trains run on time, and that people who conform can have secure lives, some societies of this sort can score high. Nevertheless, there is reason to believe that the possibilities for good lives in such societies are generally constricted, that many people have distinctively unenviable lives (even if they do not know what they are missing), and that all in all there is likely to be less value within the society. In both cases we give more weight to the testimony of some witnesses of value (especially people who are intelligent, perceptive, and have some wide experience of life) than to that of others.

This does not add up to the strongest possible claim about the epistemological status of perfectionism. To review: the perfectionist thesis is that there is, generally speaking, more value in societies in which there is strong awareness of cultural traditions, and also vital new work in the arts and sciences, than in societies that lack these features. There is no suggestion of anything like demonstrative certainty or even the very strong grounds for confidence that we have when all of the eyewitnesses to an event agree. Along similar lines, the grounds for confidence in perfectionism are not quite as strong as the grounds for confidence (chapter 4) that (in normal cases) excuciating pain over a considerable period of time will have negative value. On the other hand, there are experiential grounds of some strength for thinking that the perfectionist thesis is correct. If we take seriously the testimony of intelligent, perceptive people about what it is like to be in a setting in which cultural vitality is entirely lacking as opposed to one that is culturally alive, and if we give some weight also to the thought experiment represented by a revised *Brave New World*, it does look as if the grounds for confidence are strong enough that we are entitled to claim that we know that it is correct. We know (or, at least, many of us know) the value of cultural vitality. But, all the same, this is not one of those matters in which the truth is so luminous that reasonable people could not disagree.

It may help the reader here to think of a scale at the bottom of which is entire ignorance or guesswork, rising to something a bit better than guesswork, then through modest grounds for confidence to strong grounds (with little reason for doubt), and finally to grounds so strong that only someone who was ignorant or significantly impaired in the abilities to discern truth would reject them. My contention is that our position in relation to the correctness of perfectionism is at the next to highest of these levels.

It may seem disappointing that, while the argument supports a claim to knowledge, the claim is not so very strong that it approaches anything like demonstrable or inductive certainty. This is added to (what might seem) an earlier disappointment, that the position about value that is argued for is far from precise. Let me suggest that these unappealing features are fairly typical of the degree and kind of assurance we can have of values, in relation to various goals and risks, in making public policy decisions. Indeed, the degree of confidence in the general perfectionist claim that we are in a position to have is much greater than the assurance about values that we often are able to have in relation to particular public policy decisions.

Such decisions change people's lives, and usually do not change everyone's life in the same way. Some changes can be readily (although not very precisely) evaluated: we know that it is awful not to have minimally adequate housing or enough to eat, even if we cannot put a number on how awful it is. But many other changes, which people may feel make life better or worse, are less easy to weigh even if we are tolerant of imprecision. How much better is someone's life, for example, if traffic on highways generally moves about ten miles an hour faster and he or she can get to destinations more quickly? There is no reason that we should equate the degree of preference with the degree to which life is made better, although there is no reason also to assume that the two are entirely unrelated.

This imprecision helps to limit the degree of confidence that we often are in a position to have that a public policy decision is the correct one. A further limitation is this. The consequences, including unintended consequences, of public policy decisions are notoriously difficult to predict, even in the short run. Even if we have a reasonable degree of confidence that the goals promoted by a policy promise significant value, there is the worry that in the end they may not be effectively promoted by the policy. There is room also for worries about risks, either negative reactions to the trend that the policy represents or unintended results of other kinds. Thus, even if we have a rough sense of the values at stake and are pretty much right about this, the policy that we are led to favor can turn out to be a mistake.

Because of these complications, it seems unusual for anyone to be in a position to claim to know that a public policy decision will be a good one. It is important to recognize this, both as a matter of honest realism and also because its recognition will be conducive to the tolerance and openness to dialogue that are so important in democratic societies. The point, however, should not be overstated. That it is unusual for anyone to be in a position to claim to know what is good (or bad) public policy does not mean that no one ever is in such a strong position. There are some policies that are predictably ruinous to the fundamental interests of many, with few redeeming features; we can know that they are wrong, much as we can know that certain forms of direct disaster relief are right.

Also, we should not equate the (usual) absence of grounds for confidence so strong they they amount to knowledge with an entire absence of grounds for confidence. Reasonable opinions occupy a middle ground between knowledge and guesswork. In short, there can be reason to think that the goals of a public policy involve major positive values, and also reason to think that the policy will promote these fairly effectively without major undesirable side effects, even if we cannot claim total assurance on either count.

It may be tempting to say that, unless we have total assurance that what we are about to do is good, we should do nothing. But it is not clear what logic supports this very timid strategy. If it were applied to personal life, no one would ever get married, form long-term relationships of any kind, or make major career decisions.

My contention is that there is a range of perfectionist public policies in which one can have a reasonable degree of confidence. These are policies that provide modest amounts of public money to support preservation of cultural monuments and dissemination of materials related to a variety of cultural traditions, and development of new artistic and scientific projects. The experiential basis for thinking that there are positive values involved in having more, rather than less, vital new work in the arts and sciences and awareness of cultural traditions has already been outlined. This provides grounds for a degree of confidence in the values of the goals of perfectionist policies that is high enough to justify a claim to knowledge. The remaining question is whether the policies effectively promote these goals with little risk of undesirable side effects.

This is largely an empirical question, and here especially nothing like entire assurance is possible. In the end everyone must arrive at her or his own judgment of what the real world of the arts and sciences is like. It is often argued by perfectionists that government patronage is needed to replace the aristocratic patronage of the past. How effective or fair the latter ever was is debatable (cf. Hildesheimer 1983). Fundamental scientific research of the sort that is unlikely to yield any immediate practical benefits has become increasingly expensive, and here there is a strong case for saying that government support makes possible what otherwise would largely not exist. Something like this case can be made also in relation to grants that support individual artists, composers, and playwrights, in that their projects can be very time-consuming with (in many cases) little likelihood of much financial reward. Such grants also have the advantage of being far cheaper than the grants that support scientific research.

The case for support for novelists, poets, and those doing research in the humanities may be somewhat weaker. The prospects that good work will bring financial reward seem in general brighter in the case of novelists than in that of, say, composers, although it is hard to generalize. Poets and humanists could be argued to be, by and large, in a better position than, say, artists and playwrights to combine creative endeavors with paid employment without cost to the quality of their creative work. Certainly artists and playwrights often contend that the habits of mind required for academic employment are subversive of those required for creative work, a claim less likely to be made by humanists, although here again one needs to be cautious about generalizations. In any event, to say that the case for modest grants to novelists, poets, and humanists seems on the whole slightly weaker than that for artists, composers, and playwrights, and for scientific research, is not to say that there is no case at all. Not all poets could function in other jobs the way Philip Larkin and T. S. Eliot did; not all good serious novels sell; and some humanistic projects are exceptionally time-consuming and unlikely to attract non-public support.

One complication is this. Even if it is granted that there is a need for public support for projects in the arts and sciences, in that vital new work will contribute value to the society, it may be questioned whether the administration of such support (including the selection of scientists, composers, artists, etc., to be supported) generally accomplishes its goal. This doubt is more likely to be raised in relation to the arts than the sciences. Not so long ago there were English press reports of a policy, at the onset of World War II, to protect gifted young men in the arts from what had happened to some of their predecessors in World War I, by assigning them to desk jobs. The press reports suggested that it much later was clear, given hindsight, that by and large the wrong men had been protected. What good is public support of artists and composers, it may be asked, if there is not much assurance that what will turn out to be the best ones will be helped?

This concern should be taken seriously as a doubt about perfectionist policies; but even so, we need to bear in mind that it applies mainly to support for new work in the arts, and that similar doubts would have much less force in relation to support of scientific research or of programs to preserve and disseminate material related to cultural traditions. Perhaps this doubt should be left as a question mark. It can be argued that, given the modest amounts of money required for grants to individual artists and composers, we might reasonably take some chances at hitting the target of someone who turns out to have a major talent. It also can be argued that even when aid goes to someone who, in the long run, turns out regrettably not to be entirely first-rate, all of this contributes to a milieu of artistic vitality.

Let us return to the general argument for perfectionist policies. In a society that is increasingly dominated by the most popular forms of culture, and in which most college students have difficulty in reading much that was written before 1900, institutions designed to maintain and to disseminate the great cultural achievements of the past increasingly need help, as do those concerned with new work in the arts and sciences that is not immediately easy to understand. I have suggested that there can be difficulties in targeting aid to individuals in the arts. These difficulties, however, should not be taken as implying that it is hopeless to try to encourage those who will be the best new artists and composers, nor need we downgrade the effects of public support on the vitality of the arts. It seems highly plausible to suppose that public grants to cultural institutions and to individual artists and scientists generally further (more reliably perhaps in some cases than in others) the values of cultural vitality and of awareness of cultural traditions. Are there significant negative effects?

One could *imagine* major negative effects, such as a widespread revulsion against the arts and sciences and culture generally. Perhaps an exceptionally heavy-handed and narrow-minded perfectionist policy might lead to such a backlash, especially if very large amounts of money were in involved and if some cultural traditions were systematically slighted. Perfectionist policies that have been followed in countries like Britain and America on the whole have not been like that, and in the real world significant negative effects have not been discernible.

There remain the obvious negative effects: government programs that require money take money from taxpayers. Even if the amounts per taxpayer are fairly small, this cannot be disregarded. A very small cost is still a cost, and multiplied by a large number of people will emerge as a disutility that is not entirely negligible. Perfectionist government policies, like any other government policies that require money, must be assessed in terms of benefits as against costs. How serious the costs are must be viewed in the context of the lives of those who pay taxes. If virtually all of them are very close to the edge of not being able to afford housing or medical care, then even small costs can look serious. If some are very close to the edge but most are not, then small costs look less serious. Furthermore, in this case any worry about the costs to the less well-off of relatively inexpensive cultural programs can be met effectively by rewriting the tax code in order to protect the less well-off.

Let me sum up the argument for limited perfectionist policies. Such policies will be designed to promote a strong sense of cultural traditions and also vitality of new work in the arts and sciences. There is some strong experiential evidence that these goals involve important values. One may assume further that reasonably intelligent programs effectively (on the whole) will promote these goals. Part of the argument, indeed, is that contemporary culture in countries like Britain and the United States is such that both people's connectedness with cultural traditions and the vitality of new work in the arts and sciences need support, that the position is especially problematic without some degree of public support. The argument claims further that there are not major negative values created by limited perfectionist programs of a reasonably intelligent sort. The results of such programs, in short, can be expected to include more gains in value than losses.

This result creates a strong prima facie case for public policies answering to a limited form of perfectionism. I do not claim that it is an absolutely compelling case. However we have seen that a priori objections of a Rawlsian sort to perfectionism have a very limited plausibility. Anyone who wishes to argue against perfectionist public policies or against perfectionism must begin by looking at the ways in which such policies work in the real world.

# Bibliography

Anscombe, G. E. M.
> 1957      *Intention* (Oxford, Blackwell)
> 1958      Modern Moral Philosophy, *Philosophy* 33, 1–10

Aristophanes
> Fourth c.
> B.C.E./1962      *Complete Plays of Aristophanes*, ed. Moses Hadas (New York, Bantam)

Aristotle
> Fourth c.
> B.C.E./1962)      *Nicomachean Ethics* trans Martin Ostwald (Indianapolis: Bobbs Merrill)

Armon-Jones, Claire
> 1991      *Varieties of Affect* (Hemel Hempstead, Harvester; Toronto, University of Toronto Press)

Asch, S. E.
> 1952      *Social Psychology* (Englewood Cliffs, NJ, Prentice-Hall)

Ayer, Alfred J.
> 1936      *Language, Truth, and Logic* (London, Gollancz)

Baier, Kurt
> 1967      Fact, Value, and Norm in Stevenson's Ethics, *Nous* 1, 139–60
> 1973      Reason and Experience, *Nous* 8, 57–77

Bennett, Jonathan
> Unpub      Consequentialism; What is Consequentialism? Consequences vs. the Behavior Itself

Brighouse, Harry
> 1995      Neutrality, Publicity, and State Funding of the Arts, *Philosophy and Public Affairs* 24, no. 1, 35–63

Camus, Albert
   1955        *Myth of Sisyphus*, trans. Justin O'Brien (New York, Vintage Books)
Confucius
   fifth c. B.C.E./
   1938        *Analects*, trans. Arthur Waley (New York, Vintage Books)
Csikszentmihalyi, Mihaly
   1990        *Flow: The Psychology of Optimal Experience* (New York, Harper & Row)
David-Neel, Alexandra
   1929/1971   *Magic and Mystery in Tibet* (New York, Dover Books)
Davidson, Donald
   1970        Mental Events, in Foster and Swanson, eds. *Experience and Theory* (Amherst, University of Massachusetts Press)
de Sousa, Ronald
   1987        *The Rationality of Emotion* (Cambridge, MA, M.I.T. Press)
Donagan, Alan
   1977        *The Theory of Morality* (Chicago, University of Chicago Press)
Feinberg, Joel
   1975        Rawls and Intuitionism, in *Reading Rawls*, ed. Norman Daniels (New York, Basic Books
Fields, Lloyd
   1994        Moral Beliefs and Blameworthiness, *Philosophy* 69, no. 270, 397–415
Findlay, J. N.
   1963        *Meinong's Theory of Objects and Values* (Oxford, Clarendon Press)
Foot, Philippa
   1958–59    Moral Beliefs, *Proceedings of the Aristotelian Society* 59, 83–104
Franklin, Alan
   1990        *Experiment Right or Wrong* (Cambridge, Cambridge University Press)
Frijda, Nico
   1993        Moods, Emotion Episodes, and Emotions, in *Handbook of Emotions*, Emotions, ed. M. Lewis and J. M. Haviland (New York, Guilford Press), 381–403
Gaus, Gerald
   1990        *Value and Justification* (Cambridge, Cambridge University Press)
Gibbard, Allan
   1990        *Wise Choices, Apt Feelings* (Cambridge, MA, Harvard University Press)
Glendon, Mary Ann
   1991        *Rights Talk* (New York, Free Press)
Griffin, James
   1996        *Value Judgment* (Oxford, Clarendon Press)
Hardimon, Michael O.
   1994        Role Obligations, *Journal of Philosophy* 91, no. 7, 333–63
Hare, R. M.
   1963        *Freedom and Reason* (Oxford, Oxford University Press)
   1981        *Moral Thinking* (Oxford, Clarendon Press)
Hildesheimer, Wolfgang
   1983        *Mozart* (New York, Vintage Books)

Hume, David
 1739/1978     *Treatise of Human Nature*, 2nd ed., ed. L. A. Selby-Bigge, rev. P. H.
               Nidditch (Oxford, Clarendon Press)
 1751/1975     *Enquiry Concering the Principles of Morals*, in *Enquiries* (3rd ed.), ed. L.
               A. Selby-Bigge, rev. P. H. Nidditch (Oxford, Clarendon Press)
Hurka, Thomas
 1993          *Perfectionism* (Oxford, Oxford University Press)
Hutcheson, Francis
 1728/1972     *An Essay on the Nature and Conduct of the Passions*, section 1, in *A Guide
               to the British Moralists*, ed. D. H. Munro (London, Fontana)
Isenberg, Arnold
 1953          Critical Communication, in *Aesthetics and Language*, ed. William Elton
               (Oxford, Blackwell)
Jackson, Frank, and Philip Pettit
 1995          Moral Functionalism and Moral Motivation, *Philosophical Quarterly* 45,
               no. 178, 20–40
Johnston, Mark
 1989          Dispositional Theories of Value, *Supplementary Proceedings of the Aris-
               totelian Society* 63, 139–74
Kagan, Jerome
 1984          The Idea of Emotion in Human Development, in *Emotions, Cognition,
               and Behavior*, ed. C. Izard, J. Kagan, and R. Zajonc (Cambridge, Cam-
               bridge University Press), 38–72
Kagan, Shelly
 1989          *The Limits of Morality* (Oxford, Clarendon Press)
Kamm, F. M.
 1992          Non-consequentialism, the Person as an End-in-Itself, and the Signifi-
               cance of Status *Philosophy and Public Affairs* 21, no. 4, 354–89
Kant, Immanuel
 1785/1981     *Grounding of Morality*, trans. James Ellington (Indianapolis, Hackett)
 1797/1964     *Metaphysical Principles of Virtue*, trans. James Ellington (Indianapolis,
               Bobbs Merrill)
Kierkegaard, Søren
 1846/1941     *Concluding Unscientific Postscript*, trans. David F. Swenson and Walter
               Lowrie, (Princeton, Princeton University Press)
Korsgaard, Christine
 1996          *The Sources of Normativity* (Cambridge, Cambridge University Press)
Kuhn, Steven
 1996          Agreement Keeping and Indirect Moral Theory, *Journal of Philosophy* 93,
               no. 3, 105–28
Kuhn, Thomas S.
 1962          *The Structure of Scientific Revolutions* (Chicago, University of Chicago
               Press)
 1970          Reflections on My Critics, in *Criticism and the Growth of Knowledge*, ed.
               Imre Lakatos and Alan Musgrave, 231–78 (Cambridge, Cambridge Uni-
               versity Press)

Kupperman, Joel J.

| | |
|---|---|
| 1970 | *Ethical Knowledge* (London, George Allen and Unwin) |
| 1981 | A Case for Consequentialism, *American Philosophical Quarterly* 18, no. 4, 305–13 |
| 1983 | *The Foundations of Morality* (London, George Allen and Unwin) |
| 1991 | *Character* (New York, Oxford University Press) |
| 1995 | An Anti-essentialist View of the Emotions, *Philosophical Psychology* 8, no. 4, 341–51 |
| 1996 | Axiological Realism, *Philosophy* 71, no. 276, 185–203 |

Leibniz, G.W.

| | |
|---|---|
| 1710/1951 | *The Theodicy: Abridgement*, in *Selections*, ed. Philip P. Wiener (New York, Scribner's) |

Lemos, Noah

| | |
|---|---|
| 1993 | Higher Goods and the Myth of Tithonus, *Journal of Philosophy* 90, no. 9, 482–96 |
| 1994 | *Intrinsic Value: Concept and Warrant* (Cambridge, Cambridge University Press) |

Lewis, David

| | |
|---|---|
| 1989 | Dispositional Theories of Value, *Supplementary Proceedings of the Aristotelian Society* 63, 113–37 |

Mackie, J. L.

| | |
|---|---|
| 1977 | *Ethics: Inventing Right and Wrong* (Harmondsworth, Penguin) |

Malcolm, Norman

| | |
|---|---|
| 1958 | *Ludwig Wittgenstein: A Memoir* (London, Oxford University Press) |

Meinong, Alexius

| | |
|---|---|
| 1917/1972 | *On Emotional Presentation*, trans. Marie-Luise Schubert Kalsi (Evanston, Northwestern University Press) |

Mill, John Stuart

| | |
|---|---|
| 1834/1984 | Reform in Education, in *Collected Works of John Stuart Mill*, vol. 21, *Essays on Equality, Law, and Education*, ed. John M. Robson (Toronto, University of Toronto) |
| 1843/1884 | *A System of Logic* (London, Longmans Green) |
| 1859/1978 | *On Liberty*, ed. E. Rappaport (Indianapolis, Hackett) |
| 1861/1979 | *Utilitarianism*, ed. G. Sher (Indianapolis, Hackett) |

Moore, G. E.

| | |
|---|---|
| 1903 | *Principia Ethica* (Cambridge, Cambridge University Press) |

Nagel, Thomas

| | |
|---|---|
| 1975 | Rawls on Justice, in *Reading Rawls*, ed. Norman Daniels (New York, Basic Books) |
| 1991 | *Equality and Partiality* (New York, Oxford University Press) |

Ni, Peimin

| | |
|---|---|
| 1992 | Changing the Past, *Nous* 26, no. 3, 349–59 |

Nietzsche, Friedrich

| | |
|---|---|
| 1883–91/1978 | *Thus Spake Zarathustra*, trans. Walter Kaufmann (New York, Penguin Books) |

Nozick, Robert
   1974        *Anarchy, State, and Utopia* (New York, Basic Books)
Oldenquist, Andrew
   1966        Rules and Consequences, *Mind* 75, April, 180–92
Pettit, Philip
   1984        Satisficing Consequentialism, *Supplementary Proceedings of the Aristotelian Society*, 165–76
Plato
  Fourth c.
  B.C.E./1937   *Dialogues*, trans. Benjamin Jowett (New York: Random House)
Rawls, John
   1971        A *Theory of Justice* (Cambridge, MA, Harvard University Press)
   1993        *Political Liberalism* (New York, Columbia University Press)
Rozin, Paul, et al.
   1993        Disgust, in *Handbook of Emotions*, ed. M. Lewis and J. M. Haviland (New York, Guilford Press), 575–94
Rundle, Bede
   1993        *Facts* (London, Duckworth)
Ryle, Gilbert
   1949        *The Concept of Mind* (New York, Barnes and Noble)
Scheffler, Samuel
   1982        *The Rejection of Consequentialism* (Oxford, Clarendon Press)
   1992        *Human Morality* (New York, Oxford University Press)
Searle, John
   1995        *The Construction of Social Reality* (London, Allen Lane)
Sennett, Richard, and Jonathan Cobb
   1972        *Hidden Injuries of Class* (New York, Knopf)
Sidgwick, Henry
   1907        *The Methods of Ethics*, 7th ed. (London, Macmillan)
Siedentop, Larry
   1979        Two Liberal Traditions, in *The Idea of Freedom*, ed. Alan Ryan (Oxford, Oxford University Press)
Skinner, Quentin
   1984        The Idea of Negative Liberty: Philosophical and Historical Perspectives, in *Philosophy in History*, ed. Richard Rorty, J. B. Schneewind, and Quentin Skinner (Cambridge, Cambridge University Press)
Slote, Michael
   1984        Satisficing Consequentialism, *Supplementary Proceedings of the Aristotelian Society*, 139–63
Smart, J. J. C.
   1956        Extreme and Restricted Utilitarianism, *Philosophical Quarterly* 6, 344–54
   1977        Benevolence as an Over-Riding Attitude, *Australasian Journal of Philosophy* 55, no. 2, 127–35
Smart, J. J. C., and B. A. O. Williams
   1973        *Utilitarianism: For and Against* (Cambridge, Cambridge University Press)

Smith, Michael

    1989        Dispositional Theories of Value, *Supplementary Proceedings of the Aristotelian Society* 63, 89–111

Solomon, Robert

    1976        *The Passions* (New York, Doubleday)

Stevenson, Charles

    1963        *Facts and Values* (New Haven, Yale University Press)

Strawson, P. F.

    1950        Truth, *Supplementary Proceedings of the Aristotelian Society* 24, 129–56

    1961        Social Morality and Individual Ideal, *Philosophy* 36, no. 136, 1–17

Swanton, Christine

    1993        Satisficing and Virtue, *Journal of Philosophy* 90, 1, 33–48

Tanner, Michael

    1976–97    Sentimentality, *Proceedings of the Aristotelian Society* 77, 127–47

Urmson, J. O.

    1968        *The Emotive Theory of Ethics* (London, Hutchinson)

Waley, Arthur

    1958        *The Opium War Through Chinese Eyes* (London, George Allen and Unwin)

Walzer, Michael

    1965        *Revolution of the Saints* (Cambridge, MA, Harvard University Press)

Wittgenstein, Ludwig

    1953        *Philosophical Investigations* (Oxford, Basil Blackwell)

# Index